HEAR ME WITH YOUR EYES

Managing Editor: Greg Dawes
Copyeditor: Audrey Hansen

Hear Me with Your Eyes

Women, Visions, and Voices in Argentine Cinema

Ana Forcinito

Translated by Andrea Rosenberg and Ana Forcinito

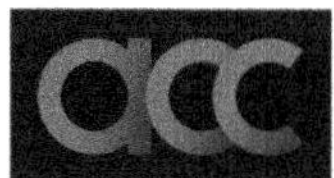

Complete Library of Congress Cataloging-in-Publication Data
is available at https://lccn.loc.gov/2022004941.

ISBN: 978-1-4696-7094-2 (paperback)
ISBN: 978-1-4696-7095-9 (ebook)

Originally published in Spanish as *Óyeme con los ojos: cine, mujeres, visiones y voces* (Havana: Casa de las Américas, 2018).

This is a publication of the Department of Foreign Languages and Literatures at North Carolina State University. For more information visit http://go.ncsu.edu/editorialacc.

Distributed by the University of North Carolina Press
www.uncpress.org

To my daughter Gabriela.

INDEX

Acknowledgments ix

INTRODUCTION 1

Women Who Dare to Look 4

Women Who Dare to Speak 6

The Nearly Inaudible on the Other Side of the Mirror 7

Theories of the Gaze and the Voice 10

1. TRANSCENDENCE, GAZE, AND VOICE: MARÍA LUISA BEMBERG 21

Gaze, Sound, and Feminism: Some Considerations 22

From the Personal to the Political 24

From Voices to Transcendence 34

From the Other Side of the Mirror 39

Hearing with the Eyes 42

2. WHISPERS IN A REALM OF VOICES: LUCRECIA MARTEL 44

La ciénaga: Opacity and Indiscernible Voices 45

La niña santa: Between Prayers and Disobedience 53

La mujer sin cabeza: The Loss of the Voice 60

Feminine/Masculine: Voices, Murmurs, Whispers 65

3. THAT SCREAM, THAT WRITING, THAT LOST VOICE: ALBERTINA CARRI 71

Displaced Voices and Narrative Authority: *Los rubios* 73

Géminis and the Voices of Senselessness 80

La rabia and the Excesses of Language 87

4. VOICES AND ECHOES 93
Echoes and Distortions: *Cielo azul, cielo negro* 95
Echoes of the Maternal Body: *La cámara oscura* 100

5. POLITICS AND AESTHETICS OF THE VISIBLE AND THE AUDIBLE 109
Gaze and Ghostliness 114
Voice and Ghostliness 116
Mourning and Ethics 119
Intersections of Voices 120

6. THE SONOROUS CRYSTAL-IMAGES OF MEMORY 123
Returns, Crystal-Images, and Remnants 126
Hearing Voices 136
Voices, Spaces, Times 139

7. THE VOICE AND THE UNLIVABLE 146
The Faded Voice 148
The Intrauterine Voice 152
The Suffocated Voice 154
The Dialogic Voice 158
Mirror Sounds: The Invisible and the Unlivable 162

Coda 164

Bibliography 169

Filmography 177

ACKNOWLEDGMENTS

To the University of Minnesota and especially to CLA for all the support it provided for the research I conducted in writing this book.

To all my colleagues at the University of Minnesota, especially to Nicholas Spadaccini, Carol Klee, Ana Paula Ferreira, Raúl Marrero Fente, Ofelia Ferrán, Francisco Ocampo, Bill Viestenz, Jaime Hanneken, Luis Ramos García, Sophia Beal, Barbara Frey, James Ron, Alejandro Baer, Lisa Hilbink, Leigh Payne, Greta Friedemann Sánchez, Patrick McNamara, Christina Ewig, Osiris Gomez, and Amy Kaminsky. My thanks to the library of the University of Minnesota, especially Rafael Tarrago, for making so many materials for this book available.

Many colleagues and friends are part of this book through our conversations (and discussions) at conferences, in e-mails, at cafés, and in many other meeting places.

My thanks to David W. Foster, who encouraged me from the start of this project and read several of the chapters in essay form. To Ileana Rodríguez for so many conversations about the voice and the gaze. And to Ana Amado, to whom this book owes an enormous debt, especially for the contagious enthusiasm with which she encouraged me to finish it.

My gratitude to the colleagues, and friends who, through conversations and readings, inspired ideas and inquiries for this project. Special thanks to Guillermina Walas, Gonzalo Aguilar, Florencia Garramuño, Mónica Szurmuk, Nora Dominguez, Claudia Bacci, Paulina Bettendorff, Agustina Pérez Rial, Bladimir Ruiz, Arturo Madrid, Antonia Castañeda, Luis Duno, Matthew Stroud, Mariana Achugar, Alejandro Solomianski, Alejandro Meter, Sergio Villalobos-Ruminott, Hugo Achugar, Cynthia Tompkins, Lucille Kerr, Megan Corbin, Eva Palma, Julia Kratje, and Agustina Paz Frontera.

The point of departure of the current book is *Óyeme con los ojos: Cine, mujeres, visions y voces* (La Habana, Fondo Editorial Casa de las Américas, 2018), which was jointly translated into English by Andrea Rosenberg and myself. All the translations of texts originally in Spanish are Andrea Rosenberg's except when indicated otherwise. To Matthew John Phillips for the copyediting and his suggestions.

To all the women filmmakers I discuss in this book and who accompanied me with their images and the voices they brought to life on the screen, because they made it possible for me to enjoy my passion for cinema in a new form.

To all my students from my film classes who allowed and allow me to share my love of cinema and who came with me on my study of voice and image. To Olga Salazar Pozos, Javier Zapata Clavería, Carolina Anon Suárez, Alejandra Takahira, Juan González, Natalia España Defiel, Guillermo Fajardo Sotelo, Nicolás Ramos Flores, José Aguirre, and Emma Jasnoch for fascinating conversations and insightful comments.

To the Casa de las Américas for giving me the opportunity to share this book that encourages us to hear with the gaze, and especially to Myrna García Calderón, Saúl Sosnowski, and Luciano Castillo, and to the Fondo Editorial Casa de las Américas.

To Silvana Di Meo, Ana María Caula, Thérèse Tardio, Marisa Kalbermatten, Meritxell Mondejar Pont, Rosa Rubio, Silvina Casen, Hilda Frisari, Lizzie Millar, and Marcela Agnese, for our many discussions of the things that matter to us so much. To Osval. And, of course . . . to Gabriela, for everything.

Introduction

THIS BOOK TAKES AS its starting point a poem by Sor Juana Inés de la Cruz, the seventeenth-century Mexican nun, poet, and writer who is one of the pioneers of Latin American feminism. In "Sentimientos de ausente" ["Sentiments of Absence"], she addresses the distance of a faraway beloved through a juxtaposition of visual and aural dimensions. The synesthesia ("Óyeme con los ojos / ya que están tan distantes los oídos" [Hear me with your eyes / since your ears are so far away]) highlights the distance. Yet this remoteness, though it seems irremediable, can be diminished through the eyes that read the poem, as long as they not only read it but also, and especially, hear it. The poem is not simply about the senses; the world of emotions is also present ("Óyeme sordo pues me quejo muda" [Hear me deafly since my plaint is mute]). This is a love letter and, at the same time, a mute plaint. It overflows with echoes and whispers, which are then transformed into questions and hopes, about the possible reunion of the two lovers: her eyes meeting the beloved's and her voice brushing against his ears. The materiality of the voice and of that longed-for contact is at the center of the initial synesthesia and provides a bridge over which her sorrow and her plaint manage to get across. The poem is about absence, distance, love, desire, and sorrow. There is a longing for presence and a request to be heard. Hearing with one's eyes also points to the irruption of the voice into the gaze, and thus the irruption of touch and closeness, which dismantles the distance of the visual. Even though the eyes are focused on reading the words of the poem, there is also an invitation to close one's eyes in order to feel (and not just read or imagine or hear) that voice—an invitation to feel her voice, and to be touched by her love, her hope, her plaint.

Rethinking the juxtaposition of the gaze and voice requires understanding film as *audio*-visual and imagining that the eyes are now also ears—and hearing the voices, pleas, and inflections and the world of emotions and senses that are evoked by acoustic marks, as well as the pain, injury, and violence they attempt to reveal. The work of Michel Chion has pioneered the study of audio-vision, the audiovisual contract, and the intersection of two mutually influential forms of perception. Likewise, Chion has studied the voice in film and proposed a key concept for studying it: acousmatic sound. The term "acousmatic" refers to an unseen voice that we cannot identify nor synchronize with a body and hence refers to a disruption in the relationship between sound and space. This concept emphasizes the dislocation of a faceless voice that haunts us. Although acousmatic sound is one of the starting points for thinking about that disruption, I am proposing a feminist reading of the voice, thinking about the disruption produced both in *looking* relations and in *gendered* (and *gendering*) relations.

In this book, I examine the intrusion of the voice into the cinematographic gaze and the intersections (and ruptures) of the sound-image. I focus on the aesthetics emerging from that interplay of distances and proximities and what is revealed by different shots and different acoustic registers. Employing a feminist perspective in my approach to Argentine cinema directed by women, I examine, on the one hand, those ways of looking that affirm women as subjects of difference in the process of liberation of the gaze. On the other hand, I analyze how voices inhabit those looking relations or defy the patriarchal visual regime by foregrounding hierarchy and power.

Feminism in this book refers to an interpretive lens and not to an attempt to posit these directors as such. That is not to say they are or are not, in fact, feminists; María Luisa Bemberg was a self-proclaimed feminist. Still, that is not the case with all of the directors discussed in this book, and many of them did not identify as feminists (at least until the emergence of the NiUnaMenos movement in 2015), even if their work challenges the paradigms of the heterosexist patriarchy. My aim is not to study feminist cinema as a response to sexist cinema, but rather to analyze visions and voices that have been shaped around the poetics of a plaint, an injury, or a marginality that is, in turn, defined by escaping masculine, binary, and heterosexist parameters, even if it intermittently complies with them.

The use of sound in Lucrecia Martel's work has been widely discussed in studies of Argentine cinema, and the acoustic components in her films were vital to my examination of both her productions and those of other directors. I should emphasize, however, that this project also came out of my interest in Albertina Carri's use of voice. In *Los rubios* [*The Blonds*], for example, the articulated voice of her father (disappeared during the dictatorship) is central, yet its powerful presence can be heard only through a displacement—that is, the reading of a passage of one of his books. In addition, there are sounds associated with her mother, ones that are not articulated voices but prelinguistic utterances, especially shouts, and sounds associated with a maternal language, or at least with a voice that cannot be translated into the paternal language. Carri's installation in the Parque de la Memoria in Buenos Aires in 2015 fully embarks on the quest to "hear with one's eyes" by emphasizing voice and sound in an attempt to restore or invoke the presence or the memory of her mother, who disappeared during the last military dictatorship (1976–83). Thus, the close-up on her mother's handwriting, through a microscopic view of the images of the letters sent to her daughters, transforms the legible writing into a materiality that draws her closer to the viewer through the sense of touch rather than through sight. The close-up is so extreme that we actually cannot read it any longer, but instead it creates a feeling of proximity. On the one hand, the handwriting is captured, with lenses that allow us to get closer and closer to it. On the other hand, we can hear—through a transposition of voices—the redoubling of the mother's multiple modulations. In the installation, we hear the mother's voice revealed through letters but read by Carri herself. In addition, the installation also includes that other voice recalled through the body, as the sound of a maternal voice (as a pre-symbolic sound), a voice that Carri herself would perhaps hear (or imagine) upon reading the letter. That sound ("Recovered Sound" is the title of this section) brings her mother closer through Carri's own voice, through the sounds that remind us perhaps of intrauterine sounds, through the materiality of the handwriting. Yet it also points to her absence—a remembrance of the sound of the womb and a counterpoint of voices that come from letters written in the clandestine detention center—in a desperate attempt to recover a voice that cannot be recovered. Only memory and imagination are able to recover those sounds.[1]

1. My thanks to Ana Amado not only for providing material about the installation but also for our many conversations about this installation, and about the relationship between sound and gender.

The voices and sounds in films directed by the filmmakers discussed in this book invite us to pass over the threshold of the visible world (a concept that Lacan assigns to the mirror and that Kaja Silverman rethinks in relation to film and ethics) to invisible worlds erased by violence, abjection, and marginalization and languages that cannot be translated into the rigid grammar of heteronormative masculinity. Those worlds often remain outside the visual field and are made present as shouts, singing, distortions of the voice, whispers, sighs, and panting, which frequently indicate the dislocation of images. The acoustic presence of voices that are often invisible (though never entirely invisible because sound brings them to light) differs from the presence of the images reflected in mirrors. The voices evoke closeness and contact, and, although they might sometimes be located in the depths of the mirror, they also splinter and fragment it, thereby exposing the cracks in patriarchal dominance.

Women Who Dare to Look

When Hélène Cixous argues that women have been trapped between two horrifying myths (between Medusa and the abyss, between castration and the hole) and that these two myths are part of a sexist, phallocentric militancy that theorizes male desire, she concludes by rejecting castration and the sirens' song (the link between women and death), instead offering a new image: the beauty of Medusa. At the same time, she invites us to hear the sound of her laughter (1976: 885). Cixous describes a castrated and castrating Medusa, one who annihilates with her gaze but who also has been disempowered by the gaze of the male hero. Cixous also challenges the idea that the sirens' song leads to death (after all, she says, "the sirens were men"). Instead, she presents another image and another acoustic footprint: a beautiful, laughing Medusa who is nevertheless described as monstrous and destructive for the sole purpose of maintaining the male fantasy of domination over women and all feminine attributes. The two undergirding axes of this book (the gaze and the voice) are anchored in this detour proposed by Cixous in her attempt to rethink the mythic foundation of the entrapment of women in the male–female clash, a detour away from the images of castration and the abyss and toward a different voice (a liberated laughter) and a different model of seeing (a feminist image of beauty).

The model of the woman who looks is also central in children's stories, such as the wicked stepmother in the tale of Snow White. The voice has a significant role in dismantling the queen's supposed authority. Here we have another woman who is allegedly a wicked woman and who looks at herself in a magic mirror, thus revealing the contradictions of a narcissism marked by the articulated voice of a male, heterosexual other. It is the image of the wicked stepmother in the famous Brothers Grimm story that demands that the mirror respond and confirm her beauty. With that gaze, the stepmother keeps watch to ensure that her power is maintained. At the same time, by looking in the mirror, she reaffirms her status as an object: she is a prisoner of her image and of the imaginary of feminine beauty. However, that power is the power of the voice, a strong voice that is unseen, but which embodies the voice of patriarchal power. The ghostly voice reveals how the stepmother's power is constantly monitored, thus undermining her power. The stepmother is, despite her deference to masculine norms of dominance, a powerful woman, but she is also a woman under surveillance—one whose power, which lies in patriarchal models of beauty, is closely watched. It seems relevant that the portrayals of repudiated femininity that play out in the Brothers Grimm story revolve around the image of a woman whose gaze is tied to power, malevolence, and criminality. Gaze and power are interrelated in both cases, whether in the image of the stepmother as a powerful woman or as a woman who is subjected to a culture that suppresses her. The wicked woman looks at herself because she wants to maintain her power, but it is the mirror (or maybe her image) that in fact holds the power to answer her question: "Who's the fairest of them all?" That voice, a male voice responding from the depths of the mirror, both has the power of the gaze (it sees her from that other side) and cannot be answered or contradicted.

In both cases, vision and hearing are senses that ultimately privilege the logic of patriarchy (even if unconsciously). Both voice and image—the female voice rooted in the body and the image of women as objects—are used to bolster the identification of masculinity with power and femininity with subjugation, even when this takes place, as Teresa de Lauretis suggests, through a complex game of seduction that invites women to embrace femininity (1984: 137–44).

I begin these reflections on women's gaze in Argentine cinema with references to Medusa and the wicked stepmother not merely to emphasize the traditional relationship between the female gaze and monstrousness and evil, but also to suggest that such a construction has to do with the process of domesticating (and punishing) the danger posed by the eyes of women when they assert their ability to see. Many of the ideas developed in feminist theory regarding the relationship between women and the gaze highlight those images that create negative associations between women and their ways of seeing. E. Ann Kaplan (1983: 29), in referring to this "dangerous" relationship, suggests that in patriarchal cinematic representation, the woman who looks becomes masculine—that is, she loses her "femininity" and adopts a masculine role, and she also often becomes ambitious and manipulative. These arguments also resonate with the observations of Mary Ann Doane, who suggests that the image of the woman with glasses (as a cliché for an unattractive woman who is also, at the same time, a dangerous woman) is a cultural manifestation of the fear of and apprehension regarding women who dare to look. According to Doane, a woman with glasses is a woman who "signifies simultaneously intellectuality and undesirability; but the moment she removes her glasses . . . she is transformed into spectacle, the very picture of desire" (1990: 50).

As a starting point, then, the exercise of the gaze is anti-patriarchal, which encounters how both the gaze of the camera and the eyes of the spectator alike are shared by the patriarchal dominance of the moving image. Thus, the intrusion of sound on images can imply, at once, a return to the image (a hearing with the eyes) and an interruption of the continuity of male dominance, even when the universe of sound—and especially the voice—is founded, at least in terms of its relationship with rationality and power, on paternal language. As such, the voice can also be seen as a battlefield for the liberation of women who have been silenced, as well as for languages that have not been considered sufficiently intelligible.

Women Who Dare to Speak

Just as Medusa's gaze is associated with monstrosity, the dangers of the feminine voice can be represented by the beautiful and perilous sirens, who lead those drawn to their singing to their deaths. Once more, to explain how this danger is overcome, we must turn to the image of a hero. It is Ulysses, lashed to the mast as he listens to the sirens singing, who highlights the dangerous seductiveness of the voice and of death. The sirens represent dangerous (and subversive) femininity because they kill those who become enchanted by their voices. In an inverted form of monstrousness, they are monsters without appearing to be such, because they kill through beauty. This aesthetic twist is quite unlike other Greco-Roman divinities that inspire artists, storytellers, and historians (and are always invoked to tell the story of patriarchal heroism). The muses, for example, even though they do not always wish to do so, can tell the truth as they inspire beauty. Women's voices in Western mythology are trapped in an aesthetics founded on the articulated voice (whether monstrous or not). Like the muses, they recount heroic deeds so that poets can narrate them, and, like the sirens, they can take the hero to the depths of danger and death. The muses are, of course, in service to patriarchy—they are the acceptable voice and, therefore, the authorized voice. The sirens, however, represent the beauty of the voice and the danger of extermination: they are the ones who can tempt the hero as he returns to his home (land).

Two additional figures evoke the relationship between women and the voice in Greco-Roman mythology. Both refer to the punishment of women through the voice. The first is Echo, who falls in love with Narcissus and, in a romantic dispute that is a by-product of patriarchy, loses the ability to use language. (Hera, seeking, as usual, to defend Zeus's authority and her own authoritative status, leaves Echo unable to articulate language on her own.) Increasingly, Echo's voice becomes one that repeats and echoes; expelled from *logos* and meaning, she becomes a succession of besotted phonemes. The other figure is Cassandra, who is not just a voice, but a quasi-*logos*, a seer who tells and foretells. She is quasi-*logos* because reason is not enough: she lacks authority. She speaks an articulated language, but her words fall flat in the face of people's incredulity. No one believes her and that is her punishment. Punished by Apollo for not allowing herself to be seduced, she is permitted to learn the art of divination in his temple, but she is condemned to never be sufficiently convincing. It is not the production of the voice, as in the case of Echo, that is at stake; it is the reception of the voice where her voice grows weak. Even though she has the ability to foresee and foretell, Cassandra is doomed to a voice that fades in the face of her listeners' doubts. Echo cannot say, and Cassandra cannot be believed.

The Nearly Inaudible on the Other Side of the Mirror

Until recently, many of the discussions about Argentine cinema have focused on male ocularcentrism. While these discussions may have differed in terms of levels of sexism or heteronormativity, it is indisputable that Argentine cinema has lacked (or used to lack) a gender framework, making it a male-centric cinema (with María Luisa Bemberg proving the rule through her liberal, feminist exception). Laura Mulvey's analysis of classic US cinema is relevant to this scenario as well: throughout the history of Argentine cinema, the centrality of the male gaze has reduced women to objects "so they can be said to connote *to-be-looked-at-ness*" (Mulvey 1975 [1989]: 19). Born of this wound, the feminist's answer, upon viewing herself from the other side of the screen, might be the same as Alice's: to pass through the looking glass in order to see what the camera's framing cropped out and to listen to the voices that have been silenced.

Argentine cinema from the mid-1990s provides a framework for a variety of gazes that offer, from different perspectives, a gender-based reading of the same concerns that preoccupy the new male filmmakers. All of these filmmakers emphasize the weakening of social and political bonds as a consequence of the neoliberal turmoil of the nineties. Through new aesthetic approaches that fracture and fragment in the face of the narrative image, these filmmakers grapple with an already fractured social and symbolic reality at the end of the twentieth century and the start of the new millennium. The new cinema expresses unease in the face of the transformations that go hand in hand with the triumphant discourses of economic and cultural globalization, and points to the visible and invisible faces of neoliberal discourse. In response to both the dominant discursivity and the cinematic interpretations of the directors of the eighties and nineties, a new group of women filmmakers emerges in the ten shorts included in *Historias breves* [*Short Stories*] from 1995. They grapple with this sense of unease through a gender-based lens that makes visible how social and symbolic fissures affect the lives of women, as well as the different kinds of violence perpetrated against them.

In one of the most important contributions to the discussions of the new Argentine cinema, Gonzalo Aguilar proposes a gaze from the "otros mundos" [other worlds] that inhabit the body of work of these new filmmakers. Aguilar argues that this new cinema involves a blurring of past worlds and substitution of new ones, which, though they may lack clear outlines, are just as intense as the ones that have vanished (2006: 7). Included among these "other worlds" are those that trace gender through the splitting of the image (which is itself linked to the patriarchal realm of the visible) and through the plasticity of the sound (especially through those voices that move away from or question *logos* and the masculine rationality of language, or that, even as they strive to replicate them, emit echoes that transform them).

Many late-twentieth century and early-twenty-first century filmmakers call into question the visual realm through their fragmentation of images and through their exposure of the challenges inherent in any attempt to create visual narratives. This concern is expressed in various ways, such by cropping the image in unusual ways when framing bodies (*La ciénaga* [*The Swamp*]; *Por tu culpa* [*It's Your Fault*]); using a still camera that only records the movements that take place in front of the lens (*El cielito* [*Little Sky*]); chopping up the narrative sequence to emphasize visual images that halt the narration (*El cielito*; *El niño pez* [*The Fish Child*]); explicitly showing us images of characters or directors with their cameras (*Cielo azul, cielo negro* [*Blue Sky, Black Sky*]; *Los rubios*; *La cámara oscura* [*The Camera Obscura*]); repeating takes and going out on the street to look for a random story (*Cielo azul, cielo negro*); recording with a photograph the last moment before a suicide (*Cuando ella saltó* [*When She Jumped*]); and even highlighting their problematic relationship to the visual and visibility through constant references to seeing, knowing how to see, not being able to see, the differences between seeing and looking (*La ciénaga*; *La cámara oscura*; *Cuando ella saltó*), and characters who peer, whether literally or metaphorically, "through the peephole" (*La niña santa* [*The Holy Girl*]; *La rabia* [*Anger*]).

These narrative images are accompanied, and often interrupted, by different types of voices. Voices that are articulated and those that never are, voices that promise to tell the truth and those that lie, voices that exist outside the visual field and those that are affirmed as omniscient, as well as singing voices, whispers, the echo of the maternal body, labored breathing, and screams. So many voices, so many modulations, and so much silence in the form of noise: the noise we hear when we cannot hear the materiality of the voice, when the vocal sound does not touch us, when the presence of the voice is postponed and remains outside the acoustic field—we hear only noise that evokes silence. The acoustic realm can also mark the presence of concealed emotions. Whether through stifled shouts or through barely audible whispers; whether as excess (the tinnitus in *La niña santa* that accompanies an inability to see), as lack (the girl in *La rabia* who expresses herself only through drawings, a visual format, but who cannot speak), or as distortion (the protagonist's voice and its echoes and repetitions in *Cielo azul, cielo negro*), sound seems to point to what remains invisible in the process of visual representation. Singing also serves to dislocate the narrative image (*La cámara oscura*; *El niño pez*) and to bring into view the presence of the feminine within a maternal logic that evades the norms of patriarchy and heterosexism. In many of these instances, these voices restore what Luce Irigaray calls the "body-against-body" in relation to the mother, making visible and audible the space–voice relationship, as well as languages and modulations that were forgotten or marginalized.

Theories of the Gaze and the Voice

I would like to recognize the feminist theorists of gender and film who have had the greatest influence on my approach in this book. From them I have learned to read images, movements, voices, synchronies, and desynchronizations, and to rethink to what extent aesthetics is also political when talking about cinema (particularly a cinema dominated by the male gaze and voice).

The theoretical approaches of Laura Mulvey, E. Ann Kaplan, Teresa de Lauretis, Kaja Silverman, and Mary Ann Doane have opened new lines of inquiry regarding gender, subjectivity, the gaze/look (whether of the camera, the spectator, or a character), and the acoustic record. Feminist contributions to film studies begin with a reflection on the male gaze and on what Mulvey calls *the patriarchal unconscious of the gaze*. Nevertheless, the ways of imagining a feminist gaze vary and, as in the cases of Kaplan and de Lauretis, are also studied in relation to other spaces of otherness and marginalization.

Key in this respect is the work of Laura Mulvey in her seminal, and controversial, 1975 essay "Visual Pleasure and Narrative Cinema." For Mulvey, it is the patriarchal unconscious that defines erotic gazes and the subject/object divide in terms of gender. If the gaze is determined by male pleasure, then the spectator is fundamentally male, while women, Mulvey claims, are the depicted objects. According to Mulvey (1975 [1989]: 19), both pleasure and the reaffirmation of its subjective nature (within the patriarchal discourse) confirm the male privilege of the gaze. It is the patriarchal unconscious itself that determines the active erotic participation of the viewer as voyeur. Thus, film (as part of the ideological apparatus of the patriarchy) reinforces the position of the male subject as a dominant subject through the processes of spectator identification and meaning-making for the filmic text.

The primary critique of Mulvey's argument has to do with the essentialist nature of her approach, which in this case reflects the difficulty of categorizing the spectator in purely binary terms (male/female) and, thus, of avoiding a consideration of gender. In the 1980s, feminist theory revisited Mulvey's initial analysis and began to de-essentialize the debate about gaze and spectator. E. Ann Kaplan (1983: 19–25), for example, criticizes Mulvey's position and claims that both men and women can be looking subjects, and that, as such, the gaze is not an exclusively male domain. For her part, Teresa de Lauretis (1984: 144) suggests that women, as spectators, can adopt a masculine position even as they identify with female characters, reflecting a duality in the interpellation of the female spectator in terms of her subjectivity. Mulvey herself had already, in 1981, revised her 1975 approach in "Afterthoughts on Visual Pleasure and Narrative Cinema," referring to a masculinization process that takes place in the female viewer. In her classic *The Desire to Desire: The Woman's Film of the 1940s*, Mary Ann Doane also asks about the female spectator of movies in which female characters are represented through images of sacrifice and humiliation and rethinks the poses that women held in the face of these images, which tend to erase them as looking subjects and affirm them as merchandise. For Doane, these poses, including feminist mimicry, transvestitism, and the masquerade of femininity, manage to defy dominion over bodies, even if only sporadically.

In these approaches, the binaries of both man/woman and masculine/feminine can be considered in terms of their prevailing essentialism, which, as De Lauretis (1987: 9) suggests, is an obstacle to rethinking the cinematic gazes of historical women due to the conflict between "woman" as an essentialist representation and "women" as historical subjects. De Lauretis's pioneering works *Alice Doesn't* (1984) and *Technologies of Gender* (1987) examine the pleasure of the gaze and the empowerment that the act of looking offers the female spectator, even when the images that she identifies with are images of submission. De Lauretis examines women's mode of identifying with film, particularly referring to the pleasure and power that they obtain as spectators, and focuses on the complex identification process of the female spectator as she alternates between the two positionalities: feminine (generally associated with the image) and masculine (generally associated with looking). This identification, De Lauretis claims, is produced through the act of looking. Upon exercising the gaze (understood as masculine in feminist and psychoanalytical analyses), the woman adopts a masculine position (1984: 142–44), and, in that precise, yet paradoxical moment, the female spectator obtains both power and the pleasure of being situated in a masculine space of power and desire. Nevertheless, this repositioning of herself as a subject of the gaze is concomitant with a process of refeminization. As a spectator, she identifies with the narrative image of woman—that is, with the image of woman as object and with the negation of a feminist subjectivity, pleasure, and agency. It seems relevant here to recall this analysis because it puts into play a power dynamic. The process of feminization and masculinization takes place at once, even though they are explained as sequential processes, and this superimposition of attributes, agency, and absences is made present in the act of looking. Many of these observations go beyond the rethinking of the female spectator and are also useful for thinking about the filmmaker's gaze and her positioning with regard to the image, to the visual regime (and its heteronormative masculinity), and above all, to other women.

If the question of the female spectator was central to some of the first and most productive discussions on gender and film, then the shift from an emphasis on the gaze to the question of visibility underscores a new set of discussions about aesthetics, ethics, and politics. By the nineties, Kaja Silverman's *The Threshold of the Visible World* breathed new life into the question of the visible. In that book, Silverman takes up the image of the threshold proposed by Lacan to explore the relationship between the visual and the subjectivity-forming process of the person who looks at an image and, as a spectator, enters both a social world and a circuit of meanings. Here the visual is an intermediary between the subject and the visible world that, on the one hand, establishes us as subjects and, on the other, is constituted as meaningful by ourselves—that is, is granted a meaning that, in part and only ever in part, was previously allotted. Those images can be read as thresholds that, like the Lacanian mirror, serve as throughways between the subject and the world. The image's significance is granted through the cultural repertoire of available meanings. The act of looking cannot expose visible worlds other than those that have already been conceived. Silverman engages with the notion of identification but also invokes the possibility and challenge of being positioned as a subject in *méconnaissance*, especially when those visible worlds represent forms of otherness that attempt to break free of the hegemonic systems of representation and signification that confine them to invisible spaces. It is in this alternative to normative identification that Silverman finds an ethical way of looking as a practice in which subjects can be constituted as such through a duel with themselves, which means an identification with an other's existence in its radical difference.

The analysis of the visible implies an examination of framing and, therefore, of what remains outside the frame and is made invisible through exclusion. This discussion is central for rethinking how things are made visible in not merely visual but also political terms, as a process that inevitably produces invisibility through framing. Making new subjects or new interpretations and aesthetics visible is a work in progress and an attempt to continue to expand the place of the visible, which is, as Jacques Rancière claims, where places, times, parts and positions are distributed, and where the realm of law comes into play (2004: 20). Following Rancière (1999: 1–4, 21–24, 36–40), this expansion also implies an intersection between the voice (as *logos* and as sound) and the visible (and invisible) to try to rearticulate the two in political terms. I am referring here to the visible in the political sense given by Rancière when he states that "[p]olitics revolves around what is seen and what can be said about it, around who has the ability to see and the talent to speak . . ." (2004: 13). According to Rancière, the political is also where the articulated word may offer the key to the losses that take place in the realm of the voice (which is marginal and inaudible), providing access to the setting of *logos*. These remnants are never lost and, though they become invisible, are not inaudible in a feminist interpretation that restores not just the articulated voice (as *logos*/rationality), but also unarticulated voices, such as screams, whispers, breathing, and all those sounds that denote a maternal language.

In addressing the question of sound, Silverman's work, now in *The Acoustic Mirror*, is central for rethinking the intersection of the gaze and the voice, as well as the relationship between acoustic mirrors and fantasy. Silverman focuses on the disconnect between sound and image, as well as their perfect synchronization. In the case of women, perfect synchronization means portraying them through a voice connected to a body. In this synchronization (or entrapment), we see once more the emphasis on the physical body. As Silverman argues, the voice is represented as being anchored in the body, in contrast with the male voice, which is often associated with the transcendent voice-over found in documentaries. This transcendence assigns authority to the voice uncoupled from the body and tied to the *logos* (the voice as narrative authority, or even as reason, as articulated, paternal language).

Mladen Dolar's classic approach to the voice is also crucial in this book, not just in its relationship with meaning or in aesthetic terms, but also as a theory of the voice that pulls from linguistics, metaphysics, ethics, and politics. Dolar starts by moving away from the distinction that Jacques Derrida draws between writing and voice. Apparent are the continuities between sound and meaning, and between the acoustic record and the *logos*. These continuities also constitute an intermediate realm between subject and object. All of these aspects are fundamental in a feminist paradigm that attempts to rethink the approach to the voice through its disobedient zones. Dolar's arguments highlight numerous ambiguities and dualities of the voice as it moves in and out of politics, ethics, language, metaphysics, meaning, and aesthetics.

Works such as those of French feminism regarding the intrauterine relationship—specifically, Julia Kristeva's work on the *chora* and Luce Irigaray's work in *I Love to You* on the relationship with one's own body and with breathing as the path to a union with nature—illuminate the correspondence between sound (especially prelinguistic sound) and the maternal body. Taking these considerations as a point of departure, I understand that the voice's association with the mother (and with the prelinguistic and pre-Oedipal—or para-Oedipal) establishes a new relationship with the body and with the *logos*. Though it can be problematic to essentialize the voice or the feminine in terms of the maternal, which is so culturally loaded with the baggage of male fantasy and the patriarchal economy, I find the maternal voice useful for analyzing a number of instances of the voice, especially those that move away from the articulated, paternal norm and reinforce their ties with the body, with the materiality of sound, and with singing. Even though I may not be convinced that, as Cixous suggests, the sirens are men, I do consider the danger that the sirens represent to be grounded in a masculine projection of fear, desire, and rejection, which associates singing with the maternal voice, and with the place where the genders fuse together and symbolic and social hierarchies are dismantled. The maternal voice, as an excess of masculine rationality, turns out to be a central issue in many of the films analyzed in this book.

For its part, Adriana Cavarero's fascinating study *For More than One Voice*, in particular when she focuses on the political aspect of the voice and takes as her starting point the opposition between *logos* (rationality) and *phone* (voice), is essential to a rethinking of the distinction between the acoustic and the semantic. For Cavarero, the excess of the *logos* is the acoustic, which is irreducible and unruly. Her analysis of the acoustic surplus of logocentric thinking and the visual regime invites us to listen to the voice as something unique (or singular) beyond the meaning it indicates. Both the rhythms of the pre-symbolic and the dialogues that take place in the outer reaches of language (which still constitute language, even if minor or unrecognized as such) are likewise crucial for feminist thought (even though they are not new and can also be addressed through Kristeva's concept of *chora* or Irigaray's *body-against-body*). I would also like to highlight, in Cavarero's work, the relationship between the voice and politics, especially ephemeral, intermittent politics, including the paradoxical relationship between the voice and phallocentrism. In many cases, it is the maternal voice that rewrites, through song and through sound and without paternal articulation, women's relationship with the feminine voice as an excess. This essentialist voice can be questioned, not just because of its essentialism but also because, ultimately, it, too, is normative within the paradigms of the possibility of a maternal (or at least not-paternal) language. Nevertheless, as I hope to show in these pages, the maternal voice is used in Argentine film to give an account of that other register of voice, which is never completely crushed. It is the voice that abruptly invades the image. In various instances in this book, I refer to that voice as intermittent, nomadic, and untranslatable, and not always as pre-Oedipal or prelinguistic (and when I do use those terms, it is in order to call into question that time-based model and propose simultaneity instead). Simultaneity does not allow the voice to be listened to many times, but it does allow it to be articulated and to call into question the paternal voice and the *logos*.

I turn again to Cixous, who writes that patriarchal thought has transformed woman into a parenthesis, "always repressed or invalidated as a woman, tolerated as a non-woman" (1996: 75). Moreover, she also claims that a woman is "accepted" only if she "effaces herself, acts the man, speaks and thinks that way" (1996: 75). Though the point of departure for this assertion may be essentialist, assuming an antiessentialist position here might erase the violence on which the concept of woman rests, which coincides, as Catherine Malabou suggests, with women's place in a particular patriarchal fantasy. In an era in which essentialism is under attack, Malabou offers a defense of it, pointing to the political consequences of negating such an essence. Women are born, Malabou says, from a wound, from violence, and it is that essence that women share (2011: 92–98). Yet that wound (or that parenthesis, to use Cixous's words) is, at the same time, the center of their resistance. Analogously to the feminine lens of Irigaray, Cixous, and Kristeva, resistance is ambiguous and dual: subordination and insubordination. Malabou takes a different route and uses plasticity as a core category of her analysis to evoke both the notion of malleability (plasticity as the ability to give form or receive it) and the capacity for reconnection (the ability to restore or rebuild circuits). Additionally, for Malabou, plasticity also entails the possibility of exploding and being destroyed, after which a new form emerges. In sum, plasticity, as a concept, is linked to subordination, insubordination, and the capacity to shape new routes of relationships but also to leave behind, to be destroyed, and to explode. When Malabou refers to "woman" and defends the essentialism of the concept, she is thinking about "the minimal concept for woman," that is, "woman" as subjected to violence as a "remainder, burning, plastic" (2011: 94). In this book, I am thinking about image and voice in terms of their plasticity, explosiveness, and destructiveness (for example, in relation to screams, or the sudden intrusion of sound into the image, or the image itself that is burned and destroyed). And I am also thinking about them in terms of malleability, the reconstruction of new visual or aural circuits, and especially the intersection between the two.

This book is organized into seven chapters. I begin with María Luisa Bemberg in Chapter 1, rereading some of her films with an eye to where voice and gaze intersect, as well as to their relationships with masculinity and femininity. Bemberg studies the use of the transcendent voice, which stands in contrast to the silenced, disciplined voice, and of the image, which captures women's subordination. Her films take the initial confinement of her protagonists as a starting point for exploring possible lines of flight that are often established through the voice. For Bemberg, the realm of the gaze seems to be a minefield and, if women's gaze can have a place, then that can only occur intermittently. And, although her films explore the intersections of female gazes and looks, it is in the transcendent voice that the possibility of feminist subversion resides.

In Chapter 2, I continue with Lucrecia Martel and *La ciénaga*, *La niña santa*, and *La mujer sin cabeza* [*The Headless Woman*], three films whose aesthetics make the patriarchal gaze visible. Her emphasis on the gaze points to the difficulty of seeing, but also to an aesthetic of the visible and the invisible (the camera makes her cuts visible and exposes that which is blurry, is opaque, or cannot be seen). It is through sound and, more specifically, voices that her films hint at what has not been entirely dominated by visual and acoustic heterosexist control. These voices cannot be discerned; they are whispers or voices that are unintelligible, but which remain present, though nearly inaudible. Martel does not deny women the possibility of looking; what she denies is the possibility of seeing or hearing clearly. What is heard with more precision is the articulated language that goes hand in hand with power, either imitating or reproducing it. The key lies in what is not seen—and, especially, in what is not heard but, rather, is inaudible and suggested.

In Chapter 3, I discuss the films of Albertina Carri and the dislocations of the voice, taking as a starting point the desynchronization that she employs in an attempt to give voice to both her disappeared father and her own vision as a little girl in a past, a vision that is now beyond reach. The exploration of the voice can indicate an interrogation of narrative authority in three different instances: shouts, writing, and a voice that is articulated through displacement (sometimes suggesting a body-against-body). Although, at first glance, writing appears to be located in the realm of conventional narrative authority, it is displaced, giving the voice and its modulation a central place in the very possibility of narrating and fracturing narration. In addition, Carri's films place significant emphasis both on the shouting voice that breaks into the linear narrative sequence and on language associated with the body (whether in contact with it or as its displacement). This language is represented by sounds that are not necessarily voices, but which evoke the search for a maternal voice.

Chapter 4 explores both the echo that distorts the male voice and the resonance of the maternal body in *Cielo azul, cielo negro* (dir. Sabrina Farji and Paula de Luque) and *La cámara oscura* (dir. María Victoria Menis). In this chapter, I underscore how the voice offers the possibility of rethinking the echo as something that, rather than failing to accurately repeat the masculine *logos*, instead exposes the failure of masculine reason. I use Kristeva's concept of *revolt*, Cixous's and Irigaray's concepts of the *maternal body*, and Cavarero's and Doane's work on echoes and the maternal voice to rethink the alchemical transformation that is produced in the aesthetics of these two films. Both films highlight the gaze through the figures of, respectively, a filmmaker and a photographer. By directing the reverberation to the intimate realm and creating echoes of the mother's voice, which is associated with the maternal body and maternal language, both films show how the voice, and the effects of the voice's echoing and reverberation, leads to an interruption of the image, suggesting a switching back and forth between voice and gaze.

In Chapter 5, I approach the voice in political terms and in close relationship with testimonial statements, exploring the audible development of the voice and its possibilities for becoming intelligible. Using Mladen Dolar and Giorgio Agamben as a starting point for reconsidering the *phone*/*logos* and *zoe*/*bios* relationships, as well as Rancière's arguments about the relationship between aesthetics and politics, I analyze Lita Stantic's *Un muro de silencio* [*A Wall of Silence*] to think about the relationship of voice and *logos* to the exception and to the boundary between life and death, as well as to think about the framework of the political voice based on dissent. In considering the articulated voice, which attempts to transmit that other (lost and unrecoverable) voice—that is, the voice as delegation—I also explore the political becoming of the voice through aesthetics. The cinematography and script in Stantic's film function as a privileged space to analyze the multiple discordant and conflicting voices that are put into play and which reorganize the visible and audible realms.

In Chapter 6, I examine the aesthetics of memory and its visual and aural dimensions. To that end, I analyze five of the shorts directed by women filmmakers included in the collection *25 miradas, 200 minutos* [*25 Looks, 200 Minutes*], celebrating Argentina's bicentennial. I analyze these shorts in terms of the relationship of the visual and the acoustic to violence, tracing the circularity and simultaneity that takes place in the transformation of time and space. By emphasizing how the exercise of memory might serve as an alternative to the historian's rigid dividing line between past and present, these shorts suggest the coexistence of the past in the present. The shorts by Sabrina Farji, Lucrecia Martel, Sandra Gugliotta, Albertina Carri, and Paula de Luque shatter the relationship between image and evidence, thus producing a shift away from the documentary format. They also play out different modes of return, signaling, if not the creation of a new meaning, at least a re-vision of past and present time, like an excavation of images and voices. The silences and voices, like acoustic records absent from the historical archives, allow us, as spectators, to immerse ourselves in the surrounding space, pointing to what remains outside the visual frame. The inclusion of what has persistenly been left excluded incites a different understanding of the past by upending the interpretation of events as well as the meanings of their traces, echoes, and residues.

Finally, Chapter 7 discusses a series of tensions related to the voice and silence. The tension between the authoritarian, violent voice and the silence of suicide in María Victoria Menis's *El cielito* serves as a point of departure for thinking about the obliteration of the feminine voice within the framework of gender. Following this analysis, I explore the tension between the voice of subjugation and heterosexist violence in Lucía Puenzo's *El niño pez.* In that film, there is an attempt to nurture voices that not only resist such violence but also resume the narration about subjugation and resistance. A third point of tension is to be found in Anahí Berneri's *Por tu culpa*. In my discussion of this film, I examine the meaning that is reestablished by the pre-/post-linguistic voice amid the voices of male authority, which make sense only through the implementation of authoritarianism. Finally, I turn to Gabriela David's *Taxi, un encuentro* [*Taxi, an Encounter*] to rethink the tension between the dialogic voice and the unarticulated voice of a teenage girl who is witness to a femicide. In all of these cases, the visual and acoustic languages are used to make visible and audible the spaces in which violence remains not only outside the visual field but also outside the articulable. At the same time, this repositioning of the visible and audible takes place according to the contractual elements of grammar, narrative, and dialogue. Thus, it is important to consider both what is narrated as well as what exceeds grammar and narrative norms—that is, the parenthesis and the residues of languages, as well as the excluded, invisible, or untranslatable.

The 2014 anthology *Tránsitos de la mirada: Mujeres que hacen cine* [*Shifts in the Gaze: Women Who Make Movies*] was one of the first efforts to examine Argentine cinema created by women. The editors, Paulina Bettendorff and Agustina Pérez Rial, survey the history of Argentine cinema to explore the absence of women filmmakers prior to the year 2000 and the multiplicity of gazes represented in "discourses, experiences, modes of perception of and about film" after that date (2014: 38). In the anthology, essays by film scholars and filmmakers address the aesthetics of a number of women filmmakers, as well as their experiences as directors and producers in a markedly male world.

Hear Me with Your Eyes is an attempt to look again, after listening to those sounds that began to transform the narrative image. The aural dimension, and above all, the voice often allude to the worlds made invisible and erased by marginalization, violence, sexism, homophobia, abjection, inequality, discrimination, and impunity. These worlds, which are often invisible and unlivable, are registered through the acoustic.[2] The voice also evokes different modulations that point to a surplus in terms of image and *logos*, evoking the maternal body and its sounds, or point to remnants of the annihilation of women's articulated voice, to echoes detached from meaning, as well as to the lover Narcissus and his impossible mirror.

2. Here once again I am building on Judith Butler's work and her exploration of the abject and unlivable (however densely populated) spaces of exclusion and marginalization (1993: 3).

As we attempt to hear with the gaze, the whispers, distorted voices, superposition of voices, screams, singing, noises, and explosions suggest the presence of the feminine as a surplus that invades shots in order to transform them. A woman's singing can transform a masculine fantasy, and continued agitated breathing can be linked to close-ups in a domestic space. The feminine voice might vocalize the violence of the patriarchy, and even dismantle the meaning of masculine texts by repeating them (as echoes) with a different modulation of the voice. Whispers might babble secrets, as well as languages that are either being born or on the brink of death. And, through all of these possible transformations, the intimate voice becomes political.

CHAPTER 1

Transcendence, Gaze, and Voice: María Luisa Bemberg

MANY OF THE DISCUSSIONS that emerged in Argentina in the mid-1990s highlight the *nuevo cine* and its clear break with the cinema that preceded it, especially the cinema of the 1980s. Yet, if we consider the articulation of gender from perspectives that examine women's position as subjects of the gaze and of the audible voice, we can draw an unbroken line back from many recent filmmakers to the pioneering work of María Luisa Bemberg (1917–1995). By noting this inheritance, I do not mean to suggest that there are no new aesthetics of the gaze or attempts to expand and multiply women's visions and the voices or sounds that go with them. Instead, I wish to posit Bemberg's contribution as a vital landmark in the history of women filmmaking in Argentina and to underscore that the development of her approach to the gaze—as well as the dislocated (if only intermittently) acoustic realm of masculine, heteronormative logic—can be seen as a significant precedent for today's feminist discussions.

From her first films, Bemberg has called into question the very relevance of the masculine control of sight, instead exploring the relation between women and the gaze within a framework that, while it starts out as essentialist, eventually becomes more oriented toward an examination of difference. There is in her films a rejection of what Laura Mulvey calls women's "exhibitionist role" (1975: 19). Her work reveals a clear concern with subverting the image of women as objects of the patriarchal gaze associated with male pleasure. Though it exists within the parameters of a monolithic logic that represents all women in terms of Bemberg's class privilege, the image of confinement serves as a fundamental starting point for analyzing all those gazes, voices, and sounds that attempt to find ways to escape the suffocation created by prevailing heteronormative norms and their regulation of how women are walled in (and especially how they are walled in the home and in the convent).

In this chapter, I explore not so much the feminist, consciousness-raising gaze of Bemberg's earliest films (*Momentos* [*Moments*] from 1981, or *Señora de nadie* [*Nobody's Wife*] from 1982), which reflect a more intimate approach to the portrayal of women, but instead the articulation of a new feminist vision that starts with *Camila* (1984), and the intersection between domestic oppression and the mechanisms of public repression in this film. Then, I examine the reconceptualization of the gaze/look and the starting point of Bemberg's emphasis on difference in her autobiographical *Miss Mary* (1986), in which the protagonist's vision is depicted through different visual positionalities. The more essentialist version of the female gaze starts to fall apart, leading instead to an examination of tensions and differences and of looking relations. Her last two films—*Yo, la peor de todas* (1990; *I, the Worst of All*) and *De eso no se habla* (1993; *I Don't Want to Talk About It*)—also reflect complex, fragmentary, and varying visions, as well as sonic elements (especially voicework), to depict the intermittent emergence of images that escape the monitoring of the dominant gaze, but which are still subjected to scrutiny. The possibility (or lack thereof) of the transcendence of the feminine voice becomes in these films intertwined with the transcendence of feminist visions, a transcendence that is linked to the suspension of the synchronization of the voice-body and an emphasis on image-voice-thought.

Gaze, Sound, and Feminism: Some Considerations

The question of the place and relevance of the female gaze is central to Bemberg's films, especially as she begins to question her initial essentialism, which led to a crisis of representation in her films from the 1990s. After her first films, which exhibit a militant, consciousness-raising feminist agenda, Bemberg seems to develop a series of conflicting frameworks, which are counterposed and juxtaposed. Through these frameworks, she examines the cracks both in the patriarchal gaze and in feminist visions. One of the metaphors that Bemberg uses is the shifting of the camera from one shoulder to the other, marking a shift in perspective or angle (Burton-Carvajal, 1999: 338). Though the camera is defined as a metaphor for the patriarchal gaze, this movement (from one shoulder to the other) can begin to dismantle the rigid, gendered framework that Mulvey applies to the relationship between the gaze (which Mulvey argues is only ever male) and the image (which is only ever female).

Moving now to the relationship between gender and voice, Kaja Silverman's theory is relevant for thinking about acoustic mirrors of patriarchal representations and the emphasis on the male voice, or, more specifically, how men's voices are emphasized as subjects of interpretation (the example she provides is the documentary voice-over, which is generally a male voice). As Silverman sees it, women are always reduced to their physical image (the synchronization of body and voice), while male voices achieve transcendence and knowledge. This shift from the voice associated with materiality to the voice associated with *logos* can be seen in Bemberg's work, which affirms the transcendence of women's voices, as well as the dual use of the female voice. On the one hand, there is a more articulated and audible voice that reproduces hegemonic norms; on the other, there are other voices that question those norms, whether in whispers (such as expressions of desire that disrupt the normalizing paternal voice) or in the desynchronization of the physical image (such as transcendent voices that defy the monopoly of male transcendence of the voice). Relevant here is Silverman's warning that analyzing only narrative images (without sound) means setting aside narrative control (acoustic and visual) and the possible zones of tension that can arise between sound and image. According to Silverman, what is in play is the affirmation of male transcendence and the reduction of women's voices to mere corporeality, as if her reality were limited to the contours of her body (1988: 70–71).

Bemberg's work on the gaze seems to suggest that recovering one's sight is a nearly impossible task. There is a recovery but, at the same time, a loss. This loss is repeated in the last moments of almost all of her films, when she portrays the annulment of the central female gaze or when the male voice ends up narrating even the recovery of that gaze. The final images in *Camila*, *Miss Mary*, *Yo, la peor de todas*, and *De eso no se habla* represent a farewell to (and thus a loss of) the vision the films attempt to explore. At the same time, while the protagonist's gaze is either suppressed or departed from in these films, something remains in suspense, whether a voice that transcends the image (*Camila*, *Yo, la peor de todas*), a photographic image that never appears visually in the film, even though it is present through sound (*Miss Mary*), or a recovered gaze that moves toward the edges of the visual field (*De eso no se habla*).

From the Personal to the Political

From *Momentos* (1981) to *De eso no se habla* (1993), there is a shift from the monolithic, essentialist feminism of Bemberg's earlier films to the feminism of differences in her later ones, a transition that nevertheless remains within the cultural code of Latin American feminism of the period.[3] In the case of *Momentos*, the gender transgression (the film had to be reviewed by the censors of the last military dictatorship and was therefore limited by it) is anchored in the intimate look at a widow who remarries and has a brief affair, during which she recalls fragments from her past, especially the tragic loss of her first husband and her son. The exploration of Lucía's subjective world and of a vision tied to her sexual desire, as well as to her grief, is shaped by an exercise of remembrance. There is an affirmation of Lucía's existence as a subject of desire and memory, though her eyes (especially with regard to her lover) seem to be dependent on the transcendent voice of her husband, who provides the key to the interpretations that the film proposes.[4] *Señora de nadie* (1982), written before *Momentos* but filmed afterward because it had not been approved by the censors (King, 2000: 19), centers on the intimate exploration of female subjectivity. The protagonist, Leonor, leaves her husband when she learns that he has a mistress. Her vision, as a constitutive aspect of her identity, seems to be poised here in confrontation with her husband (for whom her identity is defined through her reduction to an object of the gaze). In this film, the voice is tied to the figure of the mother, as well as to the figures of other women in maternal roles who repeat the patriarchal discourse. In both cases, there is an exploration of the protagonist's subjectivity in the moment of confrontation. This confrontation creates a new way of looking

3. Bemberg began her directorial career at fifty-nine years old. Nearly a decade earlier, two of her scripts had been made into movies by male filmmakers, both of them part of the "nueva ola" (new wave): *Crónica de una señora* [*Chronicle of a Lady*] (dir. Raúl de la Torre, 1971) and *Triángulo de cuatro* [*Triangle of Four*] (dir. Fernando Ayala, 1974).

4. The film ends with Lucía returning silently home after her affair is over. Her husband maintains the dominant gaze and transcendent voice (which is not authoritarian but is certainly legitimated by his authority as a psychoanalyst). In fact, he is the one who reveals to the spectator (and to Lucía) how much Lucía's lover resembles her dead husband.

(marked by her stepping out of the home into the outside world) and a new voice (marked by the confrontation with her mother's voice and, at the same time, a confrontation with motherhood as the only space in which women can be defined).[5]

5. Bemberg played an important role in the development of feminism in Argentina. She was one of the founders of the Unión Feminista Argentina (UFA) toward the end of the 1970s. The work of this feminist organization ended with the arrival of the military dictatorship in 1976. Leonor Calvera makes a clear reference to the way the UFA was shaped by feminist theories from abroad—Virginia Woolf, Simone de Beauvoir, Betty Friedan, Kate Millett, Shulamith Firestone (1990: 32–37)—and, in this sense, Bemberg follows the guidelines of Latin American feminism of the time. These first films of hers attempt to give form to that internal voice of women along the lines proposed by Betty Friedan in *The Feminine Mystique*, an enormously influential text for feminism in the 1970s. In this case, there is movement in two directions: toward the exploration of female freedom and toward the critique of the feminine mystique and its mechanisms of seduction and oppression. In her study on *Momentos* and *Señora de nadie*, Catherine Grant (2000: 74) reminds us that one of Bemberg's first publications was in Sur magazine, in an issue devoted to the debate on second-wave feminist issues, where she says, "La mujer debe tomar conciencia de la 'condición femenina' o sea del estado de dependencia política, social y económica en que se encuentra" (102n13) ["Women must become aware of the 'female condition'—that is, the state of political, social, and economic dependence in which they find themselves"]. *Señora de nadie* also posits that female independence is, ultimately, economic independence. And here we can read Bemberg in terms of Simone de Beauvoir, who, in addition to identifying women with otherness (because they are defined with reference to men and humanity itself is defined in terms of masculinity), also suggests that women's liberation would mean "renounc[ing] all the advantages conferred upon them by their alliance with the superior caste" (1957: xxvii). For Beauvoir, the risk of women's freedom is as much metaphysical as it is economic (1957: xxi). Beauvoir asserts that, after rejecting oppression (expressed as privilege in terms of material protection), women would then be able to affirm their own existence. These first two films by Bemberg, though transgressive in terms of gender, reflect a foreign feminism that, as Eduardo Rojas suggests, is out of step with the disappearances, the human rights violations, and the mothers going out into the public squares and reformulating what it means to be a mother (and not through a feminist lens). Rojas repeats the famous phrase "I didn't know" that characterized the decision not to see and not to know during the years of repression and reminds us that Lucía and Leonor are uttering those

In 1984, with her film *Camila*, Bemberg shifts from a vision anchored in intimacy to one that portrays the intersections between the domestic and the political. Through a love story, Bemberg examines how authoritarianism has shaped both the public and the private spheres. With *Camila* (using the melodrama format and with the limitations on the representation of the female protagonist that such format implies), Bemberg gives a gendered historical reading to establish the connections between politics in the household and in the public space. Portraying the domestic sphere as one of confinement (Camila's mother remarks in the film, "the best prison is the one you can't see"), Bemberg sketches out an authoritarianism that is as much private as it is public by telling an impossible love story amid the battles between *unitarios* and *federales* during the nineteenth-century Rosas government. Although the gaze is represented through political surveillance (which is intertwined with surveillance in the domestic sphere) and ecclesiastical surveillance, Camila's eyes are associated with that of her paternal grandmother, La Perichona, who opens the film with the question "Tell me, do you like love stories?" introducing what will be key to the camera's gaze. Camila's eyes thus embrace the transgression of norms and she ends up being punished.[6] Camila becomes a victim

---

words "a coro con miles de hombres y mujeres que eligieron no saber del horror de la dictadura y asumir un grado de complicidad que el país entero aún no ha terminado de saldar" (2002: 72) ["in chorus with thousands of men and women who chose not to know about the horror of the dictatorship and thus took on a degree of complicity that has not yet been fully settled with the country as a whole"]. Approaching these films solely from a feminist perspective forces us to remove them from their cultural and political contexts and produces in the (feminist) spectator the following paradox: to identify as a woman, it is also necessary to identify with indifference to the terror of the Argentine military dictatorship.

6. Ana Perichón de O'Gorman appears at the start of the film, arriving at the O'Gormans' house as we hear Camila's questions: "¿Por qué la encierran, porque es espía?" ["Why do they have her locked up? Is she a spy?"]. La Perichona is an enormously controversial figure: married to Tomás O'Gorman, she had been the lover of the viceroy Santiago de Liniers. She escaped to Brazil with her children and Liniers before he was named viceroy (Tesler, 2000: 65). Later, she was exiled to Brazil over suspicions that her family was conspiring against Spain, and later still expelled from Brazil as a spy. She is a female transgressor type who ends her days a prisoner in the tower of the family home.

not only of gender norms (which place her in the private realm) but also, and especially, of the political struggles between *unitarios* and *federales*.[7] This film exposes the movement (or, rather, the spilling out) of gender norms from private isolation into the public discourse. History is interpreted here through the lens of the rights-deprived subjectivities that dwell between those spaces. In the face of the failure of the transgression represented by Camila and Ladislao Gutiérrez (in which Camila is a nonexistent historical and political subject), Bemberg represents the possibility of restoring both the woman's role as a subject of the gaze and the transcendence of her voice.

Camila's love story is narrated in whispers. In the confessional, still unaware that her confessor is the new priest, she talks about a dream in which she cannot stop looking at a moaning woman, until ultimately realizing that the woman is herself. Her whisper and the image in her dream reveal her own unconfessed desire. And, later, also in a whisper, she confesses her love to Ladislao in the confessional, a space reserved for the Church to exercise control over bodies and their excesses.

Fear of the spectacle of violence is also expressed through the gaze/look (both that of the camera and those of its characters) and through sound (as the flip side of the whisper: the shout). The death of Mariano, the bookseller, and the public display of his body are narrated through Camila's eyes, through those of her family, and through the shout that announces the horror. One of the first moments in which we see Camila looking at Ladislao is when the priest violates the norm of silence in the face of violence by speaking from the pulpit. Looking at him implies looking with him at the world around her, despite her father's warnings. The secret love story attempts to

7. The movie includes the negative commentaries that appeared in the Chilean and Uruguayan press, where the *unitarios* used the story of Camila and Ladislao to criticize the Rosas regime. Calvera adds that, after the execution, "los periodistas exiliados de la oposición cambiaron inmediatamente de óptica. Los mismos que habían calificado con machacona insistencia de 'crimen escandaloso' el proceder del cura Gutiérrez, pidiendo que se los penara con el mayor de los castigos que hubiera en la tierra, no vacilaron en afirmar que el fusilamiento de los amantes era 'monstruoso'" (1986: 153) ["the exiled journalists of the opposition immediately changed their tune. The very same ones who had, with ponderous insistence, called Father Gutiérrez's conduct a 'scandalous crime,' demanding that he be sentenced to the nation's highest punishments, did not hesitate to declare the lovers' execution "monstrous"].

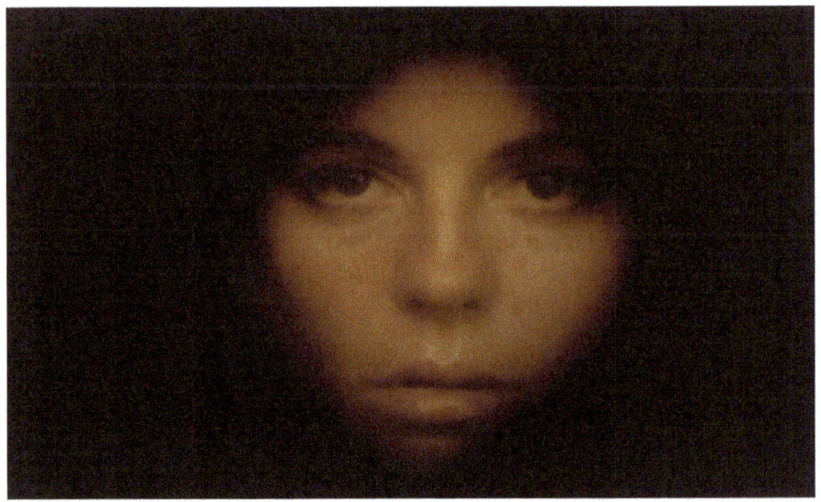

Still Image *Camila* (dir. María Luisa Bemberg, Lita Stantic Producciones, Cinematography Fernando Arribas, 1984)

elude the watchful gaze and, upon being discovered, is punished. The gaze, which is associated with masculine power (of the father, the Church, the state, and even the liberal project that begins with Rosas's defeat), is an authoritarian one. Fleeing from that gaze and thus evading it is one of the avenues of escape proposed in the film. However, such escape is only temporary. After the lovers have fled, a priest recognizes Ladislao and the couple is arrested. In the face of the nearly absolute power of the authoritarian gaze, which is encapsulated in the image of the lovers being blindfolded before their execution by a firing squad, the film points to the edges of the visual field (a space where vision remains interlinked with desire and life) and highlights those edges through sound. Through the use of the voice, Bemberg points to a surplus in the narrative image and to the constitution of the subject within the limits of the visual realm.

The film interrogates the authoritarianism and violence of the state, the use of terror, and the obligatoriness of meaning in Rosas's government. But it also offers a critique of the liberal project by revealing, lurking behind the aim of liberty and equality, the existence of certain subjects, such as women, who are conceived of as being "without rights." In the face of the promise of

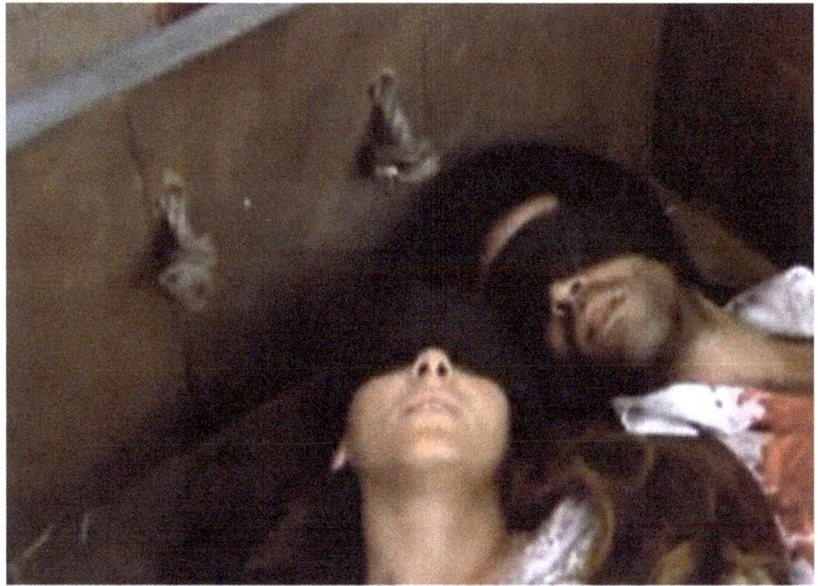

Still Image *Camila* (dir. María Luisa Bemberg, Lita Stantic Producciones, Cinematography Fernando Arribas, 1984)

freedom articulated by the liberals, Camila stands as a metaphor of the failure of that project of liberation. She remains located in an intermediate space between Rosas's watchful eye and the voices (the furious language) of the exiled intellectuals and politicians—the masculine and transcendent voices that will consolidate the Argentine nation after Rosas. Between Rosas's gaze and the voice of liberal opposition to Rosas is Camila, voiceless and gazeless in the historical account. Bemberg imagines that gaze and that voice. Although the film ends with Camila losing the ability to see when her eyes are blindfolded during the execution, the film seems to posit that she does not completely lose the possibility of speaking.

The intimate interrelation between female oppression in the domestic and public spheres, as portrayed in *Camila*, reappears in *Miss Mary* (1986). In this film, Bemberg examines the continuity between family events and national ones. Bemberg acknowledges that the film is her most personal one; while the movie is not strictly autobiographical, Bemberg's own personal experiences serve as the foundation for the film's perspective regarding the dominant class and its oppressive, fraudulent methods. The film recounts the story of the Martínez-Bordagain family from the years 1938 to 1945 and the arrival of a new governess, Miss Mary. The first shots in the film go back to 1930, when Hipólito Yrigoyen was defeated by General Uriburu. The two images from the film's opening scene present the framework of Argentina in the 1930s after Uriburu's coup: a governess prays in English with some children while their parents go out to celebrate the coup d'état. By portraying the 1930s, its dictatorships and electoral frauds, and the applauding ruling class, these two narrative images put us in contact with the coup-happy, repressive, Anglophile tradition of the Argentine aristocracy.

The final sequences refer to the triumph of Juan Domingo Perón in 1945 and depict the masses occupying the streets after Perón's release. The opening and final images present the contrast between two completely divergent historical and political moments. The first is the beginning of the dark years in Argentine history, known as the "década infame" [infamous decade], a period characterized by political persecution, fraud, and murky dealings with foreign corporations, with the attendant scandals. It was a time marked by Argentina's attempts to deepen its ties to England and by a lack of popular political participation. The second moment, however, reflects the events that led up to October 17, 1945, and the administrations of Juan Domingo Perón, with the people's presence in Argentine politics and the beginning of a story that would have a major political impact on the 1960s and 1970s. Framed between these two moments (with two very different visions of the nation), the film explores the governess's complex gaze and a voice that repeats, from the place of her marginalized position, the imperial control of the dominant classes. Located amid an interplay of mirrors that reflect European and Eurocentric gazes on family, politics, gender, and social class, Miss Mary, with her strict rigidity, represents the vision of the Martínez-Bordagains and their desire to educate their descendants in accordance with the rules of the imperial, conservative, and patriarchal order. Nevertheless, Miss Mary's imperial gaze is not that of the Martínez-Bordagains, offering us instead a distant, confused perspective—confusion that becomes evident early on in the movie, when the governess stares in bewilderment at the lady of the house after the latter shows Miss Mary her room "for crying." Her gaze, plagued by racist and imperialist formulations, not only sees commoners as "others" (as the Martínez-Bordagains do) but also extends otherness to the owners of the house, as when she reflects on her journey and says that she would have preferred to go to India because there "it was clear who the natives were."

The film opens in the Martínez-Bordagain residence. As the camera moves into the house, we hear little girls praying in English and see two girls kneeling in prayer. When their parents come into the room, they greet the little girls and announce that they are going out to celebrate the coup. Mary's arrival serves as a continuation of the supposedly stable family setting, which is characterized by rigid patriarchal norms and an imperial vision of Argentina. Nevertheless, in a scene portraying a sexual encounter between Mary and Johnny, the film brings together Miss Mary's complex positionality and her gaze. It is possible to view the sexual encounter as another part of the governess's function (one that, naturally, is not specified in her contract), and both father and son sexualize her from the very start (Carbonetti, 2002: 94–96). Yet I believe that the film also emphasizes Mary's desire, rather than her acquiescence to an unspecified but fully understood role. For example, the play of seduction can be seen when Mary scolds one of the little girls for having entered her room but goes quiet when she discovers it was Johnny who went in and rummaged through her personal effects. My intent is not to deny the existence of the family's implicit pact of submissiveness to male sexual desire, which explains why Johnny enters the governess's room in the middle of the night. Nevertheless, I want to stress that this encounter marks the precise moment in which the sexual initiative shifts from Johnny to Miss Mary. In this way, the camera simultaneously represents both the patriarchal unconscious (and the contract of submission) as well as the intermittent subversion of its surveillance. The spectator sees only the beginning of the encounter, followed by an image of the mother watching her son emerge from the governess's room. The next morning, the mother fires Mary.

The English governess's departure coincides with Perón's victory, and the final sequences in the film emphasize this connection. The atmosphere of repression, conflict, and control that dominates family (and political) life is contrasted with the explosive atmosphere as the masses flood the streets amid cheers of "Perón, Perón!" The counterpoint of past and present is accompanied by this counterpoint between the personal and the political, or, to put it another way, is accompanied by the interweaving of the political in the personal. Miss Mary, as the governess of an aristocratic family, had represented the opposite of Peronism, and her return home coincides with Perón's

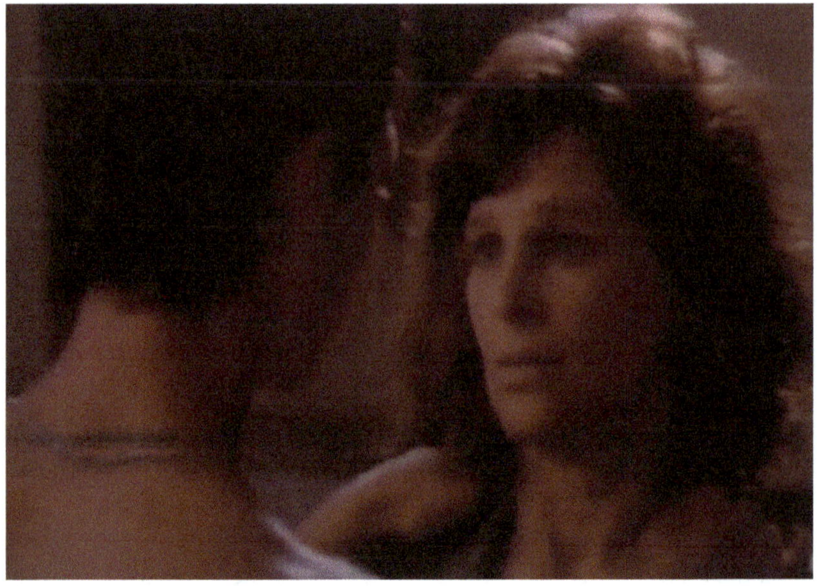

Still Image *Miss Mary* (dir. María Luisa Bemberg, Lita Stantic Producciones, Cinematography Miguel Rodríguez, 1986)

victory, marking both the end of the movie and the end of that narrative gaze that portrays Argentina in terms of an imperial vision.[8] The bifurcation of Miss Mary's vision (her watchful eyes when they monitor norms and her eyes when they express sexual desire), the dual time periods (the 1930s and the 1940s), and the bifurcation of national events (the coup-supporting tradi-

8. In thinking of the imperial gaze, I refer to the contributions of Mary Louise Pratt (1992) and E. Ann Kaplan (1997) regarding the complex othering processes that arise as a result of the dominant (imperial, male, white, and Western) gaze. In an analysis of the imperialist logic in the film, D. Jan Mennell underscores the importance of naming. Miss Mary renames the children: Terry, Johnny, and Caroline (Mennell, 2002: 107). Language is also very important; there are two versions of the film, one in English and the other in Spanish, but even the Spanish version includes dialogues in English. Bemberg herself talks about the relevance of this aspect and its connection to the imperial privilege of England and of English as a language that the colonized must learn, pointing to the scene in which Miss Mary responds, in English, that she has no reason to speak Spanish because "that's the strength of the British Empire. Even the butler is learning English" (Burton-Carvajal, 1999: 347).

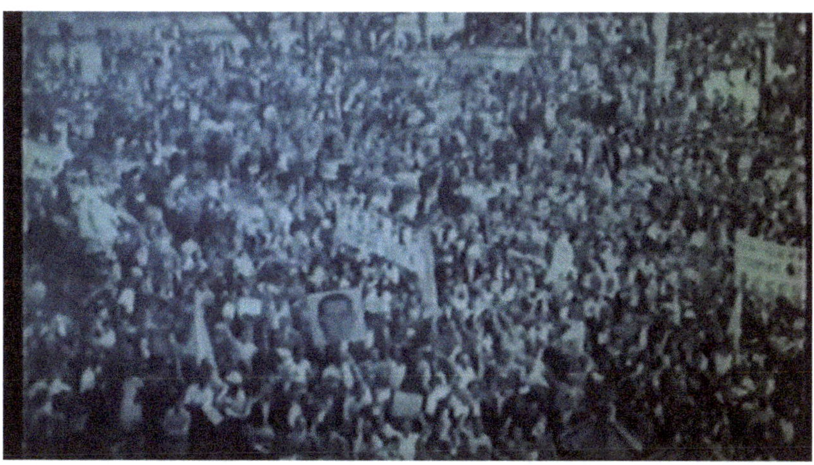

Still Image *Miss Mary* (dir. María Luisa Bemberg, Lita Stantic Producciones, Cinematography Miguel Rodríguez, 1986)

tion associated with the interests of the elites versus Peronism) and languages (English and Spanish) all serve to highlight, on the one hand, the duality in the film (an Argentine identity that strives to be English or a female gaze that attempts to be patriarchal) and, on the other, the complex interchange of differences, forces, gazes, and representations that play out in it.

The end presents another bifurcation of the gaze: Mary's departure, first from the Martínez-Bordagain family's home and then from Argentina. The final images suggest her leaving. The Spanish-language version includes a series of documentary images from 1945 that, in the English version, are substituted with an explanation of the changes in Argentine political life brought about by Peronism.

Miss Mary's departure, which may signal the end of the imperial gaze with the beginning of a new political moment, also underscores a sense of loss that pervades the entire film. Miss Mary's complex gaze is both shaped and constricted by the rigidity of prevailing norms. Revolts take place intermittently through voices and looks associated with desire, but which are unable to maintain their subversive power. The sounds that transcend the narrative images are, paradoxically, the voices of the people that Mary hears from her window in 1945, which signal the masses' presence in the streets and in political life. These are not articulated voices, responding to the language of the ruling class; instead, they mark their presence as an irrepressible sound—that is, as a mark of their existence as a residual other of the gazes portrayed by the film and as a de-structuring surplus of those gazes. The film, which started with that close relationship between domestic practices (the governess praying in English) and political ones (the Argentine ruling class's support for the coup), ends with the Perón's entrance into the nation's political life and, thus, with a new connection between the personal and the political (Miss Mary's story, which ends in Argentina with her return to her homeland after the end of the Second World War) as well as a new view of Argentina (distilled in the documentary images at the end).

From Voices to Transcendence

Through the figure of Sor Juana Inés de la Cruz, Bemberg posits the possibility of transcending eyesight by intersecting it with a voice that is articulated as poetic and philosophical. Set within convent life and shaped by different instances of control via the vigilance of the gaze and confession, *Yo, la peor de todas* (1990) positions the spectator as the one who will peer inside the confinement of the convent. This film suggests that, faced with surveillance and punishment, art and writing create spaces that enable the affirmation of subjectivity. Within this poetic and artistic space, and despite the gaze's overpowering of Sor Juana's life, the transcendence of her voice is able to perpetuate her vision.

Images emphasize chiaroscuro, and the persistent darkness of these images arises not only out of the convent's sense of confinement but also out of the increasing difficulty of seeing (and thus narrating) the nun's life. The narration is based on Octavio Paz's *Sor Juana Inés de la Cruz o las trampas de la fe* [*Sor Juana: Or, the Traps of Faith*]. The interplay of overlapping gazes begins with Paz's version of Sor Juana's life and, at the same time, serves as a starting point for Bemberg's vision. In addition to countering the characters' looks and the watchful gaze of the Church, *Yo, la peor de todas* privileges the Mexican nun's artistic, poetic, and philosophical vision, which becomes a voice through reading, dictation, and performance. The obliteration of her vision by patriarchal power is rewritten at the end of the film. Her voice survives in her writing, and, despite her supposed failure in the face of the patriarchal institution, her writing is able to put it in check.

In her study of the history of women's conspiracy in Mexico, Jean Franco notes that there were cracks in the monitoring system inside the convents

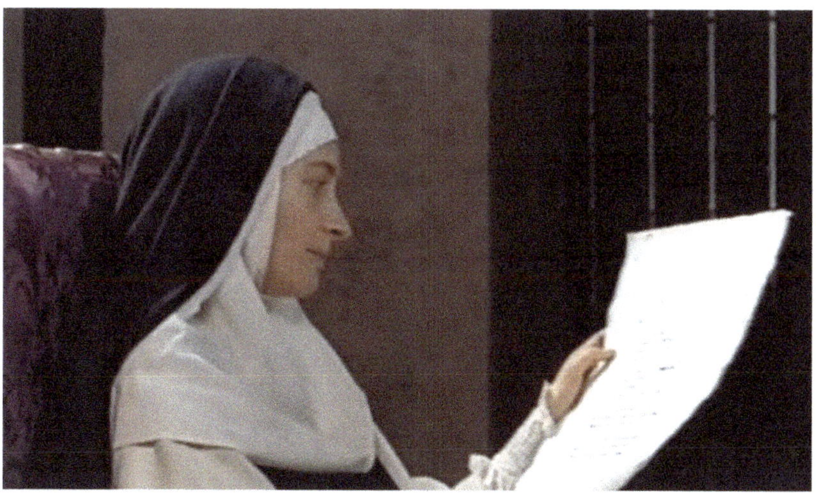

Still Image *Yo, la peor de todas* (dir. María Luisa Bemberg, Lita Stantic Producciones, Cinematography Felix Monti, 1990)

through which a new female culture was able to emerge. Franco refers to two modes of subversion. The first consists of the development of a space of resistance by female mystics and takes place within the irrationality and corporality of the mystical experience (1993: 29–51). Franco observes that, although the convent's monitoring forces the nuns to write their life stories, writing also opens up a space for the expression of desire (1993: 51). Sor Juana subverts this model of resistance (the second mode indicated by Franco) by rebelling against the emotional space upon which the mystics' rebellion is constructed, proposing instead rationality as a feminine attribute.[9]

The film also explores well-articulated voices (associated with discourses of power and the religious and patriarchal hierarchy) and whispers and inaudible, or not fully articulated, voices (situated in the marginal, untranslatable zones of convent life). The film suggests the routine silencing of these more inaudible voices (linked to sounds that are not articulated—that is, in Kristeva's terms, the semiotic). Nevertheless, suppressing these sounds does

9. "Carta Atenagórica" (1690), "Respuesta a Sor Filotea de la Cruz" (1691), and "Autodefensa espiritual" (1682) all contain this assault on patriarchal norms posited as a defense (and an exercise) of Sor Juana's intellectual abilities—that is, of attributes that are traditionally considered masculine.

not forestall a voice's poetics from leaving behind echoes of its existence. Through Sor Juana's "articulated voice" (which, if we follow Kristeva, implies the possibility of having a voice within the parameters of masculinity—that is, of having the father tongue), the sounds and echoes of the language of the body (associated with desire and the mother's body) emerge. Nevertheless, voice and sound cannot be classified so rigidly, because Sor Juana herself has a clear voice, one that is respected and well-articulated. Through this voice, she expresses that other, more intimate voice, the whisper and laughter of her interactions with the vicereine. These two voices sometimes seem to meld in poetic language, and though the film ends with the silence of her room and with the silencing of Sor Juana's voice (that is, with the stamp of the Church's authoritarian voice on her own when she says, "Yo, la peor de todas"), it simultaneously suggests that Sor Juana's voice remains in force in her writing.

This film also explores the gaze through desire, as a subversive rewriting of the Church's control of people's bodies and its patriarchal, authoritarian, and heteronormative paradigms. The reimagining of the nun focuses on desire and looking relations with the vicereine. This intimacy between the vicereine and Sor Juana, highlighted by the camera, grows, starting with the first narrative sequence, and the visual field displaces everything around it, even the articulated voice of her more philosophical texts. For example, when Sor Juana reads paragraphs from her *Primero sueño* to a male audience and is interrupted by the vicereine's arrival, the camera stops capturing Sor Juana and the clergy from an oblique angle and instead pans to show the vicereine's entrance, beginning an interplay of close-ups of the vicereine and Sor Juana. With these shots, everything else disappears from the frame. Later, the encounter between Sor Juana and the vicereine continues to emphasize the erotic tension. The camera starts showing Sor Juana from the vicereine's perspective. At the same time, we hear the question that drives the vicereine's desire: "What is Juana like with herself, when she's alone, when nobody's watching her?" The camera moves away from the vicereine's gaze and captures the two women in a medium shot as Sor Juana removes her veil. Yet that clarity regarding Sor Juana gradually disappears, and we see her in profile, as if in darkness, while we see the vicereine and her desire-filled gaze clearly. On the one hand, what is underscored is the action of looking and desiring rather than the object of desire. On the other, there is an exploration of the gaze and of desire, as well as of the exercise of power implicit in this looking relation.[10] This scene, somehow, unsettles the patriarchal norms of the camera's gaze and a clear differentiation between the gaze's male subject-position and its female object. Here the camera emphasizes a female subject who looks and feels pleasure, while also pointing to power relations in the deployment of the erotic gaze.

Sor Juana's voice is multiple, sometimes audible and sometimes completely inaudible. It is a voice that seeks to affirm a subjectivity within the parameters of a patriarchal institution (and in that sense is in line with paternal law). At the same time, it is unable to pass for an acceptable voice (that is, one that is either sufficiently masculine or sufficiently submissive). Her poetry is the voice that modulates her passions, that dismantles and puts in check the powerful voice of the patriarchy of the Church and the viceroyal culture of the seventeenth century. There is also important work with silence, especially in long shots that show only the image of a silent Sor Juana, which is contrasted with the superimposed laughter or voices of the nuns. As with Kristeva's maternal voice, sound in this case can guide us to the semiotic—the prelinguistic realm, the pre-Oedipal order—and to a shift from thinking of the process of identification based on the image in the mirror to one based on the edges of the visual frame and to a questioning of the visual through the audible (in this case, rhythms, whispers, or silences).[11]

Nevertheless, the relationship with the maternal sometimes seems somewhat ambivalent, and the figure of the mother in the film (and generally in all of Bemberg's films) serves to reproduce the patriarchal voice. Unlike the distorting echo, which calls into question the order of words, the reproduction of the patriarchal voice articulates a paternal mandate. I will return now

10. Omar Rodríguez analyzes the film in terms of the axis of power and, above all, the film's emphasis on the difficulty of successfully confronting institutionalized powers and their mechanisms of coercion. See Rodríguez, "Poder, institución y género en *Yo, la peor de todas*," *Revista Canadiense de Estudios Hispánicos* 27.1 (2002): 139–156

11. For a discussion of the maternal body and the voice, see Kristeva's *Desire in Language: A Semiotic Approach to Literature and Art* (New York: Columbia University Press, 1980), and *Revolution in Poetic Language* (New York: Columbia University Press, 1984).

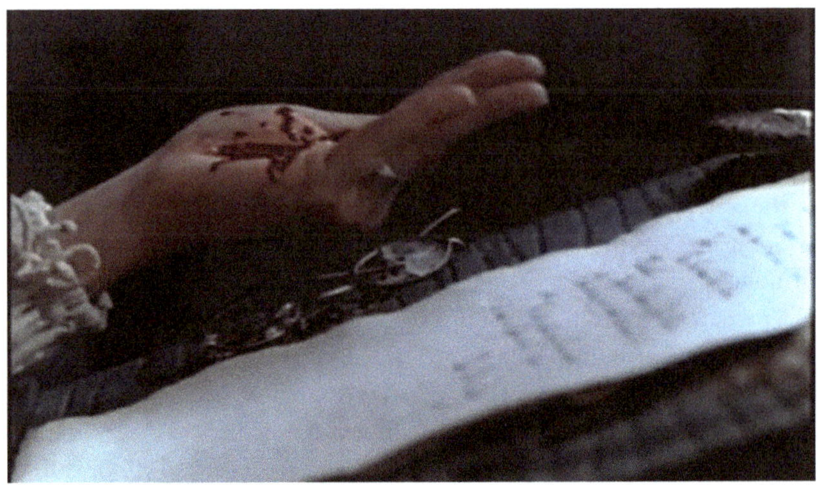

Still Image *Yo, La peor de todas* (dir. María Luisa Bemberg, Lita Stantic Producciones, Cinematography Felix Monti, 1990)

to maternal language and to Kaja Silverman, who argues that, in Irigaray's and Kristeva's respective works on the pre-Oedipal stage and the pre-language stage, the maternal voice remains grounded in the physicality of the body. Because Silverman's approach highlights the transgressive possibilities of desynchronization between sound and body—that is, the disembodiment of the voice and its relocation (off-screen) and resignification as transcendent—the centrality of the body in Irigaray's and Kristeva's theories impedes the possibility of transcendence.[12] Nevertheless, we might argue that *Yo, la peor de todas* offers an articulation of both manifestations of the voice, practically overlapping. The intimate babbling persists outside the articulated instances of language, and poetic language is able to express different modulations of the voice. There is a desynchronization of the voice, through which the voice is separated from the image, thus signaling its transcendence. When Sor Juana's poetry or fragments of her letter are read by others (whether members of the Church or of the royal court), we see the rebellious mark of the transcendence of her voice, which is monitored, punished, and undermined. And, in

12. If we follow Kristeva, that voice is transcendent because it continues to be a masculine, or masculinized, paternal voice—that is, one associated with the dominant language, the only language of transcendence.

the end of the film, with her confession, it is finally silenced. The final shots of the film depict her as mute and unmoving, her death imminent. The end suspends and extinguishes Sor Juana's gaze through the cessation of her writing, but it also invites us to reflect on this loss (the loss of writing, loss of the gaze) and her living on as her writing becomes public. In any case, the vicereine's question remains, "What is Sor Juana like when nobody's watching?" Though there is an attempt to answer it, Bemberg's visual exploration reinforces the limits of the visual realm and points to the difficulty of seeing. The film affirms the impossibility of visually recovering those spaces that resist exposure. This impossibility problematizes the pertinence of the cinematic image, while also pointing to the transcendence of the voice, a voice recorded in writing that, though it goes quiet in the final silence, manages to persist.

From the Other Side of the Mirror

In *De eso no se habla* (1993), her last film, Bemberg suggests the possibility of restoring the gaze even within a narration marked by a male voice.[13] The movie examines the mechanisms of difference and repression, focusing on the story of Carlota, who grows up under the suffocating protection of her mother, Leonor. Carlota, who has dwarfism, is inculcated with her mother's attitude ("I don't talk want to about it"). Even the title suggests a norm that regulates language. Language does not manage to make Carlota's difference invisible, but it does make her nearly inaudible, and it is in this film that Bemberg exposes language (and voice) as a matrix of social exclusion. The movie has a marginalized male narrator who tells the story that the mother "doesn't want to talk about." Bemberg depicts the restoration of the protagonist's gaze, even though that restoration also implies a departure. While Carlota leaves, moving away from the other side of the mirror of the patriarchal code, or from the normalizing logic of difference, without recovering the narrative voice, she remains untranslated by the normalizing codes of the visual narration. The gaze, which produces otherness, is at the center of what this last film scrutinizes. The gaze is swathed in a male, though also subordinated, narrative voice, and the authoritarian voice of the protagonist's mother; and the murmurs of the townspeople that encircle the production of otherness mark

13. Based on the story of the same title by Julio Llinás.

her difference. The murmurs about Carlota, as well as uncontained sounds, like shouts and her mother's hysterical laughter, all reveal the inability to sustain normalizing language beyond its authoritarianism.

David William Foster has read Carlota as an allegory for everything queer —"torcido" [bent], "raro" [strange], or, in a word, anti-heteronormative—even though that queerness is not exclusively sexual (2002: 179). Bemberg herself says, "Charlotte is a metaphor for anybody that's different" (Bach, 1994: 27). The film focuses on difference and, in particular, on how differences are reinforced by the mechanisms of power that are at work in the very act of representation. According to Bemberg, Carlota's mother embodies "a metaphor of repression and intolerance" (Newman, 2000: 183). Her silence is portrayed not as an innocent, or even ignorant, silence but as violence and violent complicity. She burns the books that might remind her of her dwarfism and also tries, at the end, to prevent the circus from coming into town. The interplay between what is seen and what is unseen, as well as between what is said and what remains unsaid, constitutes the central axis of the story.

The other gaze that comes into play is that of Ludovico D'Andrea, a mysterious male figure who arrives in the town of San José de los Altares and marries Carlota. The film rarely presents Carlota's gaze, and, when it does, it generally does so with shots that show how Carlota sees Ludovico (similar to how the film shows how Carlota keeps dancing in front of the mirror, even after she sees her mother's disapproving gaze). As D. Jan Mennel notes, at the end of the film, the camera explores Carlota's gaze ("Eloquent Elisions," 2002: 173), an exploration that takes place when the circus arrives in town and Carlota leaves her house to see it. We then cease to see Carlota and instead see what she sees. The camera shows us her gaze at the moment in which she catches sight of that which she has previously been forbidden to see. With that subversion, she becomes a subject of the gaze.

The film ends with the suspension of that recovered gaze. When Carlota leaves with the circus, we do not see the town she is leaving behind; we see her say goodbye to her friend Mohamé (who narrates the story). Later, the camera shows Leonor as she shuts herself up in her house for good, and we then see the images that accompany the account of D'Andrea's possible suicide. In other words, at the end, the camera alternates between spaces in which the characters exit the story: the mother's confinement in her house, the place where D'Andrea drowns, and the circus caravan moving into the distance. Carlota's gaze leaves us, too. We were able to see what she was seeing in only one sequence, and now we watch her move away. As Teresa de Lauretis wonders in rethinking the image of Alice from the other side of the looking glass, we can see this departure as the moving away from the mirror that once reflected her as an other.

Carlota was the object of multiple gazes: she was constructed as an object of her mother's repressive gaze, the equally oppressive gaze of the townspeople, and D'Andrea's romantic gaze. At the end, she finds a different way of looking and, instead of an object of the gaze, becomes a looking subject, and leaves the scene. Carlota abandons the space that questions her and silences her identity.[14] At the same time, however, the camera captures her movement from the townspeople's perspective, and it is from that perspective that the camera places us as spectators.

The end of the film might be understood as a reflection of the spectator's gaze. Is the gaze at the end the same as at the beginning? Do we return from Carlota's gaze without experiencing any transformation, or does that passage through the eyes of the other, the colonized, the marginalized, the excluded, the unsaid, give us another way of looking? E. Ann Kaplan indicates that subjectivity is unsettled by the sight of otherness (1997: xix). If we agree with Kaplan, we might think that it is possible to consider the transformation of the spectator and his/her/their positionality with regard to difference. When the camera moves away from Carlota's gaze, it does so both from her previous gaze, which is dominated by the silence imposed by her mother, and from D'Andrea's gaze. The new vision that is produced at the end, with Carlota's departure, is marked by absence. We are left with the vision (and the voice) of another marginalized character, Mohamé, who must turn into a witness and who becomes the narrator of a story that was silenced because, as the title indicates, no one wanted to talk about it. However, the end of *De eso no se habla* suggests the absence of Carlota's vision (the camera, and with it the spectator, had brief access to that gaze, but it is now gone) and the affirmation (perhaps even the affirmation of the calling into question) of the spectator's vision. The spectator's eyes can now explore the processes of identification that take place among spectators, camera, and characters and can scrutinize their own view of difference, as well as their own complicity in the marginalization and exclusion of those constructed as others.

14. See Mennel and Newman for their analyses of silence in the film.

Hearing with the Eyes

The words that inspired the title of this book stress the importance of understanding the intersections of the visual and aural dimensions. With a clear reference to the act of reading, they point to both seeing the words and hearing the transcendence of the voice ("Hear me with your eyes / since your ears are so far away"). Exploring these intersections might also mean reflecting on their limitations and failures. And this is what Bemberg does in her films, taking her protagonists' initial confinement as a starting point not so much for the possibility of affirming feminist transgressions, but instead for exploring the intersections and fragmentations, impossibilities and intermittences, of those transgressions.

Bemberg's class privilege is not unrelated to her ability to advance as a filmmaker. In addition, that very privilege marks her gaze through the lens of her own social class, as it does her concept of feminism and women's liberation. De Lauretis's cautionary note can be useful here for rethinking the visual regime in general, and that of the camera in particular, as metaphors for social processes of visibility and invisibility, even within feminist practice. As De Lauretis underscores, not only are there women who are invisible to men, but there are also some who are invisible to other women (1994: 149). The moving image, then, is a tool for dismantling invisibilities and implementing a feminist exploration of forms of privilege and marginalization. Bemberg's later films include a reflection on her own privilege or, at least, an investigation of difference and marginalization—that is, of those spaces and historical subjects that are left out of the very notion of gender and the struggles for women's liberation. The limits of the visual are also demarcated by the voices or sounds that, from beyond the visual field, gesture with their presence toward what has been excluded by the camera or toward what resides on the other side of the mirror. Like the voices that Miss Mary hears through the window she closes in 1945 (an action that speaks loudly of her remoteness from those historical subjects whom she was not able to see), the voices in Bemberg's films can be understood as marks of the invisible. Unlike Sor Juana's transcendent voice (or the lovers' final whisper in *Camila*), the voices through the windows in *Miss Mary* remain almost entirely outside the visual record of Bemberg's films. Nevertheless, her films entail an attempt to reveal the battlefield of competing visions, as a result of which the gazes that filmmakers attempt to restore or imagine are either lost, nullified, defeated, or banished These are battles that are also processes. Bemberg herself suggests seeing the fragmentation of the gaze as being like shards of memory—that is, seeing it in terms of its incompleteness and in terms of what, therefore, requires effort to assemble and reconstruct.[15]

María Luisa Bemberg has had a significant impact on women filmmakers today. They are especially indebted to her repeated attempts to explore women as subjects (and not merely as objects) of the gaze and of the voice, and to rethink the possibility of new forms of looking and hearing. Hearing with the gaze is a core aspect of Bemberg's feminist aesthetic. First, in her films, images are never enough to tell the stories of women and their struggles. Their voices interrupt or question these images, erasing the outlines so clearly traced by the camera. Their voices also interfere with the other outlines of the powerful, watchful gazes of the dominant logic (or, we might even also say, the blurrier outlines of the "speculum" of feminist gazes, which attempt to delve into women's bodily pleasure). Second, Bemberg points to the possibility that aesthetics might transform subjectivities through the poetics of the moving image. Instead of remaining trapped in their designated places, women go beyond their initial confinement, beyond the framing that traps them in their bodies. By making use of transcendent voices or gazes that pass through the mirror, Bemberg manages to call into question the patriarchal premise that women in film can exist only within the boundaries of the visual regime.

15. Bemberg, referring to *Miss Mary*, notes, "The film's gaze is broken up, like memory itself, with weaves in and out" (Burton-Carvajal, 1999: 342).

CHAPTER 2

Whispers in a Realm of Voices: Lucrecia Martel[16]

THE USE OF SOUND in Martel's films, which has been the subject of numerous essays, constitutes one of her most important innovations in the aesthetics of the Argentine new cinema and opens a path to a new understanding of the relationship between sound and image. Even when the emphasis on the aural dimension does not interfere with the importance assigned to the gaze in her films, the recurring allusions to what is not seen suggest that the key to interpreting what is invisible (or, at least, opaque or unclear) often lies in the acoustic realm.

Since her 1996 short film *Rey muerto* (*Dead King*)—and the silence of the female protagonist (a victim of gender violence) in contrast with the audible voices of the men of the town—Martel sets in motion not only dialogues among different characters (or dialogic sounds stripped of their meaning) but also the interpretive framework within which the violent events portrayed in the short take place, a framework made of voices that replicate gender norms and their complicity with violence. The female protagonist thus ends up being hemmed in and assaulted by sexist codes of interpretation, which either perpetrate violence directly or use paternalistic excuses to distance themselves from it. In this realm of voices, the victim is silenced and it becomes impossible for her to find her own voice. The final gunshots serve, in part, to bring an end to the domestic abuse, but they also suggest that language itself is marked by an irrepressible sexism that inevitably subjects women to violence (whether within intimate relationships, in the media, or from the public ru-

16. In an earlier work, I discuss the dilemma of the gaze in *La ciénaga* from a gender perspective (Forcinito, 2006).

mor mill). There is no space outside of violence, either in the visual regime or in articulated language. In Martel's films, only the invisible flickers and the nearly inaudible whispers are able to interrupt, intermittently, masculine and heteronormative domination.

La ciénaga*: Opacity and Indiscernible Voices*

La ciénaga (2001) is one of the films from Argentina's "new cinema," a movement that first emerged in the late 1990s.[17] The film takes place in Salta and tells the story of two families through their women: Mecha and Tali. The camera explores their gazes and perspectives, and the differences between them. Yet the masculine gaze continues to be present in this "feminine universe." And even as the film underscores looking relationships between women, women's eyes and visions are never fully disentangled either from male desire or from patriarchal logic. Mecha, the protagonist, is an alcoholic who gradually becomes bedridden. This domestic confinement is one instance of the film's portrayal of women and the annihilation of their desires. While she can be seen in terms of traditional gender norms (femininity associated with confinement, for example), her masculine and violent side is also apparent in her interactions with her husband, Gregorio, and her four children, Momi, Vero, Joaquín, and José. As a counterpoint to Mecha, her cousin

17. It is relevant to highlight some aspects of the production of the film. The film received a small grant from the Instituto Nacional de Cinematografía in 1997, but it was not enough to fund the production (Peña, 2003: 116). While more prominent directors continued to receive the highest ratings, some important movies for discussing this *nuevo cine*, such as *Rapado*, were declared "sin interés" ["without interest"] (Batlle, 2002: 25). As a result, Martel decided to go to the province of Salta to seek financial backing. It was there that she did her casting, initially planning to use nonprofessional actors. These interviews—1,600 of them, according to Martel (Quintín, "Lucrecia Martel": 2)—allowed her to choose the extras and explore more deeply this melding together of short, interrupted stories, everyday conversations, and sometimes unidentifiable voices, which forms a substantial portion of the film. When Lita Stantic became interested in the screenplay and suggested that Martel send it to Sundance (Peña, 2003: 119), it began a change in direction that came to fruition when *La ciénaga* won the prize for best screenplay in 1999. Thanks to the prize and Lita Stantic's production, Martel's debut was not a low-budget production, unlike most directorial debuts during this era.

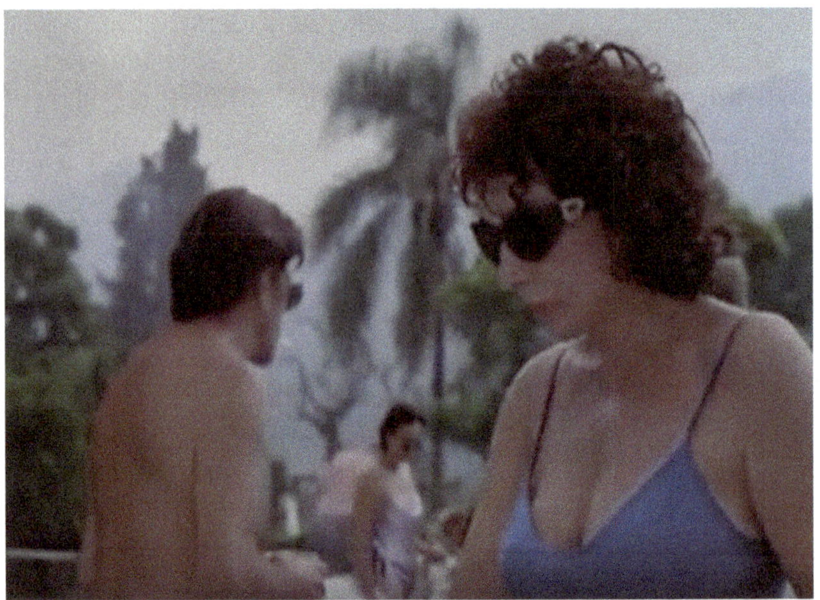

Still Image *La ciénaga* (dir. Lucrecia Martel, Lita Stantic Producciones, Cinematography Hugo Colace, 2001)

Tali is portrayed in terms of her traditional femininity. She is submissive and defines herself as a wife and mother, without making visible either her confinement or her frustration with her powerlessness. In both cases, masculinity is present: in Mecha as a mimicry of the logic of domination, and in Tali as a mimicry of the patriarchal gaze.[18]

La ciénaga problematizes the gaze from the very start: neither the charac-

18. It is important to note that, even when considering Martel's work from a feminist perspective (and by "feminist" I mean cinema by women that attempts to rethink the cinematic gaze from an antipatriarchal perspective), the visual exploration of women and their gazes is never unencumbered by masculine paradigms of representation. This can also be considered in feminist criticism. E. Ann Kaplan wonders, with regard to female entrapment in the logic of patriarchy, whether, "when women are in the dominant position, are they in the *masculine* position?" And she adds the following question, quite relevant here: "Can we envisage a female dominant position that would differ qualitatively from the male form of dominance?" (Kaplan, 2004: 28).

ters nor we, as viewers, can see fully. Martel proposes rethinking vision and the possibilities it offers: the film ends with the image of one of the protagonists (Momi) saying, "I didn't see anything," in reference to the supposed apparitions of the Virgin in the town. Allusions to the limitations of sight abound: from conversations between characters (Tali suggests to her friend Mecha, "Well, we each see what we can"), to the recurring scenes about the Virgin's apparition in contexts where different witnesses claim to have (or not to have) seen her, to the sequence near the end that recounts the tragic death of a child through shots that never show his fall and through sounds that point to what the camera refuses to record. In calling the gaze into question, Martel offers a counterpoint between image and sound, producing a dislocation between the visual and aural dimensions. The visual record seems inadequate: images encapsulate a family tedium in which nothing seems to happen because everything is simulated, hidden, and repressed. Gonzalo Aguilar suggests that the "opacity of transparency" is key in Martel's film: it affects not just the water (the *ciénaga*, or swamp, of the title) but also the windowpanes and mirrors (2006: 51), thus calling eyesight itself and the ability to see clearly into question. Opacity and a sense of calm conceal a form of violence that emerges only in sound. Auditory elements narrate what images refuse to recount, thereby becoming the marks (or the traces) of the invisible or the repressed. On the one hand, the gunshots and loud noises interrupt the tedium and slowness with which the family's everyday life is portrayed. Martel herself refers to the explosion we hear when Tali is unable to explode in front of her husband (Peña, 2003: 121). Thus, sounds give voice to what is not portrayed through language. On the other hand, sounds like the telephone that keeps ringing because nobody answers, Mecha's shouts and insults, the thunderclaps, gunshots, barks, and a blaring television all reveal a contrast with the articulated voices that can be heard and understood. We hear different voices, and not all of them are articulated and audible; sometimes they are nearly inaudible and function as a background noise; and at other times they are whispers that express all that cannot be clearly understood, and what is nearly inaudible and clandestine. These whispers express people's most hidden emotions, desires, and tensions, as well as all of the violence and invisible and unlivable experiences that seem impossible to translate into language.

The spectator here comes into contact with voices and with their limits, injuries, and excesses. Many of the conversations take place outside the visual field, which emphasizes what remains not fully articulated and thereby dislocates the image. These conversations remain out of sync or overlap with other voices that are synchronized with the image. The conventional sense we ascribe to the dialogues might not be as important as the way in which the voices make sense but stray from their traditional connection with meaning. The confusingly audible and not-always-discernible voices produce an intermittent rupturing of coherent or always synchronized representation. David Oubiña suggests we understand the polyphony of voices as "continuous, noisy, often constant," which mitigates the main action (2007: 32). For him, this film is a progression that does not move forward, an elusive progression (2007: 24). Sound—and those overlapping voices in particular—accents this dissolution of the narrative core and its intensity. The voices and dialogues, which are often disconnected, have the effect of bringing us, as Martel says, "that particular language that develops in families" (Peña, 2003: 122). These dialogues make clear reference to the existing bond between the characters as well as to the dislocation and fragmentation of language, which points to the isolation of the social subjects portrayed. Martel indicates that the polyphony produced through the superimposition of voices and family conversations can be understood as a rupture between voices and bodies: "Sometimes a conversation's voices have nothing to do with bodily position" (Bernades, Lerer, and Wolf, 2002: 74–75). Desynchronization serves as a key to the existence of those more anonymous and marginalized subjects, whom we hear speak but in a way that is splintered from the narration. In contrast to this desynchronization of the polyphonic voices, Mecha speaks, shouts, and repeats, as if she were a recording. Her voice is associated with her body (though the body is sometimes fragmented by the camera, recorded through its wounds and scars), but her audible voice (brimming with racist and classist insults) simultaneously stifles the articulation of her own voice. In something resembling ventriloquism, Mecha repeats shouted insults against everything that she perceives as otherness, shattering her fragile coherence even further. These shouts are like a spilling over that reasserts the existence of a voice that is apparently lost and vanquished and reflects an inescapable violence (her own), which is directed against the whole world and against herself. Her voice is never fully articulated because it is the voice that repeats the paradigms of the dominant discourses without ever managing to express them in a rational form. Her voice points to *logos*, but it is unable to echo it. In performative terms (and following Judith Butler's understanding of gender

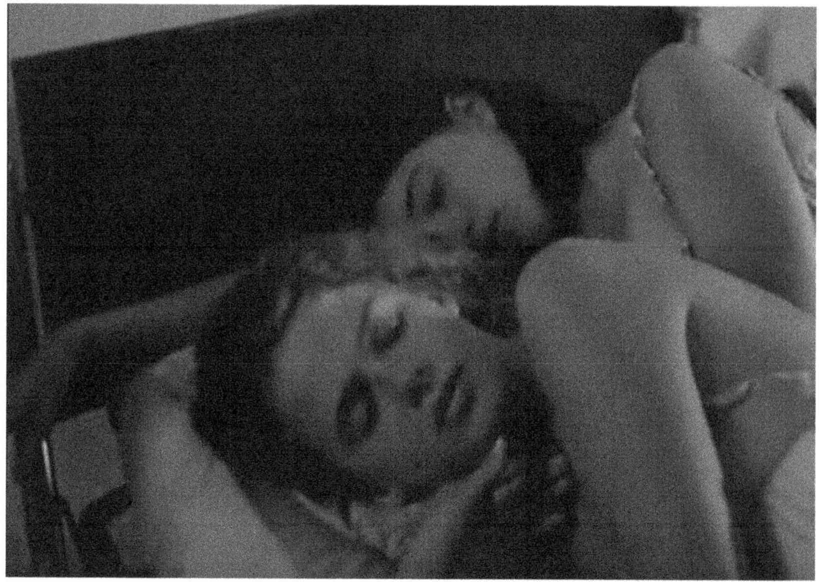

Still Image *La ciénaga* (dir. Lucrecia Martel, Lita Stantic Producciones, Cinematography Hugo Colace, 2001)

as performance), the citing of the masculine *logos* is a failure.[19] Those shouts hide overflows and excesses, but only in the register of the voice and not in the words does the voice endlessly repeat.

Her shouts stand in contrast to Momi's whispers, which reinforce the idea that the feminine (more marginal) voice is hushed by dominant voices, including Mecha's. At the same time, the subtlest and most imperceptible voices reveal stories that are not told aloud, whispers that express almost silently

19. In her famous discussion on gender performance, Judith Butler argues that social/sexual subjects are constituted through the reproduction and repetition of regulatory norms of sexuality. These norms are ideals, so individuals attempting to repeat them are never completely successful in citing them exactly but instead transform them. Performativity has to do with that repetition of standardized norms of sexuality and gender and with the possibility created by the difficulty of repeating them exactly, which enables the transformation of the norms and performative practices and which reflects both the instability of the norms and the possibility of rearticulating them.

the difficulty of listening. Momi prays in nearly inaudible whispers, "Lord, thank you for giving me Isabel." And, then she says to her sister, very quietly and weeping, "I don't want to be with anybody but Isabel." It is only in the register of that tenuous voice (which is tenuous but also quite articulate and intimate) that we get a clue to Momi's anguish, her desire for Isabel — invisible not only for the family but also for Isabel. This eroticism, which is silenced by her surroundings and only ever expressed in whispers, defies the rules of the heteronormative patriarchy. However, without a publicly articulated voice, this eroticism is nonetheless quelled by the dominant language. Martel thus highlights (and continues to do so in subsequent films) what is murmured and nearly inaudibly, and she calls on the spectator to recognize the record of what remains unarticulated, but which is nevertheless marked by sound. It is Momi's stifled weeping that points to her desire for Isabel. As a faint trace in the soundscape, that whisper reveals that Momi's recurring glances at Isabel are concealed but nonetheless filled with desire. It is Momi's stifled and silenced weeping that marks Isabel's departure when she leaves the house with her boyfriend.

Characters' bodies gesture to the fragmentation of social ties and the process of social deterioration. As a result of this gesturing, Oubiña suggests differentiating between adult bodies (bereft of desire and defeated) and adolescent bodies, which, though wounded, still harbor an eroticism that is a possible way out (2007: 51). Martel portrays forms of invisible violence, such as the violence that regulates bodies (even adolescent ones) with rigid heterosexist norms (intertwined with class prejudice and racist views) and that create unlivable spaces in which an individual's subjectivity emerges only through nearly inaudible whispers that bespeak desire. And while it is the gaze that still governs desire (Momi looks at Isabel through the bathroom window as the latter leaves with her boyfriend; Momi watches without being seen; Momi spies and desires), it is through her imperceptible, never fully articulated voice that she makes it known. The prayers that Momi whispers in *La ciénaga* are transgressions of the heteronormative gender discourses of domination. When women's voices appear as incomprehensible voices, as murmurs rather than as voices that can be clearly made out, the sound emphasizes not so much silence as the silenced nature of those voices. This silenced nature is doubled: the whisper is simultaneously a symptom of women's silencing and a space of rebellion, because it is its "nearly inaudible" nature that turns the whisper into a zone free from well-articulated language and its oppression, a zone where it seems possible to find a voice that is one's own.

The construction of the feminine takes place in the presence of a worn-out, useless model of masculinity (represented by Gregorio, Mecha's husband) that is nonetheless present within the representational dynamic. I do not mean to suggest that the model of femininity proposed by Mecha is not also worn-out and useless. Over the course of the film, we witness a shift in the narrative, as Isabel, the maid who is constantly humiliated by Mecha, leaves the house after being called racist, derogatory names and being falsely accused of stealing towels. Isabel's departure is, in some ways, secondary to the tedium of La Mandrágora, but it is nonetheless very relevant to Momi and, especially, to the racist violence represented by Mecha. The intersection of gender and racial violence, as two closely related and juxtaposed elements, involve a more complex approach to the feminine, and places power relations at the forefront. These two elements also reveal how women, as social subjectivities, are shaped by a binary system: the dominant, violent woman (Mecha) on the one hand, and the oppressed woman (Tali) on the other. The film explores the failure of those two models, whether through Tali's clear domination by men or through Mecha's domination as a woman. While Mecha's domination seems to replace the perpetrator of violence (shifting from man to woman), it does not necessarily call into question the hierarchical, violent structure of the patriarchy and its institutions (in this case, the family).

La ciénaga presents the dilemma of the power of the gaze and its limitations by examining the cinematic gaze as a tool of representation and knowledge (who looks, who exercises the power of looking, who is the object of looking, who or what remains outside that gaze and excluded by it). In addition, the film also proposes a rethinking of seeing as a metaphor. *Being able to see the Virgin*, for example, is one of the key metaphors in the film. As Tali suggests in her conversation with Mecha, this metaphor has to do with the need to rethink the limitations of perception and interpretation ("Well, we each see what we can").

In the film, there is an exploration of the visual realm, both a problematization of what is seen and what is not seen and a problematization of the ability to see. At the start of the film, when the accident sequence shows Mecha's perspective on the fall, the camera simulates a gaze that loses its balance, as if it were unable to find a stable point of reference. Later, Mecha's black glasses (which she wears all day) emphasize the difficulty of seeing, or that refusal to see (and be seen). While Tali's gaze toward Mecha is tender and compassionate, it also excuses Mecha's violence, and Tali silently stands by her. In short, it is a gaze that also refuses to see, either Mecha or herself. And even when Tali is able to see Mecha's scar on her chest from the fall, she helps her conceal it. Yet the entire narration of the Virgin's apparition revolves around looking, around the possibility of seeing (and not seeing). The film ends when Momi claims *not to have seen* the Virgin in the place where she was supposedly appearing ("I didn't see anything").

The tension between seeing and not seeing is encapsulated in one of the film's key recurring themes: falling. (There are falls we see and those we do not, those that the camera decides to show and those it does not.) The film opens and closes with a fall. In the opening sequence, Mecha has an accident: she is drunk; she falls with a glass in her hand and cuts her chest. Because of this mishap, her daughter takes her to the hospital, where Luciano, Tali's son, is also being treated by a doctor for a cut on his leg. The final shots of the movie also depict a fall—in this case, the fall and death of Luciano. Nevertheless, and despite the centrality of falling within the story, the camera does not show us the moment of his fall. Instead, the film narrates it through shots that keep it outside the visual field. Mecha's fall is narrated through sound (clinking glasses, rain) and through images that represent her inebriation, with the camera's movements mimicking the clumsiness of the people around the pool. Later, we see the glass on the floor and a sprawling body (Mecha's). In the sequence of the final fall, the camera is trained on Luciano as he climbs a staircase against the courtyard wall. We see him reach the top of the stairs, lose his balance, and, as he falls, exit the visual field. In the next shot, we see the door onto the courtyard with an empty tricycle and, in the distance, a body on the ground (Luciano's). The stagnation in *La ciénaga* is accompanied by a growing tension that leads to the blowout following the boy's accident and death. This tension can be associated with the sequences of waiting for the Virgin and the growing sense of expectation. These sequences initially seem like a subplot, but they are slowly incorporated into the story of the characters of La Mandrágora and La Ciénaga. The Virgin supposedly appears near a water tank and the media interviews the woman who saw her. The film emphasizes this mediation and consumption via television, with regard both to the Virgin's apparition and to her media coverage. The constant repetition of the media outlets reporting on the Virgin's apparition, and thus of a subjectivity that is waiting for a miracle, is also repeated in the (futile) expectation of a trip to Bolivia that never materializes. Endless postponement is a key part of the swamp metaphor and serves to redefine the atmosphere of tedium around the (false) expectation of change. This wearying atmosphere coexists with a sense of tension that builds and accumulates throughout the film, creating a sensation of slowness. It is as if something (if not many things) is about to happen, but never does. This waiting produces a sense of tension, which ultimately peaks with Luciano's death.

Surrounded by those tensions, Mecha's shouts, like a desperate mimicry of the oppressive and dominant discourse, release the violence that is inscribed on her body. It is as if she were irrationally bursting her own banks in the face of her oppression, not just by the norms that regulate her but also through the injuries she suffers. The falls and accidents (which in a sense serve as a foil to the tension that waiting produces) are rooted in corporeality. The film is full of images related to the body and especially to scars and wounds: Luciano's first accident, Mecha's fall, Joaquín's accident, José's injuries after the fight at the dance. Blood is also a crucial part of the film's representation of bodies. It is a representation of the body associated not with pleasure, but rather with pain, laceration, and loss. Nevertheless (and here we begin to shift to the generation of Tali's and Mecha's children), there is also another aspect of corporeality as a space of enjoyment, a space that operates through an interruption of the accumulated tension, confinement, frustration, and boredom that all reign in La Mandrágora. The dance between José and the sisters is one of the most eloquent scenes in the film, and it manages to disrupt the atmosphere of claustrophobia and tension through the pleasure of touch, music, and the body. The dance scene serves as a reminder of the intrusion of desire; it is here that gazes, bodies, and contacts map out another story, one that somehow remains repressed, frustrated, or nullified in a domestic space defined by suffocation and oppression. The contact between the siblings and Tali (Mecha is the only one who does not dance) generates a space of freedom in the bog of everyday life. And in these ephemeral spaces, where desire resides, the oft-whispering voice becomes body and intermittently dismantles the onslaught of violence and its tragic consequences.

La niña santa: *Between Prayers and Disobedience*

In *La niña santa* (2004), Martel presents desire that persists in spite of the institutional discourses that attempt to quell it. The film narrates a family story through a triangle in which a mother and her teenage daughter are both unwittingly involved. At a medical conference in a hotel in Salta, the arrival of one of the doctors (Dr. Jano), and his evident attraction to the hotel's owner Helena, kicks off a story that is constantly interrupted. These disruptions highlight conflicting desires and sexual tensions in the film that are never resolved. In narrative terms, the element that disrupts this first outline of a possible triangle (Helena, Dr. Jano, and his wife, who does not appear until the end) is the desire of Amalia, Helena's teenage daughter, and her attraction to Dr. Jano. The film explores Amalia's sexual desire alongside her participation in a series of Bible readings that promote sexual repression and consecrate narratives of chastity and purity. Once more, as in *La ciénaga*, the film intensifies the characters' secret erotic tension. Another disruption of the growing closeness between Helena and the doctor comes at the end of the film, with the arrival at the hotel of Dr. Jano's wife and children. Nevertheless, every element that points to the repression of desire and poses a disruption of the narrative of seemingly inexorable progress toward the sexual encounter between Helena and Jano seems also to increase the erotic tension. At the same time, the sexual encounters between Josefina, Amalia's teenage friend, and her boyfriend; the sexual conversations between the two friends (Amalia and Josefina); and even Amalia's desire for the doctor are all interwoven with a repressive religious discourse—not just as a vehicle for dubious ethical values but also as a necessary counterweight to the swelling eroticism. The final interruption takes place at the end, when the mother of one of Amalia's schoolmates comes to the hotel to tell Helena that one of the doctors has sexually molested Amalia. Nevertheless, the ending remains suspended in the final scene of *La niña santa*.

The film emphasizes the pleasure of looking within the triangle: one of the first sequences captures Jano looking at Helena's body through a window in the hotel. Thus, Jano's gaze is presented as a forbidden one, a gaze that spies on the object of its desire. In these shots, Helena is depicted several times without a head. This image of a decapitated woman points to the power that the male gaze possesses in the film. This power is further referenced by the fact that the person looking at Helena (whose name also goes back to Greek mythology) is Jano, evoking the two-headed god of Roman mythology, with his two faces and four eyes, who can look in opposite directions.

From its opening sequences, the film suggests a relationship between pleasure and vision, as well as between gender and vision and between passivity and activity. It is the heterosexual male gaze that plays out in the scene just men-

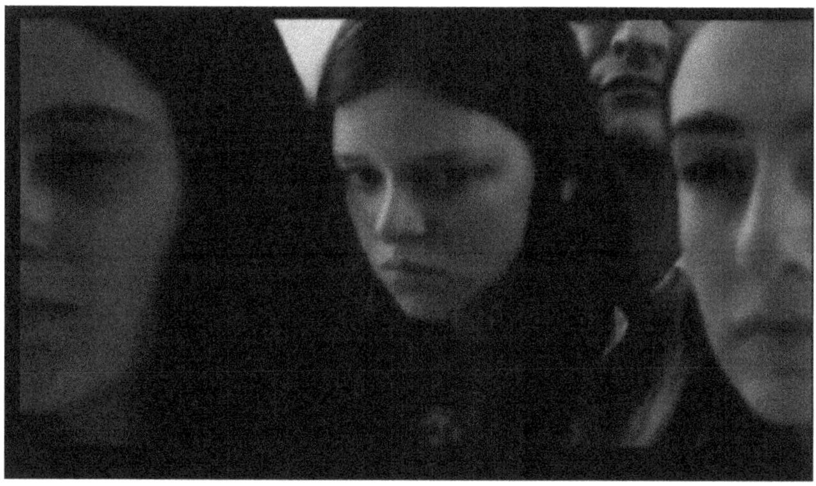

Still Image *La niña santa* (dir. Lucrecia Martel, Lita Stantic Producciones, Cinematography Felix Monti, 2004)

tioned, which shows Jano's eyes as he spies on a woman's body, thus emphasizing Helena's existence as an object of his gaze and pleasure. The camera relates this sexual tension through Jano's initial gaze, as well as through her body, only a part of which is shown but which we can identify and "complete" by assigning her the identity of Helena.[20] The camera's gaze comes into contact with this narrative image of Helena: not just her bodily image but also, above all, her bodily image as it is looked at (spied on) by Jano through a gaze that is sexualized, unconsented to, and, most of all, heterosexual and masculine.

For Jano, Helena is depicted as an object. In contrast, Amalia is depicted as a subject of the gaze. Amalia looks at and spies on Jano on numerous occasions. One of them takes place in the hotel pool, when Amalia peeks out at him from behind a screen and makes noises to get his attention. When Jano realizes he is being looked at, Amalia leaves. In another sequence, she opens

20. I say "complete," thinking of the Lacanian mirror and of the illusion of bodily unity through the image that stands in contrast to the fragmented quality of the body at an experiential level. I think it is relevant that the film does not show us Helena's entire body, only her torso (and a dress that we later see her wear on other occasions), and that the spectator must complete her body upon producing the Helena-torso identification.

his room door and, through the half-open door, sees him sleeping. When he wakes up, Amalia flees once more. Jano's role as an object of teenage desire shifts him out of his status as a subject (and possessor) of the gaze with Helena. The film produces an interplay of gazes (and desire) through two subjects of the gaze: the doctor and the "holy girl."

According to Mulvey, one of the central issues in feminist film criticism has to do with the dichotomy of passivity and activity that the cinema, as an ideological apparatus of the patriarchy, confers on women and men, respectively, and how this dichotomy revitalizes the metaphor of female castration (her lack) as a core aspect of the feminine (which Mulvey associates with the lack of the gaze). Men, Mulvey says, are subjects and possessors of the gaze, while women are only its object. Mulvey ponders the possibility of constructing the spectator in terms of gender and concludes that women must be excluded from the category of spectators, and thus from the gaze. What is the effect of looking on the representation of women in terms of the patriarchal logic? What is this effect, whether in terms of the passivity/activity binary noted by Mulvey, the proximity/distance binary developed by Mary Ann Doane (for whom proximity is associated with femininity), or the opposition between the two types of looking (gaze and look) that Kaplan identifies when she suggests that, behind the supposed female gaze (that is, the act of looking with the eyes), lurks the powerful patriarchal gaze (that is, looking associated with power)?[21]

21. The two concepts of the gaze and the look, which originate in psychoanalysis, remain in force (though modified and reworked) in psychoanalytical film criticism. The eye that merely looks is in some way distinguished from the significations of the gaze, which is characterized by exteriority and related, in Lacan, with the mirror stage and thus with the processes of subjectivization, identification, and entrance into the visible world, language, and culture. The gaze always implies a reciprocity—that is, it does not culminate in the eye–object relationship but instead entails the possibility that the object of the gaze will look back at the subject. At the same time, though the gaze therefore seems (and is) more powerful within this distinction, the look can, as Kaja Silverman (1996: 156) suggests, resist the gaze, even oppose it, going so far as to oppose the regulatory discourses of vision and even the very logic of representation itself: "The look has the capacity to see otherwise from and even in contradiction to the gaze. The eye is always to some degree resistant to the discourses which seek to master and regulate it, and can even, on occasion, dramatically oppose the representational logic and material practices which specify exemplary vision at any given moment in time" (156).

Feminine visions are multiplied in *La niña santa*: on the one hand, Helena's gaze (a more traditional gaze and, thus, one possessed/directed by masculine logic and subordinated to it) and, on the other hand, Amalia's gaze (a dangerous and, in particular, a transgressive gaze). The camera seems to be located between these two female characters, inside and outside the patriarchal regime of the eye, and thus creates a vision that is ultimately not entirely feminine but also not entirely masculine. Analogous to colonial mimicry, which the postcolonial critic Homi Bhabha refers to as *almost the same, but not quite* (1994: 86), this other mimicry repeats the hegemonic gaze (in this case, related to gender), but not quite. In Bhabha's case, the reference has clear traces of domination over the subordinate but, at the same time, involves an interstice that has not been entirely appropriated. In offering a feminist critique, we might posit a gaze that, while it cannot be separated from the patriarchal modes of representation, nevertheless also cannot be seen as repeating the mechanisms of patriarchal representation. That is, it is not entirely patriarchal.

Helena looks at herself as an object. She sees herself in the mirror, she is obsessed with "how she looks" (on various occasions she consults with Amalia and Jano about her clothing)—in short, she embodies the patriarchal representation of the woman-as-object. Amalia, though, sees herself as a subject (of the gaze, of erotic action, of the reinterpreted and transgressed narrative of divine salvation). We should recall that Amalia's declaration of herself as a subject is based on an anonymous and nonconsensual contact with Jano at the start of the film. He touches her on the street in the middle of a crowd while she watches another man play an odd musical instrument in a shop window. The person who approaches Amalia's body sexually with his own is, as the holy girl herself will discover in the subsequent scenes, the doctor who is staying at her mother's hotel. First constituted as an object (an object of assault and of desire marked by violence), Amalia rewrites herself as a subject of desire, of seeking, of touch (she is the one who touches him when, on another occasion, they run into each other in the elevator), and as the subject of Jano's "salvation." The doctor, for his part, refuses to be reconstituted as an object of desire, constituting himself instead as a subject of the gaze and of active desire for Helena. Nevertheless, the patriarchal narrative of desire is perpetually interrupted by Amalia, whose behavior has a dual valence (she is the holy girl, but she is also transgressive). Her "holy" part plays (deliberately?) at the feminine masquerade as described by Irigaray: it is an ostentation of femininity, which transgresses that forced repetition of what is understood as "traditionally feminine" in order to subvert it.

When Irigaray refers to the feminine masquerade, she understands it as a deliberate form of assuming the female role. But, at the same time, the feminine masquerade is distanced from that role, because the ostentation of femininity is a pose and not an acquiescence to the patriarchy's rules: "One must assume the feminine role deliberately. Which means already to convert a form of subordination into an affirmation, and thus to begin to thwart it" (1985: 76). Femininity, then, can be understood as a rebellious masquerade—that is, as the traditional patriarchal representation resignified as a subversive strategy that repeats the rigid norms of the patriarchy in order to parody them in an ostentatious mimicry. Amalia is the holy girl seeking the manifestation of a divine message and trying to understand her religious mission. Jano, in some way, enters into this masquerade of virginity/holiness and femininity upon becoming, in Amalia's narrative, the object of her salvation. Her salvation implies an unleashing of her erotic desires but also involves a disruption of the rigid structure of patriarchal (and Oedipal—Jano has a daughter Amalia's age) power.

"I know what I have to do," Amalia tells her friend Josefina when the latter suggests she tell somebody about the incident with Jano—that is, about how Jano molested Amalia in front of the shop window. But Amalia thinks of Jano as her mission, her revelation. There is an overlap between this religious discourse and the sexual transgression within the religious discourse. One clear example is the film's constant repetition of a scene where a group of young people read texts about divine revelations. In this scene, Inés, who is leading the group, is moved as she sings praise to God, and she talks about divine signs and the importance of knowing how to interpret them. Meanwhile, Amalia and Josefina laugh and whisper their fantasies about the instructor's sexual exploits. Sexuality interrupts the religious discourse, and, at the same time, religion serves as a context for sexual exploration. It is here that Aguilar goes back to Chion's concept of acousmatic sound to examine the "noisy confusion" produced by sounds without a visual source (the voice that is heard without being seen). As Aguilar argues, this confusion exists in the conflict between visual and auditory in the discourse of the Catholic Church (2006: 102). Yet, in *La niña santa*, it is used to rethink the causal relationship between sound and image, especially when sounds anticipate what the image later reveals.

What does the voice tell us in this interplay of reflections on looking? The acoustic frame can also be understood as *logos*, which will be transformed in the dispute between the religious and scientific discourses. Through the figures of the doctors, another space of oppression is emphasized: scientific discourse, and, specifically, the discourse around bodies and adherence to traditional gender terms. Only men participate in the conference, and women are in charge of cleaning and taking care of the hotel. Religious discourse is present through the stories and prayers, which Amalia transgresses, thus leading her to become holy. This same religious discourse is present as an echo that seems to lack any meaning, to be mere background noise, and to serve, like the conversations in *La ciénaga* [*La Ciénaga*] and *La mujer sin cabeza* [*The Headless Woman*], as an acoustic framework and interpretive key. The institutional discourses (religious and medical) are presented as the norms that eroticism calls into question. These discourses also have an aural dimension in the film. We hear both prayers and religious and mystical readings as well as scientific lectures and conversations; the former suppresses the physicality of the body and the latter explains, regulates, and "cures" it. The religious discourse might recognize Amalia's subjectivity as a "holy girl" but not in the way she envisions her holiness. Amalia "gives in" not to the religious call but to her own pleasure; her mission consists of "saving" the doctor; her own reading in the group is about a woman who would rather save a woman than be with God. In Helena's case, it is the medical discourse that ends up enveloping her and turning her into a patient (the doctors, for example, perform a test to detect an auditory disorder). Furthermore, at the end of the film, Jano and Helena are about to act out a dialogue between doctor and patient. With this scene, the movie comes to a close. We never see Helena and Jano's play-acting nor the consequences of Josefina's mother bursting into the conference to accuse Jano of abusing the teenage girl.

The film's abrupt ending puts an ellipsis on the patriarchal reappropriation of women's dangerous gaze and, thus, on the narration. We do not hear the voice that accuses him, but it is that voice (mute to the spectator) that brings to a halt not only the conference but also Amalia's exploration of desire. The voice that breaks in at the end condemns Dr. Jano. Yet Amalia is presented not as a victim but as a holy girl who performs a subversive mimicry of the patriarchal account in order to reclaim agency after an assault that positions her as a victim. Nevertheless, it is that mute (to the spectator) voice that expands like a murmur in the final sequence. It is that voice, which we first hear as a whisper and which gradually turns into a voice capable of articulating the denunciation that we cannot hear, that, in the abrupt ending, interrupts the medical discourse. It is that voice that interrupts the doctors who are discussing sounds that are heard, but which do not exist (such as tinnitus). It is that voice that, perhaps, translates and appropriates (maybe even betrays) the voice of Amalia's whisper. It is that mute voice of what remains unsaid that now falls silent in anticipation and that thwarts and dismantles the heteronormative patriarchal power of the gaze in order to lay bare its abuse and violence.

La mujer sin cabeza: *The Loss of the Voice*

Not seeing is also a key theme in *La mujer sin cabeza* (2008). Not seeing an accident, but feeling the impact with the body. Hearing it, but not seeing it. Or, simply refusing to see it. The main character, Vero, has an accident. While driving, she leans down to grab her ringing cell phone and feels the impact. She does not know whether she has run over a person or an animal, but she does not look back to find out. The plot of the film spools out from there. We never learn exactly what happened. There are some visual cues, but they are contradictory. Vero believes she has killed somebody. She moves like a zombie, now headless (*sin cabeza*), disconnected from everything. At first she is mute, but when she starts to talk, she only repeats what the men in the family are saying.

The camera gives us clues. It begins with voices and shots of children running and playing near a highway, drawing a connection to a theory that terrifies Vero: she has hit a child. But the camera also shows the car driving off, and what we see on the highway does not look like a child, but rather a dead animal in the middle of the road. The story offers information, too. We later learn that a dead boy has been found near the highway. In addition, we can look for clues either in this film or in Martel's work in general, such as the accident in *La ciénaga*. Both examples are possible: the accident with a car on the highway, the accident of a boy climbing a staircase. We see the highway. We see the children clamber up, go up, go down, run. The accident is the place of return. There are numerous connections among Martel's films: Vero is now the headless woman. (Cabeza ["head" in Spanish] was the name of the husband in *Rey muerto* [*Dead King*], who ends up injured when his wife defends herself from him.) This string of clues calls us not to solve anything,

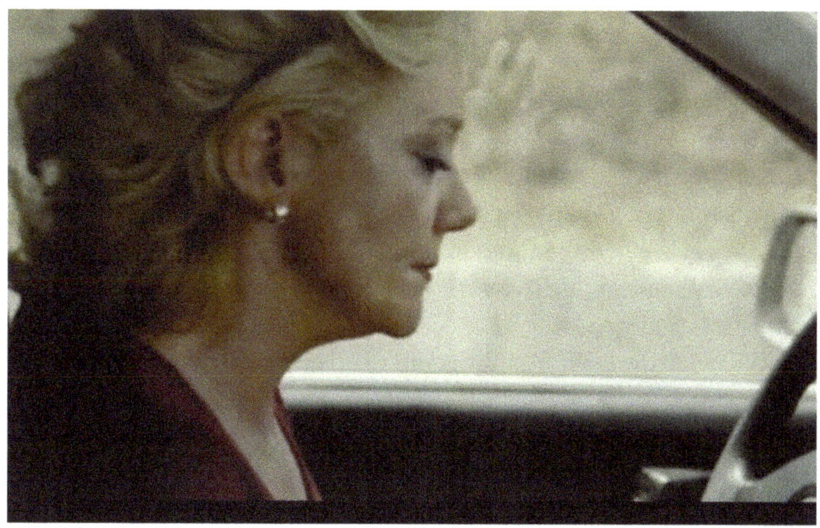

Still Image *La mujer sin cabeza* (dir. Lucrecia Martel, 2008)

but to question everything and to draw connections between everything. The emphasis on framing, traces, and doublings in *La mujer sin cabeza* reveals the simultaneity of different plots (indicated by door frames through which characters or ghosts appear or disappear); underlines the opacity that, from the start, creates a blurry gaze, obscured by rain, which makes it difficult to see; underscores sound; and especially stresses the importance of the voice. The absence of the voice is marked by other sounds, which become louder and louder. In the meantime, Vero's absent voice is monotone, locked in the same modulation and detached from meaning. Vero's ghostly presence, as she wanders among the family members, goes completely unnoticed by those around her. Only her Tía Lala—who watches dead people in old videos, hears creaks in the house, and sees ghostly presences (which she knows how to scare off, without looking at them)—recognizes how Vero's voice has changed ("That voice doesn't sound like yours").

When Tía Lala refers to the dead, she says, "Don't look at them, so they'll leave," and across the threshold, we see a boy leaving. Only Tía Lala, herself detached from logical, rational explanations, understands what she is seeing and hearing—or, to put it another way, only Tía Lala is able to give it meaning. She says, "They're ghosts." It is this voice (an articulated voice, but one that nobody believes, like the voice of the quasi-oracular Cassandra from

Greek mythology) that signals *méconaissance* (misrecognition): she does not recognize Vero's voice because Vero has become someone else. Of course, this misrecognition allows us to read the ghosts, and thus to discover the dead boy by the highway. But the figure of the ghost, which evokes a dead person whose presence lives on and who reappears, can be linked to those other characters who inhabit Martel's films (such as in *La ciénaga*). These figures exhibit characteristics of indifference and emotional remoteness, like a subjectivity that has been zombified, which has been associated with the subjectivities of post-traumatic societies and which live on, but not completely, after the weakening of social ties in the 1990s. Aguilar points to this aspect of the *nuevo cine* when he considers Martel's near-zombie characters (2006: 51), who are almost aimless in their movements, or, as the movie's title suggests, "headless."

Furthermore, Martel's movies are marked by a social and class division that is made all the more obvious because of how the film gestures to it through frames and windows, as if it were always outside, beyond.[22] Ghosts inhabit that exterior space too. But they are not alone. That outside world is populated by a multitude of excluded social subjects. They are often present in their voices, but those voices evoke not closeness but an inaudible, jumbled distance: murmurs that are sometimes clear and at others incomprehensible—and that contrast with Martel's whispers, the auditory register in which desire and the forbidden reside. In visual terms, there is little visibility, and not only of the ghosts and socially marginalized subjects. Vero, too, turns out to be invisible. Only Lala recognizes her "becoming another," her shift from Vero to "the headless woman." Vero's emotional distance is disrupted, at one moment, when she starts to cry and allows herself to be hugged and comforted by a worker who is cleaning the bathrooms. She then "recovers," thanking him and returning to her previous state.

When Vero finally manages to tell her husband that she thinks she might have killed someone, it is in the middle of the cacophony of the supermarket, which creates an atmosphere of confusion and gestures to this headless woman's mental state. She triggers a sort of "operation" around her: the men start

22. See the essay by Carla Manzoni in which she examines paraspace in Martel. In referring to *La mujer sin cabeza*, she analyzes the use of windows, mirrors, and panes of glass as the spaces in which Vero moves and which help represent, through bodily movement, both Vero's continuity with and profound separation from the reality around her (2013: 132–133).

investigating, calming her, and they even take her to the highway at night. After gathering information, they tell her she has just had a scare. When Vero comes out of her shock and starts talking incoherently about what might have happened, the narrative control is held by the men who surround her. Eventually, she starts repeating what the men say. In doing so, Vero recovers a voice that, if it ever was hers, now no longer is. It is the men (her husband, her brother, a cousin, and lover) who talk, verify, and conceal the evidence while they soothe her and speak for her. Vero starts to repeat what she hears them say: a dog ran in front of her. Even when Vero's niece, Candita, refers to the boy who was killed, Vero corrects her: "He drowned"; "The newspaper says he drowned." That is her articulated voice, the one she recovers after masculine intervention and a cover-up operation.

At the beginning, we first hear children's voices, then barking dogs, and then a group of women, including Vero, talking about makeup, eyelashes, and the opening of a swimming pool. Afterward, we hear the music in the car—the song "Mamy Blue," which recalls, as Martel herself notes, the 1970s, but which, as Mariana Enríquez suggests, is also a soundtrack of the dictatorship ("La mala memoria"). After the impact, Vero's first action is to put on her sunglasses. We continue to hear "Mamy Blue." The storm begins. The silence highlighted by the noise of the storm is, above all, Vero's silence. Or, perhaps, we should say silences. The first silence is the more traumatic one, the silence of the impact and the ensuing confusion, which is revealed through Vero's alienation from the world around her and from herself. This alienation becomes apparent when she is called in to the dentist's office where she works. Believing she is there as a patient, she seems not to understand why the assistant has put a smock on her. Finally, she speaks up to say that she has to go. Later, when she speaks again, there is another silence, one that is imposed, one that lurks behind her insistence that nothing has happened.

During Vero's silence, even after she manages to articulate what she thinks happened (that she has hit somebody), the voices we hear are other people's voices. The camera, often out of focus, allows us a glimpse of the interlocutors' bodies (even the men), whose speech evokes the authoritative voice-over or the voice of people speaking in whispers, those who remain always outside the frame and who are only ever partially made visible.

This exploration of Vero's voice affirms its destruction not only by the accident, which affects her deeply and makes her go silent, but also by the repetitions through which her voice is molded in accordance with the patriarchal logic that promises to protect her if she repeats what it says. Her voice thus emerges as the repetition of masculine voices, which sends us back to the beginning and to the voices of women talking about everyday matters who occupy a traditional position. Is it not, then, that the impact, the accident, and the silence have interrupted her voice, which already repeats the norms of the heterosexist patriarchy? Is Vero's initial voice truly hers, or is it, too, a voice that repeats the articulated voice and male logic? Is Vero a quasi-zombie only after the accident, or is the accident one more step in the process of losing her consciousness (and her memory)?

Tía Lala seems to evade the repetition of the dominant logic, as she is able not only to hear but to recognize the voices around her that operate outside of the rationality that so often surround interpretation. Candita, Vero's niece, also evades this mimicry, speaking the truth of her desires, even when she is assaulted by her mother's homophobic commentary and by an ambiguous rejection from Vero. She is portrayed as sick (she does have hepatitis but there is also a reference to her going out "zarandeando su hígado por ahí" [shaking her liver around]). When it comes time to think about the conflict of the voice, it is perhaps only Candita's voice—marginalized but not entirely—that manages to defy the norms of her family's authoritarian patriarchy. Only in her do we see an interruption of the chain of repetitions that mark the female voice as one that is complicit with and, simultaneously, a victim of the patriarchal norms. Martel herself relates it to the complicity that took place during the dictatorship: it plays out the authoritarianism (marked by '70s-era music) of the three men around Vero, who take her car, make inquiries, erase any evidence of her visit to the hospital after the accident, and send to her to bed, to rest and to forget, because, in the end, it was just a scare. Vero obeys, and her voice begins to awaken, though now she can only repeat what the men around her say. Nevertheless, when they drive by in the car with Josefina and Candita, and Vero sees that people "are looking for something" in the canal, she loses her voice again. In this juxtaposition of image-evidence and voice, what is clear is not so much that the image offers proof of reality (in fact, we see a dog on the road, so maybe the boy managed to keep walking and died in the canal?) but that the image seems to be posited as doubt, as dispute. What is visible is not always what exists, hence the presence of ghosts. But that doubt regarding the image points to a (fictional) construction of the image through narrative and silence. Rather than "I killed somebody on the road," the notion that "it was a dog" takes over, and along with it an authoritarian, suspicious construction that destroys all evidence to the contrary (such as, for example, the evidence of Vero's hospital stay). Here, again, we see the masculine realm give form to the feminine voice. Yet Vero's weeping, the different tone in her voice, and the tone that nobody but Lala notices are important components of her voice. From these interruptions. one comes to suspect that her voice is not a meaningless echo but a mimicry, performing a masquerade in order to survive. Paradoxically, the moment that Vero most resembles a zombie (just after the accident) is when she is least so; though she is in shock, she is nevertheless aware enough to later realize that she has killed somebody. That indifference—her indifference and the indifference of the people around her—that indifference to everything, even to the loss of her voice or to the nonexistence of an articulated voice of her own, her detachment from herself and others, may be the manifestation of an intermediate state. Vero is not literally a zombie—yet she is, to a certain extent. Only Tía Lala detects a change in Vero's voice and does not recognize her after the accident. And it is important to remember that it is only Tía Lala who is able to see ghosts—the dead who have not died completely and therefore are no longer residing in the past, at least for Lala, because they are visible for her in the present.

Feminine/Masculine: Voices, Murmurs, Whispers

In Martel's films, the universe of the masculine voice is a powerful, articulated, and authoritarian one. Women can repeat the male voice with considerable success, quashing their more feminine tones (as Mecha does in *La ciénaga*); they can repeat it and, at the same time, produce a subversive mimicry (as in *La niña santa*) or a performative repetition (as in *La mujer sin cabeza*, when Vero repeats the male voice and its norms, all the time marked by an anxiety about the imperfection, and unethicality, of that repetition). Nevertheless, it does not seem to be enough in Martel's films to consider the voice only in female-male or feminine-masculine terms, because the authoritarian, powerful, and articulated voice causes other lesser voices to be excluded, not only voices associated with gender but also those associated with other forms of subordination. Murmurs, too, mark those voices that are hierarchically placed in the category of inaudible, unimportant things. Meanwhile, whispers seem to be associated in Martel with the subversions inherent in desire (related to gender, as in *La niña santa* and *La ciénaga*) and through the strategic use of invisibility (as in *Nueva Argirópolis*, which I discuss in Chapter 6).

The film in which the parody of the voice as an unintelligible and distorted sound is most apparent may be *Pescados/Fish* (2010). The short begins on a highway, where a car drives by in the rain, and then the shot moves to the water, which is full of fish talking and singing over the horns and tires: "There weren't any dogs, just a car." And they seem to repeat in distorted voices, "I didn't see it, I didn't see it," until the images of the water and the colors of the fish gradually transform into what could be headlights on a highway at night. The sounds overlap, creating deformed, not completely intelligible voices. There is music and singing. The allusion to a possible conversation about the accident in *La mujer sin cabeza* is obvious. But it is not the conversation that allays our doubts; instead, it gives us hints about the same event to which we return through the distortion of the voice. Though the distorted voice is the one that contains the key, we cannot understand it entirely because it is not completely intelligible. The sound also evokes the difficulty of making sense of the acoustic realm, in another assault on the prevailing logic.

Transgression develops in the cracks of the dominant discourses (for Amalia, religious discourse; for Mecha, the patriarchal sphere; for Vero, interruptions). In these interstices, we see a mimicry play out that, as Bhabha suggests for the colonial space, exposes an ambivalence that consists of an appropriation of the other (1994: 86). In this sense, Mecha is not entirely masculine, but neither is Amalia in *La niña santa* completely feminine, religious, or "holy," and neither is Vero entirely zombified or completely indifferent. The same can be said of the camera, because Martel explores the power of the gaze and its relationships through complex plots. These plots refer to intermittent transgressions that, on the one hand, are not viable because they are confined within the dominant discourses they attempt to transgress and, on the other, subvert those very discourses through the ambivalence of mimicry and masquerade.

Martel also interrogates the gaze as a space in which power relations are explored, and explores the limitations of the gaze by calling into question the possibility of seeing (and of narrating with images). It may be this tension that is recalled when, at the end of *La ciénaga*, we hear Momi's words: "I didn't see anything." The fact that *La ciénaga* ends with these words suggests the duality articulated in the search for a new way of seing, a search that invites us to explore a plurality of gazes while emphasizing the limits of looking. In *La niña santa*, the gaze that is at work is insufficient because looking also has to do with the meaning attributed to what one sees: seeing a sign from God or not seeing it also means interpreting it, typically according to a discourse of oppression (such as religion or science, both patriarchal discourses). In addition, *La mujer sin cabeza* insists on what is not seen and on what people refuse to see—not just the accident that Vero refuses to look at in the rearview mirror, but also Vero's condition, which goes largely unnoticed by those around her. Nor is the spectator able to see clearly, with the camera thus pointing to one of the key aspects of this new aesthetic: posing questions as to the (in)visibility of those same images.

This questioning of the gaze also plays out in the contrast between image and sound. In Martel's films, there is a dislocation between the visual and aural dimensions, which leads to an overlapping of stories (sometimes they are parallel, sometimes their plot lines cross, sometimes they complement or contradict each other). The visual component tells a story, and sounds reinforce the idea that the female voice and the marginalized voice have been appropriated by hegemonic discourses, which suggests that the voice is inadequate for describing the pent-up tension. The tension is narrated through violent sounds (explosions, gunshots), which are the flip side of the accumulation of unresolved pressure. The sound of the telephone, for its part, accompanies the sense of failed communication between the characters. (In general, communication does not take place: Mecha yells for someone to answer the phone, Helena claims not to be available when people call her, Vero is unable to pick up because right at that moment her car hits something.) In this rejection of contact with the outside world, the film retreats into the closed spaces that the characters inhabit, and sounds, such as the recurrent phone calls, increasingly reveal other stories (some from the past, others from the present) that cannot be narrated in images.

Martel thus emphasizes not so much silence but, rather, the silenced nature of the female voice. The whisper is both a symptom of the silencing of women and a space of rebellion, because its "nearly inaudible" nature makes the whisper a zone that is liberated from oppression, where women can find a voice that is more their own. In both *La ciénaga* and *La niña santa*, the teenagers whisper prayers that, in reality, are transgressions against prayers, and thus against the discourses of gender domination.

In acting as ventriloquists for the dominant discourse, female voices seem to find a space of transgression. Women, as reproducers of discourses, repeat (without producing) the very discourses that oppress them. Nevertheless, there are moments of imperfect repetition, in which the female characters transform these watchful discourses and establish themselves as subjects of speaking, rather than of repetition. In *La mujer sin cabeza*, Vero loses her voice after the accident, and, as she first begins to speak again, her voice indicates her uncertainty and is replaced by the repetition of what the men around her articulate. But her repetition is monotonous, which, rather than setting out the meaning of the articulated male voice, dismantles that male voice and exposes it as a voice without any authority or logic. In the case of *La niña santa*, twice we hear the story through which the group of teenagers attempts to rethink the religious vocation. The first time, this story is read by Amalia. Later, Josefina repeats it:

> Entonces vi al Señor que tenía en brazos a un enemigo mío que estaba muerto y por el que había rezado. Me dijo: "Aquí está mi hijo. ¿A quién amás más, a mí o a mi hijo?". Yo respondí que amaba más a nuestro hijo, es decir, que prefería sufrir en este mundo por la salvación de un alma antes que estar en la gloria con nuestro Señor. (*La niña santa*)
>
> [Then I saw the Lord, who was holding in his arms an enemy of mine who was dead and for whom I had prayed. He told me, "Here is my son. Whom do you love more, me or my son?" I answered that I loved our son more—that is, that I preferred to suffer in this world to save one soul rather than be in heaven with our Lord.]

Even though they are framed within a religious discourse, the voices of these young women emphasize Amalia's reading about her "divine plan" ("saving" a man), and the ambiguity of the terms serves to disrupt the rigidity of the voice (as a norm) and to emphasize the ways it is subverted. Even Amalia herself gives her interpretation of the text: "Here the woman says she'd be ready for anything if it meant saving somebody." Amalia then tries to maintain her "holiness" through her new "mission"—that is, Amalia tries to defend her identity as saintly even as she subverts it by operating in the fissures of religious discourse. At the same time, the references to eroticism in the group's conversations interrupt the discussion of the divine plan with references to "tongues" and "kisses"—that is, to the body and sexual desire. Female voices and whispers (especially Josefina's) produce interferences in the discourses of subordination: whispers point to eroticism as a principle that disrupts domestic, institutional, and discursive confinement.

It is not a coincidence that Helena's illness is tinnitus, an illness associated with the auditory apparatus (Helena hears a constant ringing—that is, she hears sounds that are not there).[23] Nor is it a coincidence that Jano, who makes her "his" patient, is an ear, nose, and throat specialist. *La niña santa* presents issues of hearing and sound as problematic and a core element of the film (just as *La ciénaga* and *La mujer sin cabeza* grapple with the gaze). The central injury in *La niña santa* is related to the ear, an injury that does not necessarily relate to hearing, but rather to hearing sounds that do not exist and are generated in the ear itself. At the conference, there are references to the success and failure of doctors' listening (they refer to the effectiveness—or ineffectiveness—of listening to patients recount their symptoms as a necessary element of good diagnosis). That is, the focus is not just on the ear and what is heard and whether it exists or not. They also mention the ability to listen—that is, the intellectual faculty through which we interpret what we hear.

In mimicry and in the ambiguities of the gaze, Martel finds the possibility of disrupting traditional gender attributes and roles. At the same time, these ambiguities make clear the limitations of vision, highlighting what is not seen and what the camera does not capture—that is, invisible zones (and subjects). Something similar happens with sound, and Martel's films recover what is not audible, the whispers that undermine the absolute reign of dominant sounds. What repeats, like Vero's new voice in *La mujer sin cabeza*, is the articulated language of the patriarchy. Meanwhile, the voice that is never heard or understood is the key to that excess of (simultaneously subordinate and rebellious) language and all that would be said but cannot be, all that is left in parentheses and never fully made audible. If we consider *Pescados/Fish* and its references to *La mujer sin cabeza*, the voice takes on another aspect. Distorted voices are synchronized with the images of the fish, and then the short returns to what could be the scene of the accident in *La mujer sin cabeza*, evoking dogs, rain, a highway, and, of course, the difficulty of seeing.

Martel's films focus on what is outside the visual field: what is blurry and unclear, and what cannot be seen. They have to do with partial, incomplete,

23. In "La educación sentimental," Daniela Vilaboa notes the importance of sound in the film and within the narration, as evidenced by Helena's illness, which "no consiste en oír menos sino en oír de más" [consists not of hearing less but of hearing too much].

and ambiguous female gazes in which masquerade and mimicry are subversive resources that resist sedentarism. These acts of resistance allow the female gaze to move (from the feminine to the masculine, from the clandestine to the public, from the permitted to the forbidden). But they also affirm the female vision (or visions) as a threshold, one that belongs not to the visible world but to the invisible (and inaudible) one, the world that remains decisively excluded and incapable of being portrayed.

CHAPTER 3

That Scream, That Writing, That Lost Voice: Albertina Carri

THE USE OF THE acoustic register in Carri offers not only an exploration of the limits of visual representation but also a place from which to articulate narrative authority, even when that authority challenges the traditional narrative model. Voices in Carri's films highlight three different expressions: first, the unarticulated voice—for example, screaming and panting (represented sometimes by animals, as in the case of the slaughterhouse); second, the articulated voice—in particular, in the form of writing, then read and reread many times (this one is a masculine and well-structured voice); and, third, the voice as a search—one that is often fulfilled through movement and through the nomadism of the voice in flight, incapable of being recovered in the present. This last aspect of the voice can be found in the most recent work in Carri's exhibition. Titled *Operación fracaso y el sonido recobrado* [*Operation Failure and Recovered Sound*], it projects into the margins of the cinematographic image, both through intrauterine sounds and through the substitution of her own voice for the lost voice of her mother (only her mother's voice, and not her writing, was lost).

In *Los rubios* (2003), sounds—such as the characters' screams or the cries of animals in a slaughterhouse (an aspect that is explored much more fully in *La rabia*)—exceed language. Those sounds repeat, pointing both to the impossibility of recording horrors and to a reluctance to leave them unrepresented. Screams, howls, and moans evoke the domination of bodies, the biopolitical instance that finds its most systematic expression in the clandestine detention center. At the same time, these sounds remain linked to the domestic realm. Carri's first film, *No quiero volver a casa* [*I Don't Want to Go Back Home*], takes us into the family universe and its violence. This voice is

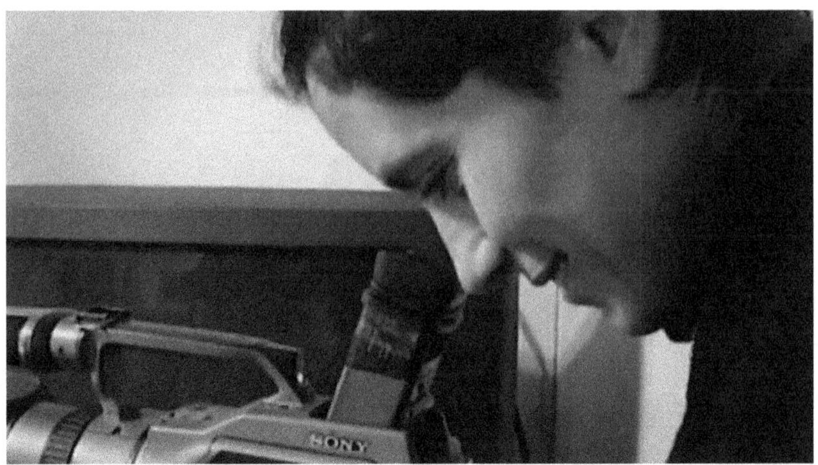

Still Image *Los Rubios* (dir. Albertina Carri, 2003)

encapsulated in the kidnapping of a man in a parking lot, which is immediately contrasted with the silent violence endured by the main character in his home. In black and white, and in a juxtaposition of fragments that refer to two families, Carri's film uses sound to represent violence. From its opening sequence, sound is then expanded over the course of the film. We see Rubén, a middle-class youth who returns home and is rejected by his father. We see him in front of a mirror, hiding a weapon. We see a parking lot, a kidnapping. We hear the gunshot. We go back.

The scream, the unexpected noise, and the gunshot all point to a form of violence that bursts into the auditory realm and the domestic space. It is the displacement of the voice that provides clues about the relationship between text and voice. (This displacement is seen clearly in *Los rubios* with the father's text, as well as in *Restos* with the text written by Marta Dillon that Analía Couceiro reads as a voice-over [see Chapter 6].) It is through voices that writing becomes modulated. The text is incarnated in the voice that reads it, in the voice that demands a certain authority (performative, rather than textual). Yet the search for the maternal voice lingers in the substance of the letters, which are filmed with a zoom lens in the installation *Operation Failure and Recovered Sound (Operación fracaso y el sonido recobrado).* As with Sor Juana's "hearing with the eyes," these letters evoke a fleeting voice, a voice that becomes (nonarticulated) sound. This maternal voice is the only refuge from a form of violence that is never exclusively tate-based, but which is also rooted in intimate relationships and in the domestic sphere. Intimate family violence plays an important role in all Carri's films, as can be seen in the explicit staging of abuse and sexual violence in her 2001 film *Barbie también puede eStar triste* [*Barbie Can Also Be Sad*]. In this animated short, Carri parodies pornography and denounces the violence of Barbie, the violence of desire and heterosexist fantasy. She takes violence and abuse as the starting point for the film and never drops the use of violence. The presence of the Barbies, as sexualized symbols of oppressive practices within the domestic and work spaces, is contrasted with the parody of voices that emphasize the panting, shouting, and cursing associated with men and male pleasure. At the same time, the film distances Barbie from patriarchal heteronormativity, exposing it as violence and domination.

In this chapter, I examine *Los rubios* and the displacement of the voice, both her father's and her own. Then, I explore the relationship that Carri establishes among childhood, adolescent horror, and violence in films such as *Géminis* [*Gemini*] and *La rabia* [*Anger*], where Carri uses shouting and panting to gesture toward the universe of what cannot be said but which is made present all the same.

Displaced Voices and Narrative Authority: Los rubios

In *Los rubios*, Carri uses the displacement of voices, through doubling and desynchronization, to explore how narrative voice (or voices) is articulated (and dismantled). The voices used to interpret the images in this fictionalized documentary (including Carri's voice) are present, but at a distance. That is to say, these voices are incorporated through a process of distancing.[24] From

24. I rely here on Ana Amado's analysis of *Los rubios*, which notes "la dificultad de seguir los avatares de recordar ahí donde esa tarea tiene 'lugar': en territorios de la intimidad, de la subjetividad" (2009: 186) ["the difficulty of following the transformations of remembering where that task takes 'place': in realms of intimacy, of subjectivity"]. Amado analyzes disjunction as a tool of representation: disjunction between word and image, "que arrastra otras distancias" ["which pulls along other distances"]. She adds, "En lugar de reunión fílmica de cuerpo y palabra, representa con su separación, una distancia definitiva" (186) ["Rather than a filmic unity of body and word, by separating them it depicts an unbridgeable distance"].

the start, doubling is embodied in Analía Couceyro's performance as Albertina Carri. Both the director and the actress who plays her engage in many dialogues, and this use of doubling indicates a degree of ambivalence with regard to displacement itself. Desynchronization takes place when the actress Analía Couceyro, as Carri, reads a quote from *Isidro Velázquez*, written by Roberto Carri, the director's father, who disappeared in 1977. Yet Albertina's voice is not absent. Instead, it becomes present through instructions—"Make sure I'm not in the frame"—thus producing an overlapping of voices, including her own, Couceyro's, and the absent voice of her father, which becomes present in Couceyro's reading. The final voice to become present is the most absent of all: her mother's.

This is the quote from *Isidro Velázquez* that Couceyro reads:

> La población es la masa, el banco de peces, el montón gregario, indiferente a lo social, sumiso a todos los poderes, inactivo ante el mal, resignado con su dolor. Pero aún en este estado habitual de dispersión, subyace en el espíritu de la multitud el sentimiento profundo de su unidad originaria: el agravio y la injusticia van acumulando rencores y elevando el tono de su vida afectiva, y un día ante el choque sentimental que actúa de fulminante explota ardorosa la pasión, la muchedumbre se hace pueblo, el rebaño se transforma en ser colectivo, el egoísmo, el interés privado, la preocupación personal desaparecen, las voluntades individuales se funden y se sumergen en la voluntad general; y la nueva personalidad, electrizada, vibrante, se dirige recta a su objetivo como la flecha al blanco y el torrente arrasa cuanto se le opone.
>
> [The population is the mass, the school of fish, the gregarious heap, indifferent to the social, subjugated to all powers, inactive in the face of evil, resigned to its suffering. But even in this habitual state of dispersion, there lies in the spirit of the crowd a deep sense of its originary unity: affront and injustice gradually accumulate resentments and elevate the tone of its sentimental life, and one day, in the face of an emotional clash that acts as a sudden fiery jolt of passion, the crowd becomes a people; the herd becomes a collective being; selfishness, private interest, and personal concern disappear; individual wills fuse together and are submerged in the general will; and the new personality, electrified, vibrant, heads straight toward its goal like an arrow toward a target, and the torrent levels anything in its path.]

Roberto Carri's articulated voice is recovered in this reading, but through a displacement. It is not the voice of her father; instead, it is both a paternal voice, an articulated one, and a quotation. As Martín Kohan notes, this quote is taken from an epigraph by Juan Díaz del Moral. And yet it is an attempt to bring to the fore the paternal voice—not biologically paternal, but masculine and articulated, standing in sharp contrast to the shouted outbursts, which are associated with the unnameable. The father (and the masculine thought that marked his generation) points both to militant activism and to the rationality of that activism during the 1960s and 1970s.

In his discussion of the film, Kohan talks about three displacements that take place in this part: the first, Couceyro's performance as Carri; the second, the fact that the copy of the book she's holding is not a first edition but a more recent one; and the third, the fact that she selects a paragraph from her father's text that was not written by her father. Kohan argues, "A fuerza de distancia y de apartamiento del pasado, en la escena de lectura de la hija sobre su padre, falta nada menos que la escritura de su padre" [As a result of distance and estrangement from the past, in the scene in which the daughter reads about her father, what is missing is, in fact, the father's writing] (29). Here I point once more to Silverman's analysis of female voices in cinematographic representations, especially her claim that, in nonfeminist representations, men occupy the space of the speaking subject (as seen in documentaries, where the voice-over is generally a male voice), whereas women are always associated with their bodily image. Through this synchronization, women are limited to their body (and thus to their representation as images), whereas men are able to represent incorporeality, transcendence, and knowledge. In the case of Carri's film, there is a clear de-corporealization in that synchronization of woman and sound, which presents female voices as transcendent subjects who both construct and question such representations.

The female narrative voice, on the one hand, and the doubling of the voices and images of Carri and Couceyro, on the other, serve to shatter synchrony in the film. The reading of Roberto Carri's text reflects how desynchronization restores voices through displacement, just as the voices of her parents' *compañeros* join in the task of desynchronizing the body–voice relationship. This desynchronization suggests that voices that take place offscreen, like voice-overs, transcend narration. (These voices are recognizable and therefore not, strictly, voice-overs.) These voices undermine any attempt to find a sole nar-

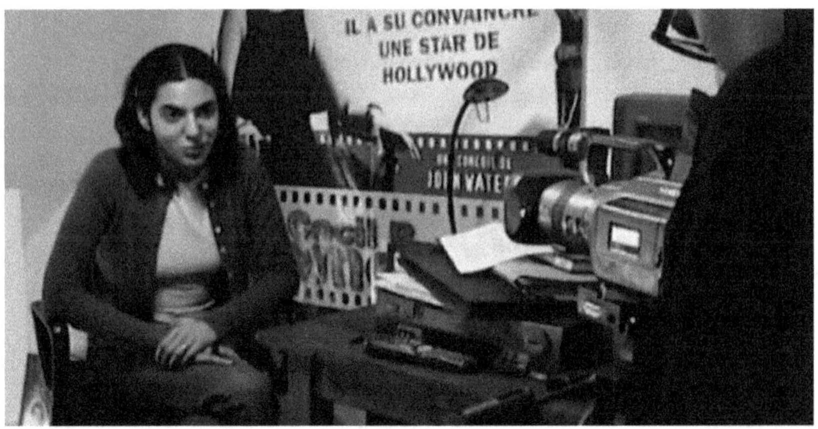

Still Image *Los Rubios* (dir. Albertina Carri, 2003)

rative voice that can bend memory to a single, linear story. The desynchronization of sound and image recurs repeatedly throughout the film, in moments that both recover the voices of ex-detainees and attempt to establish distance from those voices. Carri's project was rejected when it was presented at the Institute of Visual Arts, which objected to its lack of "documentary rigor":

> Creemos que el proyecto es valioso y pide en este sentido ser revisado con un mayor rigor documental. La historia tal como está formulada plantea el conflicto de ficcionalizar la propia experiencia, cuando el dolor puede nublar la interpretación de hechos lacerantes. El reclamo de la protagonista por la ausencia de sus padres, si bien es el eje, requiere una búsqueda más exigente de testimonios que se concretaría con la participación de compañeros de sus padres, con afinidades y discrepancias. Roberto Carri y Ana María Caruso fueron dos intelectuales comprometidos en los setenta cuyo destino trágico merece que este trabajo se realice.
>
> [We believe that the project is worthwhile and therefore should be revised with greater documentary rigor. The story as currently formulated poses the dilemma of fictionalizing personal experience, in which pain can cloud the interpretation of searing facts. The protagonist's mourning of her parents' absence, though it is the element around which the film turns, calls for a more thorough search for testimonies that would be fulfilled with the participation of her parents' comrades, with affinities and discrepan-

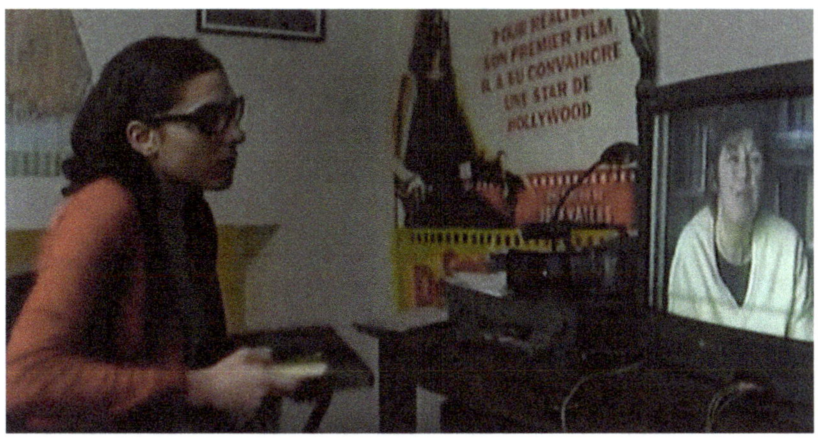

Still Image *Los Rubios* (dir. Albertina Carri, 2003)

> cies. Roberto Carri and Ana María Caruso were two politically engaged intellectuals in the seventies whose tragic fate deserves to have this work completed.]

This quotation is read and discussed by Carri's film crew, with the director herself taking part in the discussion, and it serves to highlight how *Los rubios* is made possible, as a film, through the displacement (or, even, in spite of the displacement) of the voices of a new generation, who stand in contrast to that of Carri's parents.

The displacement evoked by the Institute of Visual Arts's statement also relates to the director's approach to the voices of her parents' *compañeros*. Desynchronization relegates the images of her parents' fellow activists to the TV screens in her studio, and instead places the image of Carri at the center. We witness Carri/Couceyro working on the film while we hear voices that are disconnected from corporeal images. In his analysis of *Los rubios*, Kohan criticizes this visual postponement: "If it were excluded and left out of the film, we wouldn't see it; because she sets it aside, displaces it, we see how it is applied in that displacement" (2004: 28). Nevertheless, if we think in acoustic terms, these voices acquire the transcendent status of a voice-over, floating above other images. Whether it is a shot of Carri/Couceyro in the street, alongside the voice of one of her mother's fellow militants or the voice of Carri herself asking questions, or a shot of Carri/Couceyro in her own studio, taking notes and conducting research for the documentary, the documentary gives these voices the place of voice-over in Carri's memory-work (which, because it restores those voices' narrative authority, is a displacement and not a marginalization). The resulting effect is paradoxical: there is a visual displacement and an acoustic transcendence. Ultimately, the central project of *Los rubios* is the reconstruction of memory, and those voices serve as narrators. Carri desynchronizes sound and image. She does not link each voice to its image, but instead displaces those images to the screen, positioning them as a backdrop while privileging the figure of Carri as she studies those images, takes notes, and looks at her computer. Nevertheless, this displacement of image and voice, which seems to subordinate the presence of her parents' *compañeros* by showing interviews with them through images that are reproduced on a screen, is paradoxically accompanied by a restoration, which can be seen as an effect of desynchronization. The voices that narrate are both bound tightly to their bodies (when we do see them speak in the video) and detached from their bodies (when we hear them while seeing Carri/Couceyro), and the voices carry out the narrative and interpretive function associated with documentaries. The film distances itself from those powerful voices (of the generation of the 1960s and 1970s), while simultaneously retrieving them in the moment of distancing, and their function recalls the offscreen voice that, though it lacks the authority of the voice-over, is ultimately associated with narrative authority.

The visual privileges displacement by positioning the voices of Carri's parents' generation as a backdrop and centering her experience and her investigation of memory. The acoustic, however, prompts the opposite trajectory; the voices of the past and quotes and performances of them (in the case of her father) are preeminent, as the younger generations, even today, continue to recall and interpret the past. Those desynchronized voices function as narrative voices, and, if there is a tension, it takes place in the realm of sound. In that realm, Carri's own voice, which is usually but not always offscreen, tries to take possession of the narrative voice and, at the same time, bestows narrative privilege on other desynchronized voices. Notably, the voice that is never desynchronized, the voice that is always firmly attached to the body, is that of the neighbors. In contrast, the treatment of sound with her parents' ex-*compañeros* occupies a very different position, as sound records a testimonial dimension that can be associated with the voice—multiple voices in this case—and that has interpretive power with regard to the past and to the images presented in the documentary. I do not mean that the acoustic is Carri's only innovation. Animation is also an important and innovative element of her films (the pornographic parody of *Barbie también puede eStar triste*, the animation of the Playmobil dolls in *Los rubios*, and the children's drawings in *La rabia*). Nevertheless, Carri's work with sound in this film may also reflect the echoes of voices through which the labor of memory is undertaken. The emphasis on the voice can also be seen through the repetitions, rehearsals, and changes that Carri tells Couceyro to make as she talks about her experience (that is, Carri's experience) as a child in the first person. The take that includes this quotation is repeated three times. Via Couceyro's voice, Carri says:

> Odio las vaquitas de San Antonio, las estrellas fugaces, pasar por debajo de los puentes, las vías de los trenes, las bandadas de pájaros. Odio que se caigan las pestañas y tener que pedir un deseo cuando se soplan las velitas en los cumpleaños. Porque pasé muchos años deseando siempre lo mismo: que vuelva mamá, que vuelva papá y que vuelvan pronto. En realidad, el deseo siempre fue uno, pero yo lo estructuraba en tres partes para que tuviera más fuerza.
>
> [I hate ladybugs, shooting stars, going under bridges, train tracks, flocks of birds. I hate it when eyelashes fall out and having to make a wish when blowing out birthday candles. Because I spent a long time always wishing for the same thing: for my mommy to come home, for my daddy to come home, and for them to come home soon.]

Though in this case the voice is synchronized, Carri suggests changes to certain pauses and gives instructions to create a distancing effect, thereby disrupting the synchronization and reminding us of her presence (as a director and as a subject of memory). At the same time, she invites us to witness a process of recognition and nonrecognition, which is produced not so much through the image as through the modulation of the voice: "You can say it faster . . . . It's great if you, like, make a list and also, if you're forgetting it, it's great if you think for a second and then keep going." Or later, after the second take: "I wouldn't repeat the word 'hate' because it's really strong." In this interplay of voices, Carri shows the search for her own voice among the doublings of her own portrayal, and she affirms herself as the film's director and as a testimonial subject (an affirmation that is made based on her own displacement, analogous to the affirmation and displacement of her parents' generation).

The aural dimension could suggest that visual displacement—if we consider, for example, the controversial depiction of her parents' disappearance using Playmobil dolls—is accompanied by the desynchronization of the voice, which highlights not only the physical absence of the disappeared but also, and especially, an irrefutable presence that has left its mark on the acoustic register. This trace might be displaced, but, even with that displacement, it is affirmed as a testimonial voice. Those testimonial voices—Carri's voice, her father's "voice," the voice of her parents' generation (even in their displacement)—call for the narrative authority to be moved toward the margins and for their fragmented, opaque stories to be woven into the fabric of social memory.

There is another important and much more absent voice: that of Carri's mother. The references to her mother's voice are anchored in shouts—and shouting and screaming are central components of Carri's films. There is no agreement on the subject of these shouts. One of her mother's fellow activists says that her mother was not a shouter, while another says that, when she got angry, she could "shout things in a tiny voice." For her father, what is recovered is the articulation of the voice; for her mother, it is the shout. And though there are also references to letters, which a repressor from the Sheraton brings to the families and which make up a key part of Carri's recent installation, her mother's voice remains the searched-for voice. The activists' testimonies seem to address the question of whether her mother was or was not capable of shouting, a question that we do not hear but which can be deduced from the responses. In all of Carri's films, the voice of her mother is presented through screams. Nevertheless, these screams and shouts are not the maternal voice associated with the intrauterine voice of her most recent installation, but instead a voice that is displaced to other female characters (Carri/Couceyro in *Los rubios*, the mother in *Géminis*, the daughter in *La rabia*), a nonarticulated voice that is linked to pain, injustice, and violence.

Géminis *and the Voices of Senselessness*

An extreme close-up of skin as a syringe draws blood, followed by an image of blood slowly gathering when the needle is pulled out, is the film's opening sequence that then moves into an interior of doors and hallways. We see a man who wakes up in a bed, and the empty space next to him. Then, a young man looking at himself in the mirror. We have now entered into the family's morning routine in the bathroom, as the father (Daniel) shaves and the mother (Lucía) applies her makeup. Up until this point, the film has been devoid of voices; hereafter, and for the rest of the film until the final sequences, *Geminis* (2005) is filled by the perpetual, meaningless chatter of the mother, who talks incessantly whenever she appears in the visual frame. Her constant talking seems like an obedient repetition of the norms of articulated language, which loses meaning not in the acoustic deformation of the voice of the beloved (the masculine voice of Narcissus who rejects Echo), but in excess and endless reproduction. Her voice never transcends her corporeal presence, except toward the end of the film, when she discovers her twins' incestuous relationship and her screams engulf everything.

The film portrays an upper-middle-class family on the day that Ezequiel, one of Lucía's sons, arrives. He is returning with his bride from Spain to hold their wedding reception in Argentina to make his mother happy. Alongside this self-conscious institutionalization of family and social performance, with all its ritualistic elements, we also repeatedly see the intimate sexual relationship between the siblings Meme and Jeremías, hidden (though only barely) behind closed doors from the rest of the family. At first, their incestuous relationship is only suggested, but later it is revealed to the spectator. We get hints of this relationship through moaning and, in several shots, through reflections in a mirror. The question about what can be seen or heard seems to be central, and sound gestures toward what becomes visible or invisible. Lucía's incessant babbling, which is full of complaints, demands, recollections, anecdotes, criticisms, and opinions, conceals more than it reveals. In the face of the immense silence that is associated with blindness, articulated language is a meaningless sound. Lucía's only articulated sound is, paradoxically, her most inarticulate one: when she discovers her children's incestuous sexual relationship (first hearing their panting and then seeing them naked in bed together), she lets out a desperate cry. Though the drama and horror of the ending (amplified by Lucía's psychological and physical collapse and the return of a final calm after her desperate screaming) shape the story structure, the fact that Lucía keeps talking (now monotone) highlights once more the restoration of blindness as an inextricable core of the family institution. It also explains why the summary that appears on the DVD version says, "The influence of love endures despite any imposed morality." Lucía's initial shrieks, as well as those of Meme and Jeremías, dissolve into a silence that, once again, is expressed through the voice. Toward the end of the film,

Jeremías tells his grandmother and aunt that he does not know why he found his mother in her bedroom holding a gun, thus presenting the spectators with images to which we do not have access and that maybe never even took place. Meanwhile, assisted at first by a nurse and then by her silent husband, Lucía keeps talking about her memories.

At one moment, the moving images on a television show seem to offer a paradigm for the powerfully parodic nature of this sibling relationship. Resembling a telenovela, Analía Couceyro (the actress who played Carri's role in *The Blondes*) tells a male character that his relationship with another woman is impossible: "Carlos Alberto, you and Ana Luisa are brother and sister." This soap opera cliché, in which incest stands in the way of romance, points to the series of metonymic transgressions and displacements. In another scene, we watch a documentary about pandas who are born in captivity, which is narrated through a conversation between Meme and Jeremías. The images from the documentary have no sound—Meme is using headphones, so she has to serve as the narrative voice for her brother. We see one panda, then two. We hear the sound of a vacuum cleaner and, in the foreground, see the vacuum cleaning up the shards of a broken wineglass. Then, we hear the sound of the telephone and then Jere's voice on the phone. Meme is the one who says that it is a documentary about pandas born in captivity: "It's weird. Since the mother can't raise them both, she turns her back on one of them and it eventually dies, but first she goes crazy trying to grab them both." At play in the story are the intersecting images of motherhood, violence, and survival. In the film's ending sequence, these intersecting images reemerge in a final moment of tragedy.

In terms of voice, the mother's voice predominates in the film. Her voice is a synchronized voice, closely tied to the body. Yet, in shots with her children, her voice also occupies a spectral space that resembles a haunting. Silence is concentrated, especially, in the figure of her husband Daniel, who speaks before the final climax only to point at the sky and note that airplanes are flying overhead. He attempts to tell his wife that she should not talk about incestuous relationships in front of her children. Her children do not say much, but they are not silent either, and the sound that characterizes Meme and Jeremías is the panting and heavy breathing associated with pleasure and desire. There is very little dialogue, even when the mother is not around. Even so, one important moment of dialogue takes place between Jeremías and Meme, when he says to her, "Saying your name." (Carri has said she almost made this

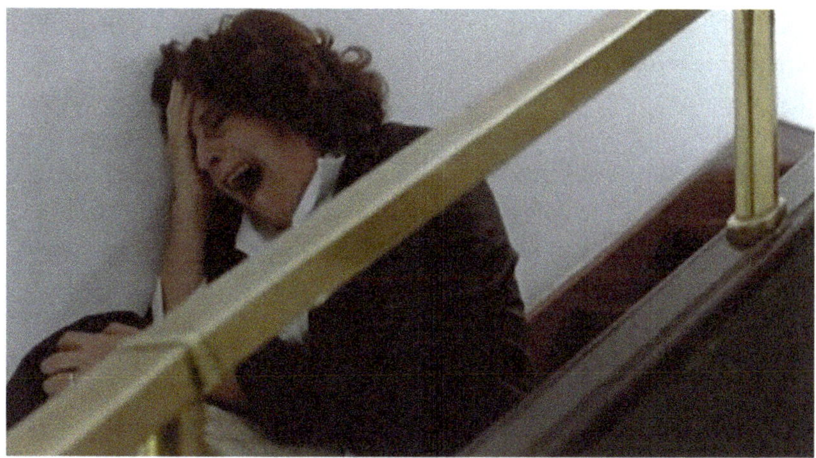

Still Image *Géminis* (dir. Albertina Carri, 2005)

phrase the film's title.) This is the only time he has ever called her by her full name, Magdalena, and he adds, "I like saying your name."

The mother's voice symbolizes a lack of communication, except when she cries out upon seeing her children. At first, she is rendered mute, but, in desperation, she screams, hits them, hugs them, kisses them, pushes them apart, and brings them back together. In that moment, her scream interrupts her usual ventriloquism, her mechanical and nervous repetition of all the norms she remembers (there are, of course, clues to be found in her repeated words). Her scream seems to suspend the realm of the supposedly articulated voice that is associated with paternal language (even though the father opts for silence in the film), and it can be read in terms of Kristeva's *chora*, the semiotic excess of the gesture, the body, and the material. Her breakdown (not the breakdown of language) expresses her displacement, a moment of exclusion or reclusion. Meanwhile, Jeremías offers a made-up version of what has happened to his mother. Still overwhelmed by the events and exchanging looks in silence, the siblings walk up and down the stairs.

The mother discovers the incident between the siblings when, guided by the sounds of sexual pleasure, she follows those sounds to the bedroom. At first, Lucía closes the door, and we see the horror on her face. Then, she opens the door again, now seemingly ready to see. After she screams, the film abandons the articulated, repeated language of echoes, which characterizes Lucía's voice throughout the film. The mother's entrance into the room as a witness highlights once more the corporeal nature of the maternal bond. Her screams point to the breaking of the paternal law and the subsequent rupture that gives rise to a new (posttraumatic) subjectivity in Lucía.[25] Before that rupture, her body plays out the conflict that is presaged by the images from the documentary that the siblings discuss. Yet the film concludes with the mother's absent and remote retreat, as she stays in her room while Meme and Jeremías walk around and retain the narrative privilege of explaining what has happened.

In her philosophical examination of the female voice, Adriana Cavarero criticizes the paternal language associated with *logos* and turns once more to the *chora*, the instance of the semiotic in Julia Kristeva. For Cavarero, the *chora* is not merely an unarticulated instinctual excess that lacks rationality. Instead, it is another kind of rationality that produces a split from the paternal law and the articulated language of phallocentrism. By focusing on the sound of the voice (and not on its meaning), Cavarero invites us to understand that instinctual excess as a collapse of the metaphysical order of *logos* and an affirmation of immanence over transcendence. This kind of sound is not associated with meaning. That dissociation (often in relation to the posttraumatic subjectivity) would not, according to Cavarero, imply isolation, though it does suggest isolation from the social realm—a realm that is governed by paternalistic laws and articulated language. Instead, dissociation implies another kind of relationship, and it is here where Kristeva's *chora* comes into play, insofar as it signifies the order of the material, embodied relationship between mother and child.

The sequence of the revelation for Lucía begins with sound and then the gaze, and it is anticipated by shots that show us doors and doorways framing that which allows itself to be seen, wishes to be seen, can be seen, and that which remains invisible but is nonetheless framed by sound that exposes (gives away) its corporeality and pleasure. We see Lucía close the door and open it, and her gaze marks the onset of the final tragedy, when articulated language is abandoned. When this happens, the film is inhabited instead by sounds that emphasize the body, and in particular, the son and daughter's

25. Here I am referring to the plasticity of the subjectivity in trauma, as Catherine Malabou understands it, both in the sense of malleability and of destruction. I am thinking of the traumatic moment as one that causes an obliteration of the subject.

physical relationship. Whereas, during most of the film, Lucía seems to repeat phrases again and again, this time she screams and cries after her encounter with her children. Later, she seems to speak as if detached from her body, dislocated in space and time, far from her bedroom and far from the past, to which she seems to refer when, in a monotone voice, she talks about the rain and horses. At the end, she repeats, in English, "All shall be well, and all matters [sic] of things shall be well." As foreshadowed in the soundless panda documentary that Meme narrates to her brother, Lucía "goes crazy." She experiences the impulse to repudiate, alternately rebuffing her children and hugging them. If we recall Kristeva's *chora*, we see a different spatiality and temporality in this scene: in the space in which one body relates to another, the mother's body acquires meaning that precedes language, the phallocentric order, and the Oedipal order. Lucía hits them, hugs them, caresses them, and hugs one while pushing the other away. For Kristeva, the *chora* is what interrupts the speaking subject, which is associated with articulated language, *logos*, and the phallic order. This interruption signals the traces of what precedes it, whether from other times or other places—perhaps what has been marginalized and excluded from the social order—or from what has been lost. We see, in the moment of Lucía's tragedy and horror, when her language is interrupted, a sort of uncertainty, as she rejects, abandons, and embraces her children, performing the corporeal bond through the excess of instinct.

Sound points to the annihilation of the maternal subjectivity and the mother's scream signals her deep wound. Nonetheless, *Geminis* does not end with her scream (we might contrast this ending with that of *La rabia*). Nor is there a return to that excessive and vigorous repetition that characterizes the mother's voice. Instead, we get rupture, an alienated and monotone voice that is removed from its surroundings and from the present. The film underscores a form of language that is not articulated, and this non-articulate language interrupts articulate language as *logos*. While the mother's scream interrupts her own anxious repetition of paternal language and its norms, the siblings' voices elude repetitions and norms. The film depicts them through rhythms, breathing, panting, and the abandonment of language. I am referring here not to narrative voice nor to dialogues, but instead to the abandonment of the articulated voice, which is also tied, in this film, to the realm of the visible.

Geminis ends with a sequence shot where, first, we see the mother standing apart from her children, who are hugging each other and crying; then the camera pans to another room, where the father is sitting; and finally, there is a time jump without a cut. A couple of days have passed in the interim. Lucía, Lucía's mother, Meme, Jeremías, and Lucía's friend are all sitting on sofas in the living room and watching a wedding video. We hear applause, like at the end of a play, and, on the screen, we see Lucía, but she is detached from the present and seeking refuge in the past.

Meanwhile, a dialogue overlays the voices in the video images. The dialogue is occurring in the present, after the moment of tragedy. The grandmother says she doesn't understand, and then she repeats herself. "I described it a thousand times," Jeremías says. "Mom was in her bedroom, Meme was in her room, I heard noise in the kitchen and went downstairs. I found Mom holding the gun to her head." We then see the father, who is sitting between his two children. The camera, in a medium shot, follows Meme as she gets up, her back to us, and walks away. The camera moves again to the place where the crisis culminated, but, this time, we see Lucía's sister talking to Olga. We follow Meme, who goes upstairs. We see a close-up of her hand on the railing, and we hear Lucía first sigh and then say, "It's stopped raining. I love rain." It is the language of shock. Now, we see Lucía. The camera abandons Meme and moves into the bedroom. Then, we hear her: "Where are the kids?" A woman replies, "Downstairs with their father." The camera positions itself behind the woman as she stares out the window at nothing. Her husband enters the room and hugs her. Lucía starts to repeat in English, "All shall be well, and all matters of things shall be well." The camera moves slowly out of the room and encounters the children as they come face to face at the top of the stairs. Slowly, we see Meme go down the stairs. The camera remains upstairs. First, we hear footsteps and then the music begins—a bolero sung by Cristina Banegas, the actress who plays Lucía. Thus, at the end, it is Lucía's voice, her singing voice, that embraces passion: "Touch me slowly, kiss me on the mouth."

The mother's voice, without a body, doubles the monotonous repetition of that voice which is relegated to the bedroom. The singing voice, Lucía's voice, is almost transcendent and sings of passion and desires. While the opening of the film consists of images of blood, close-up shots of syringes and the intense red of blood, the ending consists of the voice, both the halting, monotone voice of Lucía, which has lost all of the cheerfulness that it once displayed, and her off-screen voice, which sings about passion, perhaps suggesting that tragedy has not destroyed desire nor has it destroyed the patriarchal dominance of desire and of the articulated voice that sings about passion. The song is about the body-against-body, and it is here that the feminist dimension of the film resides. We no longer hear Lucía's voice in the bedroom. Instead, with that song, we hear her other voice, the one that remains in the rest of the house and lulls her children's passion. While one might suggest there is a weakening of Lucía's voice, through its splintering and marginalization, her voice is never her own. She is always repeating the articulated voice of paternal language. Yet, at the end, she recovers her voice through the aesthetic realm, through the musical voice that sings in praise of eroticism and of the body-against-body.

La rabia *and the Excesses of Language*

I turn once more to Kristeva and to those versions of corporeality that can express (if only intermittently) forms of resistance through semiotics, and which have to do with the register of excess, especially libidinal excess. These explosions that take place outside of paternal language (or more disconnected forms of grammar and its normativity) suggest certain counter-languages that exist on the margins of the Oedipal norm. Often that very silence highlights oppression and the lack of a voice, yet it can also act as a form of resistance to dominant language. As we will see in *La rabia* (2008), shouts function as acoustic signals that do not manifest as conventional languages. They are utterances that resist easy translation and refuse to be integrated into the circuit of comprehensible, structured, and well-articulated voices. Shouts here play a dual role: on the one hand, they represent invisible (especially domestic) violence and unlivable zones; on the other, they signal instinct, an explosion that does not fit within the structures of language and therefore shunts it aside.

La rabia takes place amid the tentacles of violence within two families and culminates in a final tragedy. Nati, the young daughter of Ale and Poldo, cannot (or will not) talk. Though the girl does not speak, she can express herself through her drawings. Those drawings rescue Nati from her isolation and therefore help her communicate her feelings, which she might not entirely understand—she is a young girl for whom puberty still seems to be a ways off. However, her drawings are soon appropriated by her father, who, from the very start, questions her, monitors her, and represses her. Those drawings become the "proof" for Poldo that his wife, Ale, is having an affair with another worker (Pichón). The girl's drawings contain sexually explicit poses, which Carri animates in order to narrate—wordlessly, voicelessly, almost silently—Nati's perspective on the sadomasochistic sexual interactions

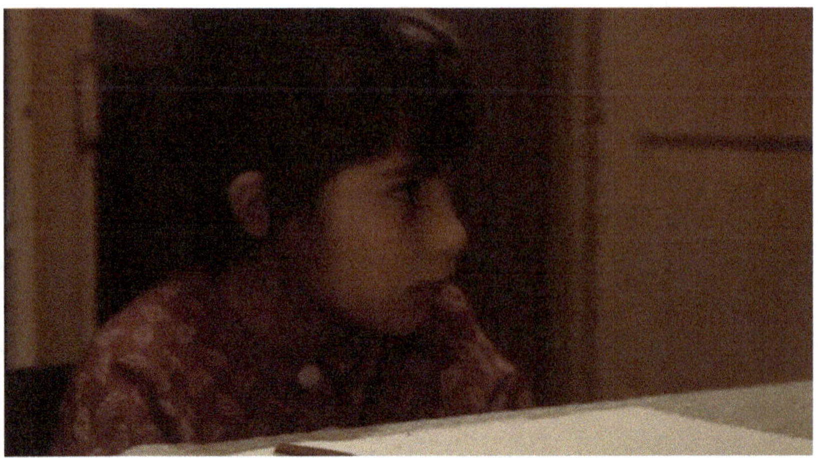

Still Image *La rabia* (dir. Albertina Carri, 2008)

between her mother and her neighbor. These animations employ visual and acoustic explosions, colorful bursts of red and black, in a montage that is interrupted by Nati's screams. The drawings lead to the final tragedy of the film. Poldo yells for his wife, and, when he cannot find her, goes to Pichón's house to look for her. There, he calls to them from outside, shouting and cursing and pounding on the door. When he goes inside, the camera remains motionless outside, and we see him go in but nothing else. Sound narrates what we cannot see. We hear noises and then a gunshot.

Nati uses screams and her drawings to express what cannot be described in words. The image–sound (drawing and scream) is an intersection in which Carri constructs a different meaning. Nati might not fully understand what is happening, but she understands enough to express it in her drawings. Her ability or talent exempts her from the contagious violence that inundates the space around her. That violence, sometimes explicit and at other times silent, is represented visually as animation and in the aural dimension as screams. There are also explosive sounds (from the sounds of animals that are about to be slaughtered by farmworkers to the sound of the final gunshot), and all of these sounds are the flip side of the film's initial placidity, represented by the image of the countryside, with its silence and muffled sounds. Nati's screams reveal the relationship between the girl and the world around her. They are her response to those scenes of violence, like the voice accompanying the animations that are splattered and flooded with black and red blotches.

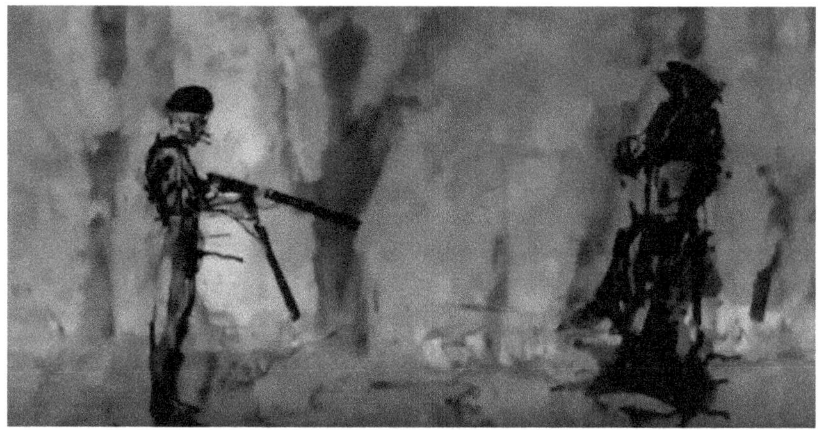

Still Image *La rabia* (dir. Albertina Carri, 2008)

Displacement is one of Carri's strategies for portraying what has been silenced, disappeared, or marginalized (or at least, the possibility of that portrayal). Displacement also plays a role in *La rabia*, with the animation of Nati's drawings. These drawings offer evidence of the connection between the violence and the sexual encounter that the girl observes, in which Pichón blindfolds Ale and watches her get undressed, before her friend Ladeado takes her away, promising to take care of her. On the one hand, the camera captures comprehensible forms of expression (the girl draws in order to express what she has seen; the father interprets those drawings and discovers the clue that leads him to find his wife with the neighbor). On the other, the emphasis on sound hints at the violence that Nati resists through her screams, which do not give in to paternal (articulate) language and cannot fully be translated by it.

The film opens and closes with a gunshot, and this circular structure points to a return to (and repetition of) the violent scene (and to the irrevocable impossibility of escape). Whether silent or explicit, violence is contrasted with the film's opening image of the countryside and with the stillness of the pampa landscape. The prevailing sounds in this landscape, apart from the gunshots, are the near-constant animal noises. Of the silence of the countryside, Carri says, "When somebody says countryside, you think silence. But in fact there's a noisy movement of bugs, crickets, chickens, cows audible in the distance, a presence. . . . On the other hand, there's the idea that sound is to-

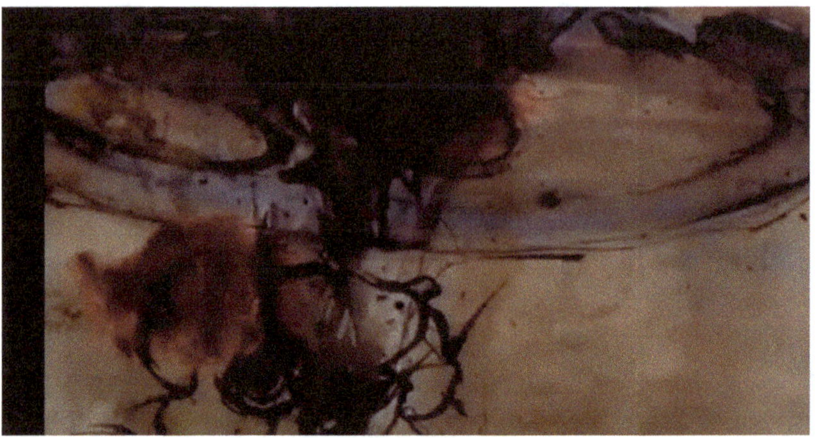

Still Image *La rabia* (dir. Albertina Carri, 2008)

tally subjective, that the ear chooses what to hear" (Pinto Veas, 2011: 5). Animals also represent violence, despite the film's initial warning ("The animals that appear in this movie lived and died in accordance with their habitat"). From the weasel that kills the chickens to the dogs that kill the sheep, animals represent a form of violence that is always present, even when characters try to avoid it (Ladeado does not want to kill the weasel and traps it in order to save its life). Many of the arguments between Poldo and Pichón about the dogs seem to morph into a battle over masculine power, which is the power over life and death, whether the death of animals or of human beings.

Nati's eyes alone are able to give meaning to this atmosphere of violence that surrounds her. She screams and compulsively takes her clothes off. Her father and mother lecture her about how to be a "good girl": "Good girls don't take their clothes off," her father says, while her mother says, "Good girls don't make that kind of drawings." The film encapsulates this paradox: Nati cannot talk, yet of all the characters in *La rabia*, she is the most capable of expressing herself, so she remains untouched by the contagion of violence. Her friend Ladeado, Pichón's son, also lives immersed in that atmosphere of abuse and will end up consumed by it. Pichón's death at Ladeado's hands is also narrated through sound, but, unlike Poldo's death at Pichón's hands, the sound is synchronized with the image. We see Ladeado with the shotgun, and we see Ale yell, "No," when Pichón goes over to Ladeado and insults him.

We see the teenager fire and we hear the gunshot while the image freezes on a shot of Ladeado.

Nati, however, can scream. The editing duplicates her scream by superimposing it over the animation of her drawings, with its bursts of color. That scream is her voice, the voice of someone who cannot speak. It is a disrupted voice striving to describe what exists, whether beyond language or beyond the images of her drawings and, thus, beyond what can be visually portrayed. The scream can therefore be understood as a ripping, in the sense suggested by Hélène Cixous when she describes the relationship between writing and voice as being like the destruction of comfortable rhythms. This dismantling of representation plays out through excess and its residues, or what remains perpetually unsaid in writing or in the narrative image (1976: 881). As Cixous suggests in her analysis of Lispector, the voice–scream associated with grief is the shattering of the discourse that ignores it, oppresses it, and abuses it. That voice–scream points to what remains outside the circuit of representation. It is a plaint associated with a physical body that, while it cannot break free, never stops resisting. That scream is also where her authority resides—a narrative authority that paradoxically does not accommodate narration but instead expresses trauma, violence, and her own role as a witness.

In *La rabia*, as well as in *Géminis* and *Los rubios*, the voice (or voices) allows Carri to portray the ambiguity of instinctual excess and, at the same time, to disrupt agreement about what language articulates. The voice engages in modulations that allow for examining narrative authority: who has it, who relinquishes it, who appropriates it, and who interrupts it to seize agency, however briefly. This description of the voice stands in contrast to writing, which fixes things in place and reflects an articulated language, such as in her father's writing in *Los rubios* or in her mother's letters in Carri's installation. Whether in the form of a letter or a publication, writing, which also reveals an absence (that is, the writing that remains after her parents' disappearance), comes to life through displacement. It is other voices that read it, that make it present. It is precisely in this displacement and in these modulations that Carri seeks both the voices of her missing parents and her own vision as a little girl in a past (a vision that can no longer be recovered). Writing might seem to be, perhaps, the space of narrative authority, yet the displacement of writing also gives the voice (and modulations of voice) a central place in the possibility of narrating and of shattering narration. The displacement of the voice dislodges the fixed quality of writing and yet embraces it. The scream, for its part, disrupts articulated language and the violence it conceals. The interruption of the scream points to what language and its rigid grammar are unable to articulate. The paternal language is abandoned, but voice survives and regains meaning in another form, even mutating into sounds that are not necessarily voices, but which evoke the search for a maternal sound.

CHAPTER 4

Voices and Echoes

THE QUESTION OF THE gaze in feminist film criticism not only implies an effort to make women and the paradigms that subordinate them visible, but is also anchored in the attempt to interrupt the visibility to which women are assigned in their role as objects by the patriarchal visual regime. The same could be said about sound. It is not merely a question of making women audible, but of reworking the aesthetics of sound and distancing women from the place they occupy in the aural regime, as mere Echoes. The story of Echo and Narcissus offers a useful starting point for this chapter. Echo, the nymph whom Hera punishes by taking away her ability to produce language, can only repeat what others say. Echo can no longer articulate her own voice. Her articulated language is destroyed, replaced by the echo of parts of the sounds of others. Yet she cannot repeat everything that is said, only a part, which leads both to misunderstandings and to the possibility of subversion. In her study of the voice, Adriana Cavarero emphasizes the misunderstanding between Echo and Narcissus, when Echo partially repeats what he says, driving away the one person who will never love her because he is capable only of loving and looking at himself. In losing material form, Echo becomes a voice without a body: "Without a mouth, or throat, or saliva, without any human semblance or visible figure, the beautiful nymph is sublimated into a mineralization of the voice" (2005: 166). This voice allows Cavarero to discuss the female voice, not only as the singing of the sirens or the muses but also as a materiality without *logos*, divorced from meaning (2005: 166).

For her part, Gayatri Spivak (1996) thinks of Narcissus and Echo through a gender lens (masculine and feminine) and also in postcolonial terms. Narcissus is placed at the center, looking at himself in the mirror and talking to his reflection, while Echo is placed at the periphery, repeating the last part of his sentences. Spivak uses this allegory to discuss the profile of the woman (periphery) in love with the man looking at himself (center) and to evoke the transformations that take place in the very act of repeating central paradigms. Echo, doomed to repetition and unable to produce her own articulations, is able to create new sentences thanks to her incomplete repetition of Narcissus's utterances. Despite her fate, she is able to produce new meanings. When Narcissus, who not only looks at his image but also speaks about it, complains that his image is rejecting him—"Why do you leave me?"—Echo repeats the last part of his complaint, "Leave me, leave me," as if she were pleading for Narcissus to go. This repetition, which is at the same time not a repetition, distorts the dominant, masculine meaning. For Spivak, it is a postcolonial echo, a mimicry that is never complete but which, in its incompleteness, becomes subversive.

If we are to think now about the echo as the sound of the resonance of the maternal body—the echo not of the male voice but of the sound of the mother's material existence—it is possible to think that the evocation of the mother's body through the voice comes out of a restoration of the relationship between the maternal body and pleasure. In that relationship with the body (through sound and touch), Kristeva, Irigaray, and Cixous see the possibility of conceiving of a pre-symbolic and pre-paternal language. The semiotic excess that cannot be salvaged at the limits of language, which is lost in articulated language, destabilizes the linguistic order and subverts grammar. This destabilization produces what Kristeva calls a *revolt*, which is always rooted in intimacy, and what Cixous and Irigaray think of as an *écriture feminine*, or the projection of the intimate into the public sphere. This chapter explores the echoes of the repetitions and resonances of the maternal body. It looks to the way the figure of Echo in love is rewritten, proposing instead more subversive instances of the resonance of the voice, first in Sabrina Farji and Paula de Luque's *Cielo azul, cielo negro*, and then in María Victoria Menis's *La cámara oscura*. Both films explore the gaze through the camera (the video camera held by a woman in the former, the photograph of an artist and former war reporter in the latter) and what this gaze makes visible. At the same time, in both films, the soundwork is key to the portrayal of the invisibility of women and the feminine. It is also key to the revolt that distorts the echo and produces the resonance of the maternal body in those languages associated with masculinity. Sound helps us to answer not only the question about what we do not see but also the question of what we can hear. It does so without relying on the way the invisible is made to *appear* through sound, thus disrupting, rather than destroying, the visual regime and its grammar. In both films, the question of the gaze cannot be formulated without the question of sound—more specifically, the sound of the voice that is also resonance.

Echoes and Distortions: Cielo azul, cielo negro

In *Cielo azul, cielo negro* (2003), directed by Sabrina Farji and Paula de Luque, Violeta, a character in the film, is also the desynchronized voice narrating a story in circles, repetitions, and echoes. She also provides some of the images captured by her camera, as she is often shown holding a camera while being filmed by another camera. The narrator's voice (Violeta's voice) is affirmed and diluted in distortions and echoes of quotations from *Alice in Wonderland* and *Through the Looking-Glass*, especially the segments that revolve around the Queen of Hearts. The two stories (Violeta's and Alice's) are blended and juxtaposed, and the repetitions and disruptions of language ultimately assault the very possibility of narrating, of respecting the chronology of events and the grammars that give them meaning. Instead, the film privileges images as white and red battle it out on the screen. These are the colors of the Queen of Hearts, and they are not only mentioned repeatedly (with changes and deviations) but also appear in much of the dance choreography, during which images leap and move in a succession of metonymies (from flowers to toilets, from caterpillars to the train station) and of mirrors (the person who films is being filmed, as we realize at the end, when Violeta finds tapes about her life in the house of the man she has met "by chance" and whom we later discover is the one who has been secretly recording her while she records other stories).

The film does not tell a linear story, but if we had to summarize it, we might say that it tells the story of four people whose lives intersect. In the narrative sequence that stretches from beginning to end, Violeta is the character who walks around filming everything, and her voice narrates offscreen. There are two additional stories: the first is the story of Abel, who is injured after he is shot and who, amid the hallucinated sounds of his dripping blood, reassembles the fragmented memories of his love story, including the details of how his lover left him, his pain, and then his crime and his agony. The other

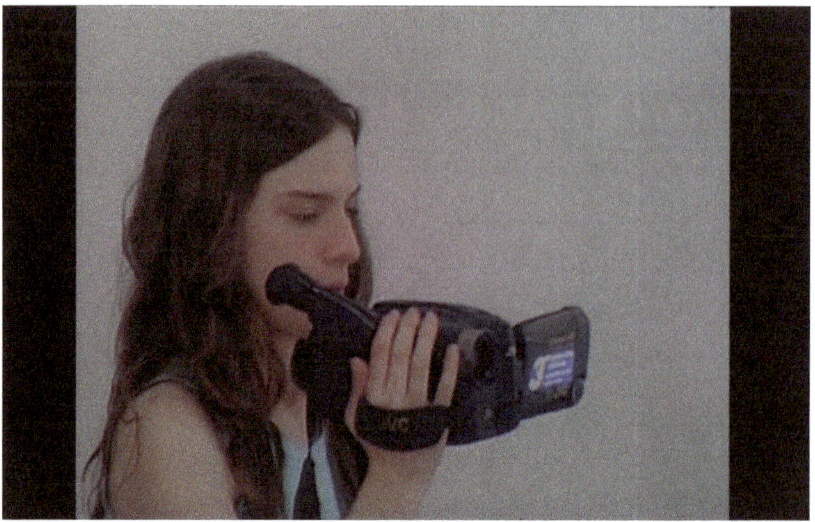

Still image *Cielo azul, cielo negro* (dir. Sabrina Farji and Paula de Luque, Barakacine /Cooperativa de Trabajo Kaos, DP Alejandra Martín, 2003)

story is about Ana, the dancer who expresses herself through the movements of her body and who dances on a stage full of white toilets set a couple of feet apart from one another. She also visits her mother in the hospital, where she meets Gabriel, who refuses to leave the hospital after the loss of a loved one. The framing of the shots points to boundaries and limitations of the visual order. The visible world (though it is portrayed through fragmentation, lapses, and jumps) excludes anything that remains outside these boundaries. As I will discuss below, it is also often accessible to us only through the voice. As such, acoustic narration (less associated with language than with the rupturing and distortion of language) opens up the boundaries of one or several worlds, revealing what the narrative image leaves out.

The film's narration is articulated (or disarticulated) through Violeta's voice, an offscreen voice that seems almost automatic and unconscious, a voice that repeats and distorts texts by Lewis Carroll: "Caterpillar game: a race in a circle. You just have to run and run and keep running until at some point somebody says stop." This description may be a good way of summarizing the film, which begins and also ends at a train station. Meanwhile Violeta repeats, with echoes that seem to dilute the first statement, "Things travel backward. A race inside a circle."

Here again I turn to Silverman's theory to discuss Violeta's voice and the way in which it dismantles the idea of a cohesive story, presenting it, instead, in fragments. More specifically, I want to reconsider this desynchronization through the theory of the body linked to *l'écriture fémenine*. Silverman's work focuses on Hollywood movies, and she claims that sound plays a crucial role in the embodiment of women through the synchronization of image and voice. The female voice, Silverman argues, is trapped in the diegesis and in the woman–body, and this voice speaks "out of the 'reality' of her body" (1998: 70–71), thereby keeping her firmly attached to her physical corporeality. The contrast that Silverman suggests points to the use of the desynchronization of the voice as a strategy of rupture in feminist cinema.

The shattering of body–voice synchronization in Farji and de Luque's film takes place in the diegetic space. Violeta's voice is untethered from the diegesis and narrates intermittently in circles and echoes. We see her image many times, but we do not see her speak. Instead, her voice recounts her disordered thoughts. The initial desynchronization resides in this displacement of the female voice to the realm of the mind, thoughts, and immateriality. In addition, her voice serves as a narrative voice—that is, as a voice that transcends the story and has the authority conferred by her gaze and her interpretive power. The near absence of dialogue is apparent in the film. The narration relies on visual images, particularly symbols (especially in the choreography). The fragmentation generates a zigzagging narration that does not seek to move toward a denouement but, instead, and as the offscreen voice foreshadows, builds a circular story that is affected by the echoes of Violeta's voice. Only in the hospital sequences is there dialogue between the characters. The offscreen voice narrates and describes: "A man alone in a deserted room. The caterpillar was the one not moving." Meanwhile, the characters talk to one another. In the hospital, Ana's image overlaps with Violeta's offscreen voice: "This hospital is like the train. The waiting rooms are like the train. I'm the only one who can come and go—everybody else lives there, waiting." And later, "Could you please tell me which way I should go from here?" Echoes of *Alice in Wonderland* also interrupt the film's narration.

Violeta's voice at first transcends the narrated story before finally entering it. Nevertheless, Violeta (Alice?) is not telling a story but instead interpreting it, either giving clues that echo and repeat quotations from Lewis Carroll's classic tale ("Things travel backward"), giving instructions ("recognize the difference between real life and dreams"), or attempting to define words

("Turn: to change direction. Show: to expose something to view. Move: To make a body change position. Relationship: correspondence between one thing and another"). The echoes and distortions from Alice's story accompany the camera's movement. This voice is an articulated voice, but never completely. It is a voice that seeks to affirm a different subjectivity, one that defines itself not through an echo of a children's story, an echo that not only repeats but also transforms and creates. It is the female voice, superimposed on the echo of the text, which subverts the text, transfigures it, and appropriates it. The voice moves through images—the caterpillar and its circles, colors (especially red, the color of the Queen of Hearts)—and then formulates a question about which way to go, even though the answer does not seem to matter. Her voice narrates other stories, too, in an effort to act as the architect of her own: "And when I come across two guys wearing the same color of suit, I stop there and he has to be there and he will be there." Violeta's offscreen voice narrates, asks, wanders aimlessly, accompanies, and questions the video camera and the meaning of the stories it records. There is an approach to and a distancing from language and its regulations. The bodily and emotional excesses that surpass the limits of the structured paternal language are expressed through the voice (Violeta's voice as the flip side of Alice's voice), the same voice that quotes in resonances and inhabits the outer limits of language, in all of its surplus. It seeks the norm through a near obsession with definitions: "Look: the act of looking." Her voice also abandons norms by panting alongside the definitions, and the sound of panting, which is anchored in her body, indicates arousal. Thus, Violeta narrates through her body in order to distort the limitations of definitions and the norms of language.

This conflict with language takes place in Violeta's voice. She incessantly repeats the stories of the caterpillar and the Queen of Hearts, but she transforms them each time: "the caterpillar was on drugs but still elegant; it kept its balance." The effect of this endless repetition is that it creates a gap between Alice's story and Violeta's, and this gap is, at the end, reflected on a mirrored surface that deforms her image. In the bedroom of the man she has just met, she finds the gaze that has been recording her. There, she finds videos labeled "Violeta," and, when she watches them, she sees herself. It is her story, now without her voice, but shown from another perspective. The videos show a gaze of which she is the object. As spectators, we have already seen her image, but it was accompanied by her narrative voice, and now that we see her in silence, she has become someone else. This video, without her voice, is not complete. Then, we hear, "Things travel backward. A race inside a circle." This phrase is repeated several times before we discover that we have returned to the start of the film, and so the ending has come full circle to the beginning, just as the caterpillar predicted. Violeta's voice (as offscreen narration) appropriates Lewis Carroll quotations, repeating and transforming them. The film affirms Violeta and her narrative and interpretive authority as a subject, which transcends the visual image, by appropriating and transforming the text's words in the form of echoes and distortions. Violeta does not repeat everything but only parts. Carroll's text is changed too. A text like *Alice*, associated with the image of the mirror and the visual realm, a Northern Hemispheric text that is repeated from the periphery in the voice of a woman/echo, is now transformed through the voice. But this voice is not associated with language and phallocentrism; instead, it distorts and dissipates language.

There is a continuity between Violeta's offscreen narration and the voice-over (here I am following Doane [1980] and her distinction between voice-off and voice-over). The offscreen voice is a voice that is outside the visual field, but which is recognizable as a character and thus exists within the diegesis. The voice-over, however, is located in another space, an external realm that, according to Doane, gives it authority. Yet the echoes and distortions of *Cielo azul, ciel negro* create a dual exteriority. The radical nature of the voice lies in the way it remains outside both the text, which it repeats and transforms, and the story itself.

The power of the gaze also plays out through the conflict between look and gaze. Even though Violeta carries her camera and tells the stories of the other characters, and even though Farji and de Luque are associated with the camera's gaze, we learn at the end that Violeta's whole story (as a character and not as a narrator or filmmaker) has been recorded by the camera of a man who returns her to the position of an object. (Violeta finds the videos after a sexual encounter with this man, whom we can recognize in one of the earlier shots, where he is seen holding a camera that is obviously not hers). There is a clash of gazes. Even so, the narrative voice, which gives the images cohesiveness or inconsistency, is Violeta's. Her voice shifts between obsessively defining words and distortedly echoing bits of Carroll's original text. These bits are repeated and broken apart, displacing the story of Alice for the fragmented, distorted story of Violeta, who not only looks at and records narrative images of other people, including her own romantic encounter, but also seeks to find her own voice in the quotes (or ruins) of the children's story.

Echoes of the Maternal Body: La cámara oscura

Based on a short story by Angélica Gorosdicher, *La cámara oscura* (2007), directed by María Victoria Menis, reflects on the gaze, especially the photographic gaze. In this film, the question about how the invisible becomes visible seems even more essential than the concern about what remains invisible. The answer to this question involves taking an artistic path. The film's exploration of the photographic gaze (Who is looking? What does the looking subject desire, remember, see?) is interrupted by an animation sequence and by a sequence narrated through a surrealist collage, both of which can be seen as reflections on the cinematographic gaze. The film's approach to the visual regime moves from the figure of a male photographer to that of a female director. As I will discuss in this section, it is in this movement that sound, and especially singing and rhythm as the echo of the maternal body, points to what cannot be explained in solely visual terms. This movement toward sound is accomplished not through dialogue, but through a "sonorous envelope"—a concept used by Mary Ann Doane to refer to the maternal voice as "the first model of auditory pleasure" (1980: 44).

La cámara oscura tells the story of Gertrudis, the daughter of an immigrant Jewish family. Gertrudis's family arrives in Argentina in the late nineteenth century, and, shortly after their arrival, they move to the countryside. Instructed by her mother from a young age to look down when her picture is being taken, Gertrudis accepts her own marginalization and her supposed lack of beauty. She tries to hide in photographs, but she also (secretly) establishes herself as a "looking subject" when she gazes out at the natural world around her. We see her hide from the camera, but we also see her looking at the river. She learns to make herself more and more invisible from others and, once invisible, starts a family with a widower named León who quashes her voice. Not only does this widower not see Gertrudis, but he does not see what she attempts to makes visible (and the way she expresses herself through the combination of colors of fruit and flowers). Unlike León's first wife, whose beauty is associated with a rebellious, carefree temperament that was punished by León's watchful gaze, Gertrudis is labeled a good wife and mother, and "accepted" because of it.

The film takes place between 1910 and 1930, with Gertrudis and her family in the Argentine countryside. The camera captures both her and her invisibility. We often see her alone and silent as she completes the domestic chores associated with her role as a wife and mother: setting the table, cooking, and gardening.[26] Yet Gertrudis does not have a weak voice; she has a negated voice. Her voice is clear and well-articulated, but, in general, she is silent, often shown staring at the river, as if waiting for or remembering something. In one of the few moments in which we hear her voice, she says that her father also used to gaze at the river, pining for his homeland.

The arrival of a French photographer (Jean Baptiste) begins to transform Gertrudis and the looking relations around her. He comes to photograph the entire family, but as he starts to become aware of her and her marginality, he begins to focus on her through his photographic lens. He starts to see her. He initially sees (notices, perceives) her garden and her stores of jam, and only then does he see Gertrudis. The first time he sees her is when he takes a family photo and she refuses to participate. Jean Baptiste goes over (she is with her flowers in the garden) and speaks to her. He says, "I know very well what it's like not to want to be in any photos." His voice and these words pull her out of her invisibility. These words also rewrite the gaze of Gertrudis's mother, which is a key contributor to her invisibility (her maternal voice is here associated with the rules of the patriarchy). The photographer talks to Gertrudis (he "sees her"; for once, Gertrudis has not gone unnoticed), and, with his words and voice, he both recognizes her and calls on her to let herself be seen. Gertrudis then approaches the rest of the family to take the portrait.

The second key moment for understanding the revelation produced by the photographer's gaze is when Jean Baptiste develops the photos. In the dark storehouse where he works, the photographer sees the color-inverted image of Gertrudis on the wall, and he goes up to touch it. The gaze is ineluctably at the core of this scene. The darkroom is the place where the gaze awakens beauty, but a beauty that implies a new way of looking. (There is a third moment in which, as spectators, we see all the power of revelation concentrated in him, but I will discuss that later on.)

This reflection on the gaze and the visible does not preclude a reflection on the aural dimension. The movie reflects not only on the invisible but also on

26. See Guadalupe Treibel's interview with the director, "La mirada indiscreta," published in *Las 12* on October 10, 2008.

the inaudible, and silence becomes central. In a film with very little dialogue, we hear silence (the silenced voice at different moments) and, along with it, the various sounds of the countryside. Silence implies a hushing of the articulated voice and of paternal language so as not to succumb to it, instead allowing for an engagement with and an embrace of (rather than a dialogue with) the maternal language. The inaudible is, in this film, manifested through the countryside noises, which point to sound and to the absence of the voice. Later, I will mention another way that the maternal language becomes audible: through music and singing.

Menis proposes an exploration of the inaudible as well as of the voice. On the one hand, there is the voice of her mother, which is not a maternal voice because it is clearly symbolic and patriarchal and which defines Gertrudis as invisible. On the other, there is the voice of the photographer, who used to be a war correspondent and is looking for new ways of seeing. He calls her into a visible space, not the space of the family, but rather the space of his own visual field —and the spectator now can see her through this new pair of eyes. Through their voices (or their inaudible voices), we begin to realize that there is an intimate world shared between Gertrudis and Jean Baptiste that we cannot access, only imagine, because we see them talk but cannot hear them. Menis works with the voice and with the absence of a voice, both for us as spectators and for the rest of the family, but not for Gertrudis or the photographer.

Gertrudis notices Jean Baptiste for the first time when she hears his voice and is able to see his world. Gertrudis does not see him until she hears him. This first occurs when he invites her to join the family photo. His voice makes her visible because it makes her intelligible. Jean Baptiste's voice conveys his vision to her; he has seen her, not just because he has noticed her but also because he has recognized her. He has seen her despite her invisibility, and he has also understood her desire to remain invisible, and her invisibility will become a key element in the unfolding of the plot. When Gertrudis finally "sees him," she does so without looking; she first perceives him through her sense of hearing. During a family conversation after dinner, Gertrudis, from the kitchen, hears him speaking, but she cannot see him with her eyes. He is talking about war and suffering and about photography during war. Gertrudis is in the kitchen, listening to the photographer's voice, and she is moved by his words. When she goes to the table, she sits down next to him and looks at him and listens. But now the camera mutes the photographer's voice, while nonetheless showing him speaking. His lips move and we hear music instead of his words, which

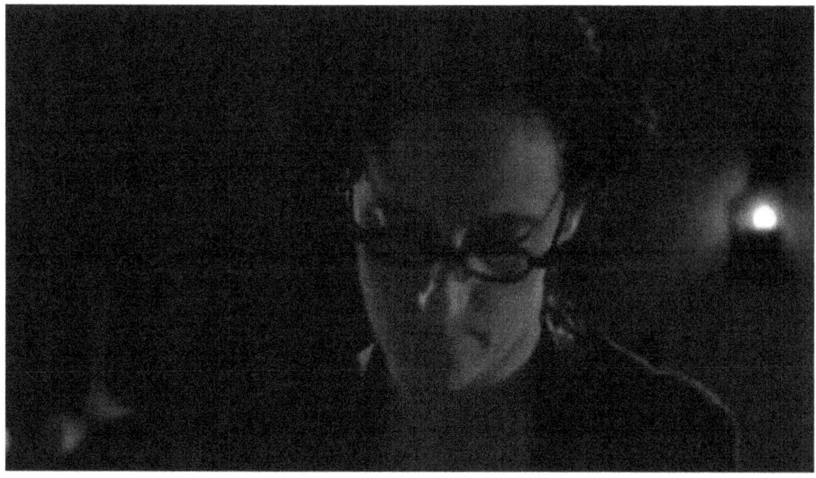

Still image *La cámara oscura* (dir. María Victoria Menis, 2007)

indicates not a conversation, because his voice is quieted and replaced by music, but a resonance and an acoustic embrace. It is also a moment of desynchronization between voice and image—she first hears him, and only afterward does she look at him. The narrative sequence places desynchronized image and sound at the beginning of their connection, and dismantles the corporeal aspect of sound and the desired object of the gaze. The film elaborates instead on a series of irruptions of the gaze and the voice, suggesting that the first flush of love takes place precisely at the intersection of a discussion on suffering, ethics, and aesthetics. While Jean Baptiste talks about his work as a photojournalist and the effects of the horrors of war on aesthetics at the turn of the century, we hear the noises of silence (not silence but thrumming crickets) and a music that evokes the resonance of language, pre-Oedipal language, outside the symbolic universe. The point of view here is Gertrudis's: now that she sees him, his voice is interrupted, but only for a moment. When we hear him again, we hear him discuss aesthetics and how war has transformed art and ways of seeing. "We had to reinvent our way of seeing," he says to explain surrealism, pointing to new ways of looking at "what's hidden from view."

The film has two interruptions that I would like to highlight. The first is the animation of a childish dream, with drawings by Argentine artist Rocardo Cohen (Rocambole). The animation shows a little girl—actually a shadow—who is freed by a beautiful woman, her fairy godmother. The girl might be a metaphor for Gertrudis herself, but the animation is also a reflection on the gaze. Discussing this sequence, Menis asks, "What does it mean to let oneself be seen, to show oneself?" At the end, the shadow breaks apart to reveal the little girl underneath. The second animation uses the photographer—specifically, the photographer's eye—as its starting point. It is a surrealist sequence that interrupts a family lunch, beginning in Jean Baptiste's eye with the bouquet of flowers that Gertrudis made. The gaze is central for Gertrudis, whom we often see staring silently at the river and expressing herself in colors, whether through food, fruits, or flowers. Through these colors, the moving image shatters and gives way to a series of images that center on the photographer's eye: flowers, petals, a family photo on each petal, and the multiplication of the photographic images. We see Gertudis, then a spiral, an eye, a waterfall, a naked woman who is barely visible, and a dreamlike sequence of displacements. Everything transforms into something else, until the image returns to the eye. In a distinctly visual sequence, we hear the voice of Gertrudis's daughter and the violin her son is playing. Her daughter is singing in Yiddish, and her voice perhaps evokes her mother. The echo is now a maternal resonance, the echo of the maternal body, an echo that is beyond masculine language. This echo overflows and points to a maternal, oral language. The echo evokes the body of that land for which Gertrudis's father longed and which now accompanies the images while also dislocating them.

Going back to the dream sequence, we can add the female voice to the photographer's visual fantasy. In this fantasy, the gaze is central, presenting a series of displacements—flowers, the female face, her body, and water—and encompassing the image of the feminine but through a male eye. The voice of Gertrudis's own daughter, however, gestures toward another language, another evocation, and another belonging. While this voice accompanies the images, it remains remote from the photographer's gaze as echo and resonance. Yet it is not Narcissus's Echo, but the echo of Gertrudis's image through her own gaze or memory or fantasy. There is an intersection between images and sound, and in this intersection, images cease to belong to the photographer and become instead the images that Gertrudis herself sees, hears, or feels, the images of the waterfall, flowers, and her own self through the artist's gaze, Jean Baptiste's eye. Thus, the dream becomes a collage of acoustic mirrors in which we can see Gertrudis not just as the object of the photographer's fantasy but also as the mirror that reflects his desire back to him and, thus, as a subject of the gaze. Additionally, we see (or hear) her as sound

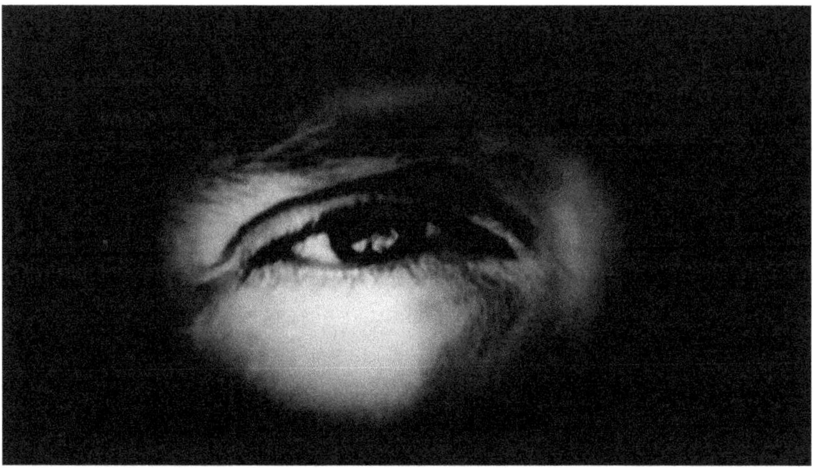

Still image *La cámara oscura* (dir. María Victoria Menis, 2007)

(as song), which her daughter echoes with her voice, and her son with his violin.

We shift from reading the echo as a distortion or subversion of Narcissus's patriarchal voice, as in Farji and de Luque's *Cielo azul, cielo negro*, to reading the echo as an acoustic relationship with the maternal body. Nevertheless, I am not discussing these two different ehoes to show a continuity between them (Echo and Narcissus and the maternal body). In her study about the voice, Cavarero suggests that there is a continuity between the maternal resonance and the distortion in Echo and Narcissus and that said connection is anchored in the pleasure of the echo as well as its resemblance to a childish game. When Echo repeats Narcissus's words and empties them of semantic content, she is doing the same thing babies do when they repeat, but without meaning, their mothers' sounds (Cavarero, 2005: 168).[27] Nevertheless, in Farji and de Luque's film, the repetition's radicality resides precisely in the fact that the distortion continues to distort and represents not an infantile gesture but a feminist one. In the case of the maternal body and its voice in Menis's

27. Of course, whereas in the former case (and here I am following Cavarero) a punishment from Hera strips Echo of an articulated voice and condemns her to only repeat others' words, the relationship established in the pre-Oedipal language is not a punitive one.

film, the repetition of the mother's sounds is the path that leads to *logos*. It is for that reason that I posit them as separate instances. Ultimately, singing and repetition evoke the maternal body and invoke the mother as music and sound. Thus, singing in the dream sequence alludes to all those images that cannot be understood, or, at least, that cannot be understood yet.

Music and the singing voice also echo Gertrudis's father, to whom Gertrudis refers in a narration that her husband silences. She remembers her father looking at the countryside: "I used to see it in his eyes," she says, referring to what is longed for and to what is—though never entirely—lost. The singing voice plays a central role in creating a new meaning for this image (what Gertrudis saw in her father's eyes). This voice is associated with the maternal body and sparks pleasure outside the realm of the paternal language (associated here with the patriarchal order of the family). Thus, there is a return to the maternal, to the maternal sound, and to the cadence and rhythm associated with feminine corporeality. The singing voice accompanies these images to make us hear what we do not see because it exists outside the visual realm. Yet it also makes us hear what cannot be heard in words: that pre-Oedipal language that exists in exile, as Irigaray suggests when she discusses the body-against-body with the mother. We cannot see it, but we can hear it, and when maternal language comes into play, so, too, does an incomprehensible sonority that has no place in the visible world.

Through photography, the film also explores what is suggested by the moving images but left outside the visual field. At the end of the film, the photographic images of Jean Baptiste and Gertrudis restore the gaze shared by them. First, the camera shows him walking toward the river. We see her sitting and look at him, and then she stands. He is taking photos, and we see him smile. Later we watch as he develops the photos, and it is here that a new revelation is presented to the viewer. (Earlier in the chapter, I referred to three revelations: the first is the gaze that reveals Gertrudis and her role in the family, and the second is the image that reveals Gertrudis to the photographer). The third revelation is a never-before-seen image of the protagonist that reflects her transformation or awakening. In the darkroom, we see Gertrudis's image appear. We see her just as she appears, wearing white, posing for the photo, looking at the camera, looking at Jean Baptiste, and looking at us.

Only at the end, when the film returns to the opening image of the breakfast table still uncleared from the previous night's dinner, do we realize that Gertrudis has left. It is then that the images, , which we previously did not see, appear. Once more, we hear her daughter's singing, and we see Gertrudis with the photographer by the river. He whispers something to her, but we cannot hear what they say. She takes a photo of him, and then they take one together, looking into each other's eyes. The camera shows us their images, but it does not allow us to hear voices. We see them whispering to each other, but we do not hear them. Instead, we hear them with our eyes. Music accompanies the ending, and the maternal voice is evoked in the moment that Gertrudis abandons that domestic space and her maternal role in the family. In the maternal voice, which evokes the mother and a fusion or harmony with the maternal body and sound, there is also a reference to loss. In her study of the voice, Mary Ann Doane calls it a "sonorous envelope," and she stresses that the relationship between sound and the maternal body is also the possibility of union between narcissistic pleasure and the fantasy of cohesion with one's own body (1980: 45). The presence of the maternal is ghostly. On the one hand, it is the voice (the resonance, the echo of a lost instance) that promises to unite one with the mother's body, and, on the other, it is the voice that dismisses the mother in the moment of separation (marked, Doane writes, by the intervention of the paternal voice that summons her with his desire). The song in Menis's film echoes this relationship and produces the illusion of a possible union with the mother and her memory, almost as an interpellation that becomes an evocation. There is an echo of the mother's sound but as if she were absent or lost, a ghostly presence.

The different instances of sound, echoes, and voices in this chapter—whether the distorted voice of the female character in *Cielo azul, cielo negro*, who narrates and renarrates *Alice in Wonderland* while trying to tell a story with her video camera on the streets of Buenos Aires, or the desynchronization of voice and image in *La cámara oscura*, in which singing and music are evoked in the moment of loss as the echo and resonance of the maternal sound—reflect the invisible and inaudible. These two films explore the acoustic realm while moving away from articulated language, whether to distort and transform it or to repeat it from outside of semantics. Although this remaining outside of semantics or against signification does not imply the absence of meaning, it does imply a questioning of articulated and therefore visible languages. The feminine, as the invisible and as all that is expressed as excess or as a dismantling of the structuring principle, is what breaks into the masculine realm, with its circumscribed language. The feminine is what operates in the folds of visual representation, on its borders and in its dark regions, and is what marks, through sound, that which remains outside its boundaries. Perhaps, one of those boundaries may be the pleasure of sound, resonance, and echoes, as well as the pleasure of positioning oneself acoustically in the otherness of articulated language. By repeating sounds that undermine traditional meaning and evoke the illusion of unity with the maternal body, one positions oneself within the sonority of the mother's voice and her singing, even if that positioning takes place in the very moment the mother and her voice are lost.

CHAPTER 5

Politics and Aesthetics: The Visible and the Audible

RETHINKING THE AESTHETICS OF memory is one of the most salient considerations for Lita Stantic's 1993 film *Un muro de silencio* [*A Wall of Silence*], which focuses on the intersection of voices and gazes through a clearly aesthetic and political lens.[28] This film tells the story of the production of a movie about the life of a detention center survivor. Going back and forth between the 1970s and the 1990s, the film-within-the-film allows for a reflection about not just the possibility of depicting disappearance and survival, but also how to give voice to intimate stories entangled with repression and human rights abuses. The film stages a range of sounds and visions that point to the visible and the invisible, toward the audible and the inaudible. There are powerful voices, for example, that are present and yet inaudible, and there are gazes that are also powerful and yet invisible. This dynamic of sound and vision is rooted in the relationship between the po-

28. Lita Stantic's work as a producer is well known, first in relation with Bemberg's films, of which Stantic produced all but the last one. Added to that list (*Momentos; Señora de nadie; Camila; Miss Mary; Yo, la peor de todas*) are her productions of more recent films by directors who emerged in the nineties—that is, the new independent cinema (Pablo Trapero's *Mundo Grúa* [*Crane World*], Lucrecia Martel's *La ciénaga* [*La Ciénaga*], Adrián Caetano's *Bolivia* and *Un oso rojo* [*Red Bear*], and Diego Lerman's *Tan de repente* [*Suddenly*]). Moreover, this public aspect of women's gaze in film deserves special attention (Stantic, for example, was president of the Cámara Argentina de la Industria Cinematográfica from 1986 to 1996 and a founder of the Festival del Cine y la Mujer). See http://www.litastantic.com.ar/unmuro/index.htm.

litical and the audiovisual, especially in terms of the political activism of the 1960s and 1970s, and the struggles for human rights and justice in the 1990s postdictatorship period, a decade marked by impunity in Argentina.

In this chapter, I examine the aesthetic and political dimensions of the voice. Specifically, I examine the relation of the testimonial voice to how it is made visible or invisible, by which I mean made intelligible and not just audible. Because testimonial voices are political voices that, in this film, attempt to explore how forced disappearances affect the lives of survivors, it is pertinent to rethink the relationship between *phone* and *logos*, which Mladen Dolar develops in *A Voice and Nothing More*, and between *bios* and *zoe*, which Giorgio Agamben develops in his now-classic *Homo Sacer* on the concept of biopolitics. Dolar suggests a relation between the concepts of *phone* and *zoe* ("Voice is like bare life" [2006: 106]) and those of *logos* and *bio* ("*logos* is the counterpart of *polis*, of social life ruled by laws and a common good" [2006: 106]). "Voice," he says, "is like bare life, something that is supposedly exterior to the political" (106). Yet that "externality" is, for Agamben, an "inclusive exclusion" of naked life, and therefore, Dolar continues, the voice is also placed in an ambiguous and paradoxical position outside and inside *logos* and politics ("the voice is not simply an element external to speech, but persists at its core, making it possible and constantly haunting it by the impossibility of symbolizing it" [106]). In Agamben, *zoe* lives on within the social realm, and is not merely the pre-social or what is excluded; in a parallel manner, in Dolar's approach, which closely follows Agamben, the voice does not occupy a space external to *logos*, which is now manifested in speech, but instead is located in a simultaneous inclusion and exclusion that contains the excluded within it (2006: 106). *Zoe*, Dolar claims, "persists, in its very exclusion/inclusion, at the heart of the social" (106). The voice, then, is not the "remnant of a precultural state" but "the product of *logos* itself," and it is also what disrupts *logos* (2006: 107). Thus, the Venn diagram that Dolar proposes shows the voice at the intersection of two overlapping circles—that is, a voice that is modulated differently in relation to bare life and life associated with community and political life. This distinction also prompts us to think of the voice in terms of what remains outside the social in spatial or temporal terms, such as in animality, which is associated with *zoe*. However, Dolar argues, this remnant persists in the marrow of social life and thus complicates any attempt to think of the voice as something external to discourse. Instead, he sees *logos* itself as producing an excess, which is the voice. The voice, whether a scream or an animal sound, is never stripped of signification but is bereft of intelligible meaning and stands in contrast to the political voice.

The aesthetic concerns about memory in *Un muro de silencio* allow us to reflect on the relationship between the visible and the audible. Moreover, it allows us to rethink this relationship in political terms, at least as Jacques Rancière defines it—in terms of a dissent and disruption that originates when an invisible, inaudible group invades the social order (1999: 26). Rancière describes a conflict between those who have an articulated voice (logic) and those whose speech is distorted and who, therefore, have a voice only as sound (1999: 26–27). Politics is governed by *logos*, words, and reason. Only bodies with names occupy the place of the visible, whereas those that lack them occupy the realm of the invisible. Rancière calls this apportioning of bodies and voices *the distribution of the sensible.* With that, the law that regulates perceptive modes comes into play. Politics exists, as Rancière sees it, because those who do not have a part (and who are denied the right to be counted) make themselves be counted. "Political activity is whatever shifts a body from the place assigned to it or changes a place's destination. It makes visible what had no business being seen, and makes heard a discourse where once there was only place for noise; it makes understood as discourse what was once only heard as noise" (1999: 30). For Rancière, the political is based on the distribution of the sensible, and thus aesthetics plays a central role in the sense that it participates in the composition of the visible and in the creation of spaces of dissent from the roles assigned by the police order.

In the tension that *Un muro de silencio* exposes between the film and the film-within-the-film, as well as between the female survivor of a clandestine detention center and her fictionalized portrayal, Stantic points to the delegation of the voice and the ethics of representation. In addition, the film poses the question of the political voice, whether confronting the voice of authoritarianism or that of redemocratization. The latter includes both the official voice that articulates democracy as accountability and justice (1980s) and the voice that articulates democracy as impunity (1990s), and reveals the tension with witnesses' voices as well as the possibility of making them visible. Because this staging of voices is a sort of performance, in the Butlerian sense, it involves the repetition of a quotation from a script that is discussed several times throughout the film. The performance also involves the modulation of the voice, referred to by the director's instructions to the actors. The voice is rooted in *zoe*, and it is also the excess, the exclusion/inclusion of *logos*, and the residual force of what cannot be made visible but can be made audible through a series of resonances and repetitions, that point to a ghostly voice, but one that cannot be articulated in terms of rationality.

Silence plays a key role in the intersection of the visual and the acoustic because it invokes the same kind of (invisible) ghostly presence as well as the impossibility of making it intelligible. In that ambiguous zone between the visible and the invisible, the spectral silence reveals its presence through an absent voice—the voice of the disappeared. Yet this presence is also rooted, as can be seen in the demonstrations calling for memory and justice, in the voices that shout, "Presente!" ["Present!"], which summon the silent and make them present.

Un muro de silencio explores the reorganization of the space of the visible through its staging of a film-within-the-film. It is the year 1990, the year in which the Presidential Pardons (Indultos) were issued to the members of the military juntas who were sentenced in 1985. In the film, the filmmaker Kate Benson travels to Buenos Aires to produce a movie, guided by a script by Bruno Tealdi, a former professor of the story's protagonist, Silvia Cassini. Silvia is a survivor of the last military dictatorship, whose husband was disappeared and who herself was kidnapped with her young daughter and later released. The tension is recorded by Kate's gaze and her camera and by Bruno's gaze and his words. Though he is Argentine and is writing the story that Kate, a foreigner, is trying to depict in her film, Bruno gives voice not to Silvia but to Ana—that is, to the fictional character that is based on his conversations with Silvia. While it could be said that Kate views things from a foreign perspective, Bruno, too, observes from a place that is external to, or at least dislocated from, Silvia Cassini's experience. The film emphasizes that tension between gazes: first between Kate and Bruno, and later between Silvia and Ana. Silvia's perspective is at the center of the film's attention, but that attention occurs at the expense of her vision—perhaps, alluding to the title itself, her vision is hidden behind a wall of silence. Yet it is within the context of that tension that Silvia's voice is modulated, as Bruno articulates her voice through Ana. But how can one talk about personal experience when confronted not only by silence but by ventriloquism? It is through that ventriloquism that the aesthetic–political considerations of the voice arise. The actress who plays Ana must employ the voice in Bruno's script, the same voice that stands in for Silvia's voice, by giving it a body and making it audible on a movie set. This ventriloquism and the not-knowing how to modulate the disappeared voice expose one of most important ethical issues related to the aesthetic and political representation of the experience of disappearance, particularly when someone from outside—who has not been held in the detention center—attempts to represent such an experience. It also reveals that bare life is made present only through the ghostly presence of the disappeared.

The intersection of different voices in the film is connected to the (paradoxical) distinction between *zoe* and *bios*—some voices are excluded in inclusion, while some others are absent but become present through siege, both in the script and the film. Thus, ghostliness in the film points to the impossibility of making present the lost voice, specifically the lost voice associated with the detention center, be it the voice of the protagonist or the voice of the disappeared husband, which cannot be recovered. At the same time, the film underscores the impossibility of allowing those lost voices to be absent. Their presence resides in that ambiguous realm of ghostliness, which Stantic explores by contrasting the emergence of a survivor's voice with the script and film that recount her story.

What are the proximities and distances between the movie filmed by a foreign director in Argentina (or the script on which it is based) and the story of a real survivor, both in terms of truth and ethics but also in the political terms of visibility and audibility? On the one hand, the film depicts the emergence of a voice that manages (or does not manage) to articulate, and especially to transmit, the personal experiences of the husband's kidnapping and disappearance. In that sense, it entails a dispute with the narratives of the terrorist state (and its crimes against humanity) and the denialist state (and impunity and presidential pardons). On the other hand, there is a tension in the film between the political voice, which is represented through artistic manifestations that make experience visible, and the articulate but more intimate voices of both mother and daughter, which offer a portrait of the intergenerational transmission of memories. While there is a gap between the articulation of these two voices, there is also a question near the beginning of the film (when the director asks the scriptwriter if everybody knew what was happening) that is repeated at the end (when the daughter asks her mother the same question). In both instances, the scriptwriter and the survivor provide exactly the same answer: "Everybody knew." This repetition suggests that, in addition to there being a gap between the artistic and the testimonial, there is also a continuity. Thus, the film explores how the aesthetic reorganizes the space of the visible and audible through the fissure between the artistic and first-person narration. Change is rooted in the shift to intergenerational dialogue.

Gaze and Ghostliness

As Kate films her story, she wonders how to observe the characters (especially Ana, Silvia's fictional counterpart), and she offers viewers a story that is both fragmented and interrogated, thus suggesting that the story cannot actually be told. The question of the gaze is therefore inextricably related to the subject of that gaze. Kate, in this case, as a subject who is located outside of Argentine history, represents the eyes of the "outsider." Though she is in solidarity with the struggles for justice in Argentina, her solidarity is not enough to grant her an "insider's" gaze.[29] The other looking subject is Bruno; though his eyes are located, supposedly, inside the recent violent past, his gaze is is revealed to be paternalistic when it seizes the right to narrate.[30] Of course, unlike Kate's, his voice is not disconnected from Argentina's painful past. Yet his is an impertinent gaze because it is emotionally close to Silvia's story but distant from her in interpretive terms. Bruno narrates from a position of not knowing. At the end, in a scene of confrontation with Silvia, when she finally relents and embraces her past through Bruno's embrace, it becomes clear that, in that past–present binary, Bruno's impertinence has to do with his not knowing and with his inability to know or imagine Silvia's perspective, in which the ghostly presence of the past is rooted.

The contrast of voices and gazes in the film illustrates the urgency of the representation of the past, or, at least, the urgency of its possible representation, as well as the urgency of an aesthetics that addresses political questions. The notion of framing serves here to rethink the visible and the invisible. In both an aesthetic and a political sense, the frame redesigns the space of the visible, where the articulated word may offer hints of what is necessarily lost for the marginalized and inaudible voice in order to gain access to *logos*. These

29. For an analysis of the "camera solidaria" in this film, see Catherine Grant, "Camera Solidaria" *Screen* 38.4 (1997): 311–328.

30. On several occasions, Bruno talks about "estos chicos" (these kids) in reference to the activist generation of the sixties and seventies, employing an authority and distance that cannot be overlooked.

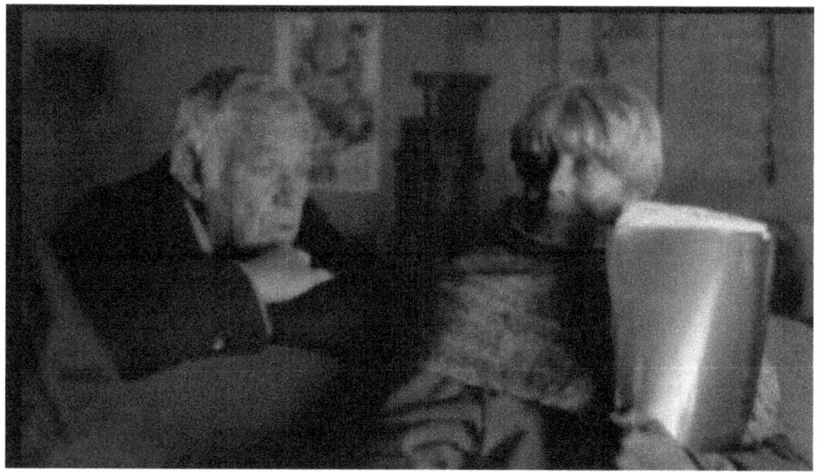

Still Image *Un muro de silencio* (dir. Lita Stantic, Lita Stantic Producciones, Cinematography Felix Monti, 1993)

never-disappearing remnants are invisible, but they continue to expand the scenario of the visible. The gap that opens between Silvia and Ana and between Jaime and Julio (that is, in the film-within-the-film) invites us to reflect on what is real and what is left out of the frame and the acoustic record, thus gesturing toward what has not yet been articulated. Silvia's concerns have to do with the intrusion of the fictional version of her life into her present and with the ghostly apparitions of her disappeared partner. In that silence of the past, the dialogue between and contrast of voices manages to create new meanings, especially in the transmission of her story to her own daughter. The film opens with the sound of the baby's laughter, and ends with the final close-up of the daughter, highlighting the role of this new generation in the transformation of the gaze and voice of memory.

Related to the question of Silvia's privileged and nearly absent gaze, one of the most revealing moments in the film takes place at the end, when the camera shows us what Silvia and her daughter are seeing: the clandestine detention center where they were once held. This sequence is related not only to Silvia's eyes but also to the signification process that looking and the gaze imply in the postdictatorship period. Silvia acquires power through her recovered gaze, but her power cannot be understood outside of gendered paradigms because she is a woman who dares to look and a survivor who proposes her own meaning in the face of her daughter's question. Her daughter asks, "Did people not know what was happening there?" to which Silvia responds, "Everybody knew." The onscreen image then freezes on the daughter. As I mentioned earlier, this brief dialogue also appears at the beginning of the film, between Bruno and Kate, and it emphasizes that the transmission of memory takes places through narration and dialogue. The repetition of the dialogue at the end poses the same questions in two different scenarios (the artistic and the familial). The construction of memory (and its aesthetics) is made of articulated voices that are able to break the silence, or at least a corner of it, and, through their modulation, they are able to transmit to a new generation the remnants of a lost voice. Through this transmission, the film creates a visible space for the survivor's daughter, both as a subject of the gaze and as a subject of the voice of memory.

Voice and Ghostliness

The film's plot takes place in two periods, the past (starting in 1976, with the kidnappings, detentions, and forced disappearances) and the present (in 1990, with the impunity that gives new meanings to the story's narration). As the title indicates, the link between these two times seems surrounded by a wall of silence. Silence, as an irretrievable sign of suppressed stories, also marks the film's reception (it went basically unnoticed on its release).[31] Silence (and its walls) evokes in the film the difficulty, or even impossibility, of recovering that voice associated with *zoe*, while also evoking the necessity of breaking the silence. Even if the attempts fail in terms of symbolization, they are able to express the residual voice left over from a *logos* and a word/gram-

31. I am referring here not just to its commercial release but also to its circulation on the festival circuit. Despite having been awarded prizes such as the Glauber Rocha from the international press at Havana's Festival del Nuevo Cine Latinoamericano and the Human Rights prize at the festival in Florianópolis, Brazil, (see http://www.litastantic.com. ar/unmuro/index.htm), the film seemed to run into a certain amount of fatigue with regard to the subject of the disappeared, even on the festival circuit outside of Latin America. One comment overheard by Stantic at the San Sebastián festival ("Otra de desaparecidos" ["Another one about the disappeared"]) is clear evidence of this market "saturation" at non–Latin American international festivals (Grant, 1997: 328).

mar/rationality that turns out to be inadequate. The film questions the powerful voice of the writer who representes the experience of a former student who was kidnapped along with her daughter and husband. As such, it invites the spectator to consider the aesthetics of political voices—that is, how that voice can be heard. The script is based on personal letters and confidences, which poses an ethical dilemma. At the end of the film, this dilemma becomes audible when the protagonist confronts the figure who represents authority in various senses, whether the authority of the teacher's voice, the writing of the script, the assertion of the correct political analysis, or the masculine voice. It is in that precise moment that Silvia finds her voice and is able to displace silence. This rediscovery of her articulated voice takes place in two moments: first, in the confrontation with her former teacher, and second, when Silvia manages to articulate the turmoil caused by Jaime's disappearance and tells her former teacher, almost desperately, that she thinks she has seen her disappeared spouse on the street. That "still seeing him," the following him on the street in her car until she eventually crashes, the search and the suspension of certainties, and the visions haunting her constitute all she must face in order to regain a voice, a testimonial voice. In this case, this testimonial voice is employed in intrafamilial transmission, to tell her (and their) story to her daughter. The fact that this voice is deprived [*privada*] of a public dimension is crucial. In the Argentina of the 1990s, following the passage of the impunity laws, the possibility of giving voice to the victims was discarded by presidential decree. These voices—which, in the trials of members of the military juntas, swear to tell the truth and nothing but the truth, thereby legitimizing their own political dimension in the context of the *polis* rather than of bare life—are now confined to the transmission of memory without official recognition.

As with other movies that center on the experience of the dictatorship, *Un muro de silencio* involves reconstructing or creating the ability to see and to hear. Yet this task implies not only reconstruction but also, as Derrida suggests at the end of *Specters of Marx*, the necessity of living with ghosts. Derrida's hauntology is useful here for reconsidering the voice because it allows us to examine it precisely, as it exists in that gap between the articulated voice and the lost voice. According to Derrida, hauntology, as the flip side and supplement of ontology and as a questioning of ontology and its being, posits the figure of the specter as a being beyond absence—that is, as being in an intermediate, unstable zone between presence and absence. Derrida analyzes

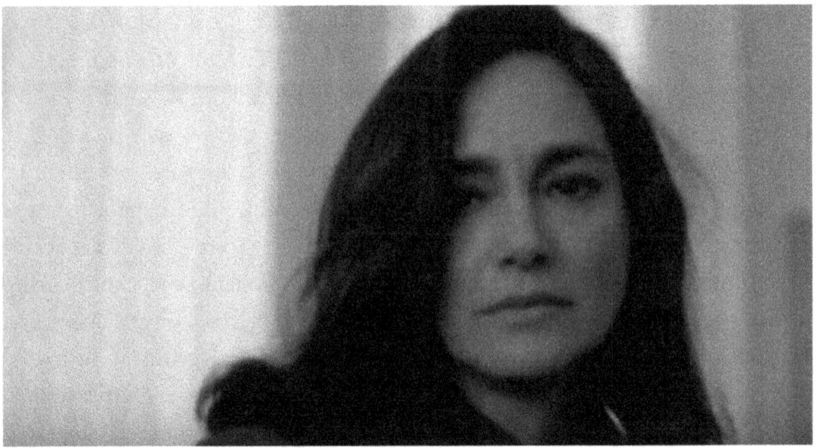

Still Image *Un muro de silencio* (dir. Lita Stantic, Lita Stantic Producciones, Cinematography Felix Monti, 1993)

the specter in terms of the gaze and the voice. With regard to the gaze, he says that the specter surveys the world from an invisible place and interpellates us; it "looks at us and sees us not see it." With regard to the voice, he suggests that it is this impossibility of engaging in dialogue with the absent other that creates the need to talk *about it*, but also *for it*, in its place. It is in that intermediate zone between being and nonbeing that we can also consider the importance of the voice and its haunting function, which points to what is invisible but never completely gone. The struggle for human rights, and with it the ritual voice that chants *Present!*, has that function and marks the ambivalence between existence and nonexistence—that is, marks its ghostliness.

In Stantic's film, voices are located, on the one hand, between the script and the film set, and, from this location, voices record language and emphasize the materialization of language. On the other hand, voices are also located between the film set and a survivor's experience, which allows us to see those ghostly apparitions and hear the multiple voices that make them more or less visible. From these two locations, the film posits a key aesthetic and political dilemma: Can a script or film represent the story of a former detainee and the wife of a disappeared person through the private letters and confidences that were sent to/made for a friend and former professor? Between writing and film, there is a confrontation of the aesthetic and the distribution of the visible, a conflict that primarily surrounds the possibility of modulating or not modulating a political voice. Yet the voice of Silvia, who is able to articulate her thoughts in her argument with Bruno, is intimate but also has a political cast. She tries to transmit her story to her daughter (and thereby to the next generation of memory) and that intimacy expands onscreen, pulling viewers, too, into a relationship that allows for her to articulate her memories. The question of the aesthetics and politics of the image and the voice runs through the entire film. Despite giving clear and definitive answers, it also portrays the fragments through which we find fissures in the wall of silence.

Mourning and Ethics

In addressing the loss and appropriation of the other that takes place in the mourning process, Derrida suggests the very impossibility of mourning. By pointing to the question of ethics, Derrida presents the failure of mourning because, even as we interiorize the other, there will be a resistance to that interiorization.[32] Derrida does not deny the cannibalism involved in the process of mourning or the way it erases the other. Interiorizing the other enables, at least according to the psychoanalytic model, an acceptance of loss. Yet Derrida emphasizes its failure and its impossibility. He thus points to a resistance to the process of interiorization of the loved one in the mourning process, arguing that it is never entirely possible to reduce the absent other to oneself.

In aesthetic terms, Stantic's film is located at the same crossroads, and it is at this same intersection that ethics comes into play. The possibility of justice begins precisely with the impossibility of mourning and with the haunting of that other who resists being interiorized. Justice emerges first as the possibility of establishing an ethical relationship with the absent other. The question posed by Derrida has to do not only with mourning but also with the betrayal of the absent other. One wonders which constitutes the most unjust betrayal, the most destructive disloyalty: the interiorization of the other within ourselves, or that impossible mourning, which "leav[es] the other his alterity, respecting thus his infinite remove," and which refuses to be the tomb in which

32. In his discussion of mourning, Derrida builds on Nicolás Abraham and María Torok's interpretation and expansion of the notions of mourning and melancholia in Freud, which draw a distinction between success and pathology, with the former depending on the incorporation of the beloved other. It is precisely this point that Derrida pulls apart in his *Mémoires*.

that other is buried as an effect of its interiorization (1989: 6). The suspension that ethics brings to the fore also makes way for the political, which now looms above the crossroads presented in the film. Representation, whether in writing or on the film set, implies an appropriation of the absent or inaudible other, who cannot speak for him- or herself. For Derrida, the very impossibility of mourning is, paradoxically, its success, because by interrupting the interiorization of the absent other, we allow space for that absent other to intrude into the setting of mourning and to remain outside the narrative subject in an exterior position that affords him or her respect as an other (35). With the confrontation between Bruno and Silvia, we are able, if not to hear a more articulated voice from Silvia, then, at least, to give that voice a place, one marked by the two images evoked by the title, a wall and silence. Silvia's articulated voice can be heard only in the private space and is, therefore, stripped of its political dimension. While that context is crucial to the transmission of memories, it is the film-within-the-film that tries to provide memory with a public reach. While Silvia is able to have an articulated voice during her confrontation with Bruno, her daughter's eyes are opened when she watches a sequence in which the character playing her mother meets her disappeared father at a coffeeshop for the last time before he disappears. Her voice, too, comes out of her conversation with her mother and, thus, out of the transmission of intimate family memories. Her voice also becomes audible when it duplicates, although perhaps with a different meaning, the question that Kate asks Bruno. The last gaze of the film is that of the daughter, as she looks at both the spectators and the camera, which freezes her face in a final, suspended gaze.

Intersections of Voices

The film opens with a baby's voice and laughter. The film ends with the voice—articulated this time—of a young woman, Silvia's daughter. The whole film reflects on the voices of silence, which are present, sometimes audible and at other times mentioned by other people. Silvia's silence is surrounded by voices: the voice of her ex-comrades after her release ("The fact that you were released didn't sit well with our comrades"), the voice of the mothers of the Plaza de Mayo demanding the return of their children and demonstrating against impunity, the voice of her disappeared loved one on the telephone, the voice that Bruno imagines when reading Silvia's letters, and

Silvia's voice when she confides in Bruno (we do not hear this voice but we know it exists). The film depicts a relationship between a mother and daughter and the growth of the daughter's voice from that of a baby to that of a young woman. (We also witness the development of her gaze as she watches the filming about her parents' experience).

Nevertheless, despite the obvious clash of voices in the film, particularly between writer and survivor, there is another voice. This voice is manifested as text, as a decree, and serves as the starting point for the 1990s as a decade of impunity. I am speaking of the pardon decrees (indulto), which came after the Law of Due Obedience and the Full-Stop Law and which clearly show that, in the 1990s, the prosecution of the military juntas had been reduced to a mere gesture, at least until the return to the accountability model in the new millennium. The voice of denunciation is understood more in terms of how it is pronounced to make itself heard (i.e., a political voice) than in terms of the official voice of the law (i.e., the police voice). This distinction applies to both the terrorist state (the last military dictatorship) and the 1990s denialist state. At the same time, this articulated voice, the voice of denunciation, points to an excess. While the voice of the disappeared cannot be articulated, it nonetheless continues to haunt the present as a ghost.

When Kate goes to the Plaza de Mayo with Bruno, she hears a voice through a megaphone demanding the return of the disappeared and condemning the impunity laws. She also hears a collective voice calling for justice ("Now, now it's imperative: Getting the disappeared back alive and punishing the perpetrators"). From the 1970s through to the voices of the Madres de Plaza de Mayo, the voice associated with human rights has initiated a new modulation of the voice in the public sphere toward the collective demand for justice. This new modulation evokes other, also collective voices, which come from the past and can be heard in the documentary that Kate watches about the Cordobazo, the popular uprising that took place in the Argentine city of Córdoba in 1969. Just as these documentary images are also guided by a male voice-over, which presents an interpretation of the images and events, Stantic's film, using a gendered lens, also works from within the confrontation between the male voice, which grants itself the privilege of interpretation and representation, and the female voice, which thwarts that privilege. Bruno's voice is one invested with authority, and, at the same time, it is a voice "in process," following Kristeva, who argues that subjectivity exists in transformation, but also under scrutiny. In his relationship with Kate, Bruno emphasizes the hierarchy between them; his is the voice of the teacher telling the filmmaker about recent Argentine history. Kate's voice is the one that asks questions and brings the issue of ethics to the forefront. At various points, we see her guiding the dialogues, adjusting the tone with which words are spoken. Kate is obsessed with the voice, as its modulations are not indicated in Bruno's script, and she feels that those intonations and rhythms belong to her interpretation of Ana and Julio's past rather than to the protagonists themselves. Silvia's voice confronts Bruno's, but hers is also a voice that allows us to confront her, as spectators, with the voice of Ana, her double in Kate's film. In the end, it is the voice of Silvia's daughter, which develops from the prelinguistic sound of laughter at the beginning of the film to an articulated voice that formulates questions about the past, that harbors the narrative memory. As Marianne Hirsch suggests when referring to "postmemory," it is through the voice that the memory of those remnants is transmitted to Silvia's daughter and the next generation. This transmission may happen silently, but the silence is inhabited by untranslatable voices.

CHAPTER 6

The Sonorous Crystal-Images of Memory[33]

As part of Argentina's bicentennial celebrations, the Secretaría de Cultura de la Nación and the Universidad Nacional de Tres de Febrero invited twenty-five filmmakers to create eight-minute shorts for a collective project. The end result was *25 miradas, 200 minutos: Los cortos del Bicentenario* [*25 Looks, 200 Minutes: Short Films of the Bicentennial*] (2010), which includes fictionalized documentaries (*Mercedes* by Marcos Carnevale, and *Fallas de origen* by Juan Taratuto); films that narrate the repetition of a single narrative sequence (*Una vez más* by Gustavo Taretto); a choreography that reinterprets a foundational legend about Argentina's national flower (*Leyenda del ceibo* by Paula de Luque); a critical rewriting of a text associated with the nineteenth-century liberal undertaking represented by Domingo Faustino Sarmiento (*Nueva Argirópolis* by Lucrecia Martel); films that rethink the history of Argentine cinema (*Gente querible* by Leonardo Favio, *Restos* by Albertina Carri, and *Más adelante* by Lucía and Esteban Puenzo); interviews (*Argentina del Bicentenario: Las voces y los silencios* by Carlos Sorín); as well as rereadings of battles from Argentine history (*Pavón* by Celina Murga and *El héroe que nadie quiso* by Israel Adrián Caetano) and of historical figures (*El espía* by Juan Stagnaro). The result is a collection of short films that highlight the aesthetic relationship between the image-sound

33. A preliminary version of this chapter was published in Spanish in *En la lente: Memoria, referencialidad histórica y documentalismo en el cine latinoamericano actual*, edited by Ana María Caula and Guillermina Walas. *Revista Iberoamericana* 251 (2015): 409–33.

and the labors of memory, rather than a documentary format associated with historical narrative.[34]

In this chapter, I analyze five films from this collection that are directed by women. These shorts rethink the link between image, sound, and violence during the two-hundred-year period that stretches from independence to 2010. They record, visually and acoustically, the transformation of time and space, and highlight repetition, belatedness, and simultaneity. This transformation implies a reimagining of the relationship between the gaze and the past. In contrast to the rigid dividing line that historians place between present and past events, these short films instead emphasize memory as an attempt to position the past as coexistent with the present.[35] Different shots

34. The twenty-five shorts, in alphabetical order, are *El héroe al que nadie quiso* (Adrián Caetano), *Mercedes* (Marcos Carnevale), *Restos* (Albertina Carri), *Leyenda del ceibo* (Paula de Luque), *Guillermina P.* (Inés de Oliveira Cézar), *La voz* (Sabrina Farji), *Gente querible* (Leonardo Favio), *Hija del sol* (Pablo Fendrik), *Posadas* (Sandra Gugliotta), *Malasangre* (Paula Hernández), *Intolerancia* (Juan José Jusid), *Ser útil hoy* (Víctor Laplace), *El abuelo* (Alberto Lecchi), *Nueva Argirópolis* (Lucrecia Martel), *En la trinchera* (Mausi Martínez), *Chasqui* (Néstor Montalbano), *Pavón* (Celina Murga), *(mi) Historia Argentina* (Gustavo Postiglione), *Más adelante* (Lucía y Esteban Puenzo), *Argentina del bicentenario: Las voces y los silencios* (Carlos Sorín), *El espía* (Juan Stagnaro), *Fallas de origen* (Juan Taratuto), *Una vez más* (Gustavo Taretto), *Nómade* (Pablo Trapero), and *Para todos los hombres y mujeres de buena voluntad* (Ricardo Wullicher).

35. In his study of memory, Maurice Halbwachs proposed a distinction between memory and history that is worth mentioning. Halbwachs notes how historians attempt to generate and maintain a distance from the past. There are insurmountable barriers to understanding history, and it is historians, as a select group of specialists, who dedicate a great deal of time to reading and understanding these barriers. This small group stands in contrast with the larger social group that simply recalls the past (collectively). For the social group, the past has meaning in the present and thus has a powerful presence that erases distance and the barrier that history requires. At the same time, in thinking about temporality through Bergson in *Matter and Memory* and Deleuze in *Cinema II: The Time-Image*, Halbwachs emphasizes how duration makes us think of the past as being at once past and present. And it is this last point that many of the shorts seem to propose: not a return to the past but a return to the past as it is made present (sometimes as déjà vu, sometimes as an after-effect). Many of the shorts emphasize the two centuries, their duration, and how they are simultaneously both past and present.

and narrative sequences explore and reflect on temporality, whether through a representation of traumatic belatedness or through a de-representation of linear time. This exploration of temporality and the relationship between past and present can best be understood via Gilles Deleuze's concept of the time-image. The heft of the labors of memory in the Argentine postdictatorship period implies a reconstruction of the past and, simultaneously, a challenging of historiographical accounts. The moving image here is a privileged space for analyzing this relationship. The return to the past is achieved not with a flashback (the image located clearly in the past, which is remembered from the present) but through images that zigzag in time, or images that are simultaneously past and present.[36]

It is in the intersection between memory and history that the voice and the moving image underscore the fusing of time and space, inasmuch as history intertwines with the present (and reveals its obsessions and frames), but also refers to the past and, therefore, can be transformed only through new interpretations. In addition, this past time appears in these short films as an acoustic image, or the voice through which each film presents the last two centuries. In the first part of this chapter, I will discuss three directors' depictions of forced disappearances: Sandra Gugliotta's *Posadas*, Paula de Luque's *Leyenda del ceibo*, and Albertina Carri's *Restos*. Through these short films, I will analyze three ways of portraying temporality that move away from linear narrative and, instead, emphasize the belatedness associated with trauma: the scene of disappearance witnessed by a daughter or bystanders in Gugliotta, the interval through which the past inhabits the present and highlights gaps of time in De Luque, and the portrayal of the image decoupled from linear time to accentuate time as a becoming in Carri. In the second part of the chapter, I examine other disappearances—those of invisible communities—which Lucrecia Martel represents through the acoustic register in *Nueva Argirópolis*. In this short film, Martel goes back to Domingo Faustino Sarmiento's writing to explore the relationship between voice and literature not just in the past but in the juxtaposition of past and present that fuses spaces and times. This fusion can be read alongside Deleuze's crystal-image, even though it is important to note that Martel's film is about a *new* Argirópolis and, as such,

36. And here, Bergson's distinction between the real image and the virtual image, which he mentions in his work on memory, comes into play. Gilles Deleuze later takes up this distinction. See Deleuze, 1989: 79–83.

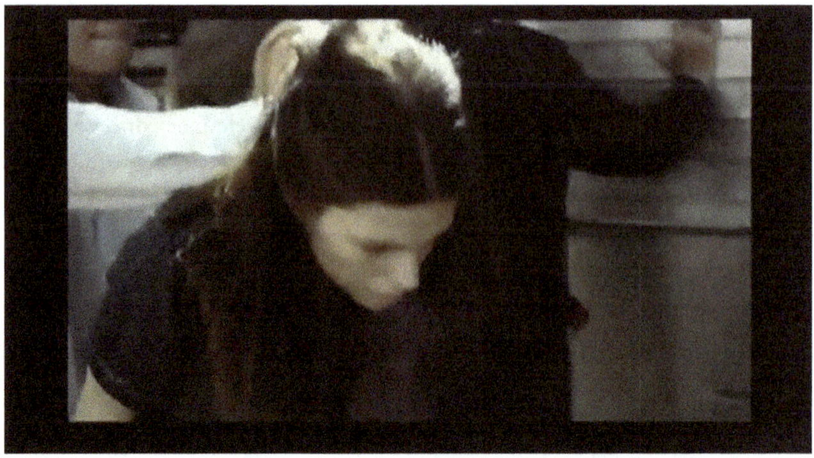

Still Image *Posadas* (dir. Sandra Gugliotta, Ojo Blindado, 2010)

past and present are not fused in the title but are differentiated. Finally, the third part focuses on an analysis of *La voz* by Sabrina Farji, which questions the very possibility of narrating recent memory without the interference of voices from the past. In this final part, I rethink how time collapses in the moment when historical voices temporarily inhabit the body of the present, only to be interrupted by other voices.

Returns, Crystal-Images, and Remnants

In *Posadas,* Sandra Gugliotta returns to the context of Argentina in December 1978, during the last military dictatorship. The short narrates the disappearance of a woman who is trying to flee with her young daughter. The kidnapping scene also portrays the little girl's fate as she is taken by another mother and continues her bus journey. The depiction of forced disappearance means a return to images that expose the traumatic event and to the relationship that the image establishes with history. In the short, disappearance, as the inescapable core of trauma, evokes the labors of memory without claiming the rigor of historiographical accounts.

In addition to depicting forced disappearance, this short's narrative images (the image of a woman who is about to be disappeared, a daughter who is about to start a new and uncertain life, a daughter who may be appropriated by another family or returned to her biological family) serve as a metaphorical encapsulation of the Bicentennial. These images move away from the act of historical representation and show the recent past as loss, focusing on how memory might be fictionalized or might incorporate aspects that are not strictly recorded within archives, more than on history. In an interview, Gugliotta explains, "We were invited to reflect on two hundred years of history, and I really wanted to talk about the construction of our country through violence" (Ranzani, 2010). The short returns to the scene of the kidnapping through images that advance in a linear narrative; the mother prepares to flee with her daughter, they leave on a bus, police officers burst in, they force the passengers out, and they take the mother away. At the same time, the final shot shows viewers the daughter watching from the bus window as her mother is taken away in a military vehicle, highlighting the relationship between the gaze and the recording of violence. As an exercise of memory, Gugliotta's short explores traumatic belatedness through a return to the moment of survival (for the daughter/witness) and disappearance (for the mother/victims of state terrorism) and through the construction of meaning. While the narrative is reconstructed linearly and the sequential images evoke the narrative sequence of disappearance, the moment of the kidnapping itself is chaotic. The scene is full of shouts, names, responses, abrupt movements, shots of hands and legs, and it ends with the protagonist's kidnapping, which her daughter witnesses.

In her now-classic study on the relationship between trauma and narration, Cathy Caruth argues that, while narration implies the loss of the (unrepresentable) event, poetic language is able to capture that unrepresentability, the gaps, time jumps, and absences. Analogously, cinematic language can produce certain cuts in narrative time to halt the narration and delve into a particular moment—in this case, the kidnapping. These images are still narrative images, but they interrupt the linear narrative. The camera focuses on body parts, and it moves rapidly. The scene is accompanied by voices that, even as they restore the relationship between what lies outside the visual frame and the diegetic space of the narration, also point to the confusion and the difficulty of restoring temporal linearity to those few seconds of repression. Then, the close-up on the daughter, now inside the bus and watching through the window as her mother is taken away, halts the linear narrative and invites us to reconsider the relationship between images and events.

While Gugliotta depicts the recent past of state terrorism, Paula de Luque's *Leyenda del ceibo* returns to past colonial violence to portray a different persecution and crime. De Luque retells a well-known Argentine legend that centers on the capture and burning alive of an indigenous (Guaraní) woman by Spaniards. The legend is about her survival in the form of a cockspur coral

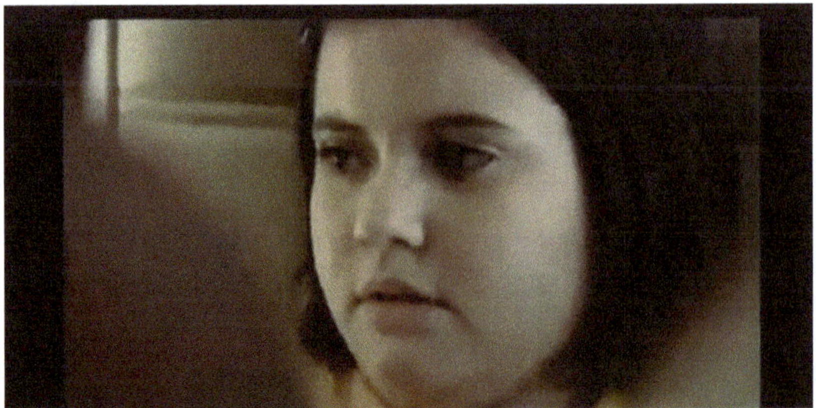

Still Image *Posadas* (dir. Sandra Gugliotta, Ojo Blindado, 2010)

tree (*ceibo*), whose blooms are Argentina's national flower. In this case, there is a dual symbolism and a dual displacement: of the Guaraní women (and other indigenous nations) and of the foundation of the Argentine nation on a substructure of violence exerted against the indigenous nations.

The short film opens with a still photographic image, a detail from Eduardo Longoni's *Marcha por la vida*, which also reappears at the end. After slowly zooming in on one of the horses from which military officers are harassing a group of the Madres de Plaza de Mayo, the film dissolves in a fade. As such, the opening of the film places us in the territory of the last dictatorship and in the record that photographic images have created of that repressive event. Therefore, one of the film's starting points is the documentary record of the image. A portion of this documentary record is shown by the camera to, on the one hand, distort it with a close-up that gets so close as to transform it into a black screen and, on the other, evoke the spectator's own (in) ability to see by trying to approach and almost touch the screen as the spectator draws ever nearer to the horse.[37] After and in contrast with the close-up,

37. For a discussion on the close-up, see Mary Ann Doane, "The Close-Up." She recasts the question of the relationship between the close-up and space-time coordinates, whether as a fragment and magnification (Epstein) or as an abstraction (Deleuze), always emphasizing what the former has that is inarticulable and supplemental as a starting point for thinking about its duality (as proximity vs. distance, as small vs. large, as proximity, as the boundary of what is visible/intelligible, and as a place of tension between detail and totality).

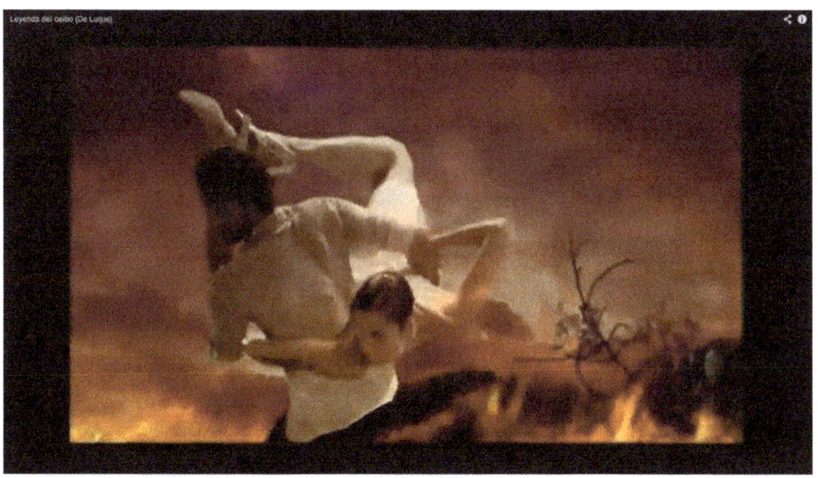

Still Image *Leyenda del ceibo* (Dir. Paula de Luque, Barakacine, 2010)
Courtesy of: Ministerio de Cultura Argentina, Barakacine, and Paula de Luque

the film shows the image of a maze. As the camera moves away from it, and then closer again, an animated chase sequence begins, and for much of the sequence the camera takes the perspective of the person being chased, a woman who is running and panting, unable to find her way out of the maze. We then see her white shoes as she runs, stops, and starts running again. The chase is followed by a dance that represents the struggle in which she will be defeated. The camera records the chase from various angles, cutting off the head of the woman, who is dressed in white, as she is chased by a man to the edge of a cliff. The woman's white high heels place her in another, much more recent space and historical time, thus emphasizing the repetition of historical traumas. The images intertwine in metonymic displacements as the maze becomes the image of a fingerprint, from which we return to the opening photo, shown it in its entirety for the first time. We then see the same (yet different?) woman, dressed in white and looking at the photo in an exhibition.

Past time intersects with other more recent times. The images zigzag, moving between images from the colonial past that survived in *The Legend of the Ceibo* (such as the fire) and images that are associated with the recent past (such as images of bodies falling into the river, and images from the photography exhibition). The legend of Anahí is recast as the story of other captive women, other much more recent chases, and other murders and disappearances. The dance and struggle between the chased woman and her pursuer

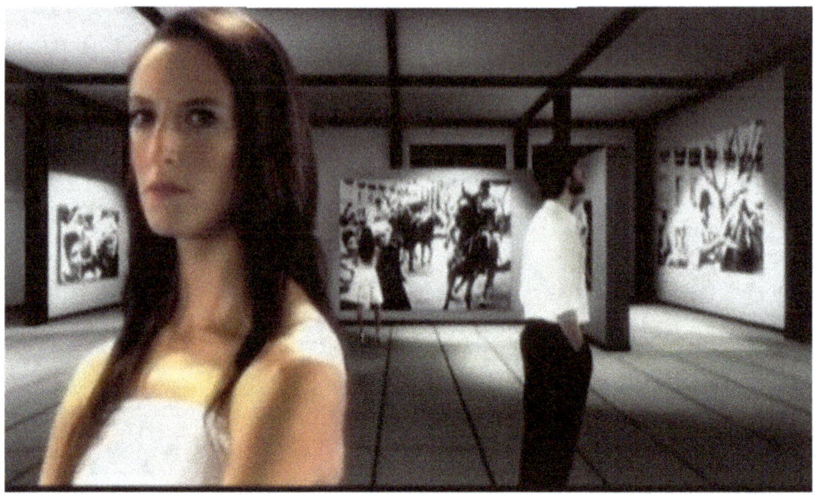

Still Image *Leyenda del ceibo* (Dir. Paula de Luque, Barakacine, 2010)
Courtesy of: Ministerio de Cultura Argentina, Barakacine, and Paula de Luque

are followed by a violent fall, which is shown first in slow motion and then multiplied in different images, both at the beginning of the fall and in the ocean. After the fall sequence, the dance continues, ending with the death of the victim by fire. The images of the sea and of bodies falling (perhaps being thrown?) into the water evoke the forced disappearance of citizens during the last military dictatorship. Nevertheless, we see the victim, or someone who represents her, the woman in white, at a photography exhibit, looking at Longoni's *Marcha por la vida*. This image crystallizes the fusion of the past and the present and its transformation, in Deleuzian terms, into the crystal-image. Yet she is not the only one who survives. The perpetrator is also shown in the same space.

The victim, who looks first at the black-and-white photo and then at the camera, and thus at the spectator, is located in history, outside of the legend of Anahí. In a sense, her survival makes possible both the short's fictional turn and its traumatic repetition. As a starting point, we see a photograph about the military dictatorship's repression, through which the camera shows us the recreated images of a legend associated with the past, which also encapsulates violence and resistance. As Ana Amado suggests, in that conflictive relationship between history and fiction, film cannot distance itself from "*mostración*" [showing or exposing] (2007: 34). However, it can move away from showing images that narrate without condensing, shattering, or undermining the outlines of the historical narrative.[38] The close-up marks the break in the linear narrative that opens and closes the story-within-the-story (the reinterpretation of the legend of the cockspur coral tree through choreography). At the same time, the close-up alerts us, as Doane reminds us in her study of the close-up, to the question "What is happening beyond what I can see?" (2003: 96). In the close-up, there is a proximity that makes the image simultaneously near and imperceptible. Close-ups of the photograph frame the legend of Anahí, beginning with the close-up that fades to a black screen and ending with the close-up of the maze that first turns into a fingerprint and then into the same photograph used at the beginning, before the camera finally pulls back and shows the protagonist looking at the photo. In this series of shots, which constantly evoke what lies outside the visual field, the optical unconscious, or the detail that leads to the story within the frame, holds the key, and more literally the fingerprint, to the two hundred years of history depicted by De Luque.[39] The final sequence and the emphasis on the

38. Amado is not referring to this film; she is talking about an inverse operation seen in films from the 1980s, during the redemocratization period. She claims the following: "Para una sociedad que con la ruptura de la oscuridad y el silencio quería saber, las ficciones cinematográficas coincidieron en añadir su cuota interpretativa, o simplemente informativa a la circulación de discursos sociales sobre los procedimientos genocidas y sus víctimas. Tras un período de no ver nada, las imágenes del cine podían permitir verlo todo" [For a society that tried to know through the shattering of darkness and silence, the cinematographic fictions added their interpretive, or simply informative, element to the circulation of social discourses about the genocidal proceedings and their victims. After a period of not seeing anything, cinematic images could allow everything to be seen] (Amado, 2007: 34). She thus compares 1980s-era cinematographic production to literary fiction, which, instead of exposing the truth, attempts to compress it (34). In 2010, Paula de Luque's short film frames that compression through the camera and by returning to the legend, but it also uses as its starting point the photographic image that serves to reveal the truth.

39. Walter Benjamin says about close-ups, "With the close-up, space expands; with slow motion, movement is extended. And just as enlargement not merely clarifies what we see indistinctly 'in any case,' but brings to light entirely new structures of matter, slow motion not only reveals familiar aspects of movements, but discloses quite unknown aspects within them" (2008: 37). For Benjamin, "it is through the camera that we first discover the optical unconscious" (37).

gaze that surveys violence bring to a close the reinterpretation of the legend and its return to the present through images that come one after the other, breaking the logical and temporal continuity. These images assert how the past intrudes into recent historical contexts and suggest that the interpretation of the recent past is key to reading history. In both cases, we observe a movement to spaces that harbor that which is remembered but forgotten, like the image of the childhood bedroom that Walter Benjamin uses to discuss memory. This childhood room is a place full of details that crowd around that which cannot be recalled because it has been hidden. Through or despite these minute details, the past becomes a story of forgetting, or of an incomplete recollection that is reinterpreted afterward and that in some form has remained latent or suspended as an image. In *Posadas* and *Leyenda del ceibo*, the undertaking of this return can be read as a search for lost memory, whether the memory of a kidnapping or the legend of the cockspur coral tree as a vestige of the photographic image. That return to the scene of the disappearance is both a revision and a delay, both a practice of re-seeing, of looking again, as well as a confirmation of the existence of silence and of belated, delayed knowledge.[40]

Disappearance, murder, and massacre as a nucleus of trauma that leaves us in silence are here reconstituted as an absence of voice. In *Leyenda del*

40. In the story, Benjamin relates how, because his father does not tell him the details of a death, he comes to see in those images a delayed knowledge. Years later, he realizes that the conversation he recalls in that room conceals a silence that is later recovered. Benjamin says, "So the room in which I slept at the age of six would have been forgotten, had not my father come in one night—I was already in bed—with the news of a death. It was not really the news itself, that so affected me" (1999: 633). He then tells the story again, with some differences: "I was perhaps five years old. One evening—I was already in bed, my father appeared, probably to say good night. It was half against his will, I thought, that he told me the news of a relative's death. The deceased was a cousin, a grown man who scarcely concerned me. But my father gave the news with details, took the opportunity to explain, in answer to my question, what a heart attack was and was communicative. I did not take in much of the explanation. But that evening I must have memorized my room and my bed, the way you observe with great precision a place where you feel dimly that you'll later have to search for something you've forgotten there. Many years afterward I discovered what it was. Here in this room, my father had 'forgotten' part of the news about the deceased: the illness was called syphilis" (635).

ceibo, there is a mute character, voiceless and unable to scream, who dies in silence. The short depicts pure corporeality without a voice, a mutism that shifts only in the images of the chase, in which we hear her breathing heavily. That heavy breathing occupies the entire space of her voice. In *Posadas*, we hear voices: the shouts, questions, and orders of the police officers who stop the bus. Somebody is asked, "Where are you going?" and responds, "To Posadas." Among the voices of the officers pointing at the protagonist as they lead her away and while her daughter watches in silence, we hear someone saying (the images show several hands surrounding the young activist), "Don't look, don't look." Then, the final silence. In the two shorts, the starting point for the acoustic realm is different: in *Leyenda*, the articulated voice is absent from the very beginning, while, in *Posadas*, the voice is lost after contact with military repression. Violence and repression represent the only universe of "the" voice, in the sense employed by Elaine Scarry in *The Body in Pain*.[41]

The images of the return in Benjamin's childhood bedroom and the details that surround and prowl about the edges of the search for an elusive memory have to do with memory as a visual practice, in the sense that those images of the past take on new meanings in the present. These metaphors are not merely spatial but also temporal, and they imply an updating process of the meaning given to the memory. Of the three shorts analyzed in this section, the one that most thoroughly explores the relationship between images, remnants, and the gaze is *Restos* by Albertina Carri. "Is accumulating images resisting? Is it possible now to restore their gesture of defiance?" These are the questions that the narrative voice, the voice-over, poses as we watch a naked man crouching in a forest. Yet the voice-over affirms not the documentary, or documentation, but its remnants. Next, the image shows flames burning celluloid film. We see the film strips twist and disintegrate. Then, the image shows filmstrips heaped on one another in piles. The narrative voice talks about the films of the 1960s and 1970s as political weapons,

41. I am referring here to the loss of the prisoner's world and voice, which, according to Scarry, takes place in the setting of torture, and to the loss of the acoustic presence of the torturer's voice and world. Scarry says, "Although the torturer dominates the prisoner both in physical acts and verbal acts, ultimate domination requires that the prisoner's ground become increasingly physical and the torturer's increasingly verbal, that the prisoner become a colossal body with no voice and the torturer a colossal voice (a voice composed of two voices) with no body" (1985: 57–58).

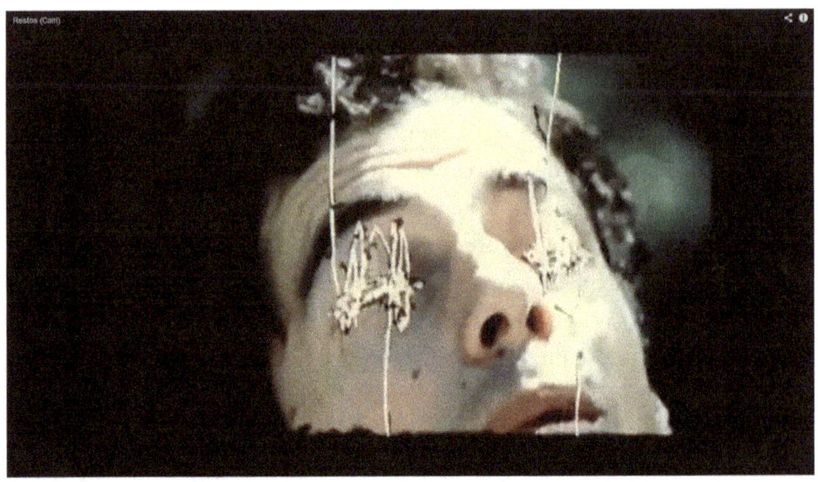

Still Image *Restos* (Dir. Albertina Carri, 2010)

films that were made in secret and which stood in defiance of repression. Next, a young man projects a film. We see the lights of the city at night shift to the image of someone who starts running. While the naked man runs, the voice-over talks about cultural repression ("eliminated like the traces of the persecuted," "burned by those who had created them"). A purple blotch mars the image, spreading until it nearly covers the close-up of the running man. Again, the close-up is used to halt the narrative, rethink the gaze, and condense meaning: an image that burns from the middle to the edges. We can no longer see anything. "They are disappeared too," the narrative says before fading to black. Carri has said of the short, "It's not fiction or a documentary either—it's an essay" (Ranzani, 2010). The transcendent voice, the voice that harbors knowledge, is a female voice. The female voice is a starting point for subverting the male transcendence of the voice in documentaries. Yet it is also doubled. The voice-over is a voice that is doubly gendered, both in its acoustic substance and in its content. The voice reads from a text by Marta Dillon, while the voice itself belongs to Analía Couceyro, who, thanks to *Los rubios*, also evokes Carri herself. The body that is portrayed, by contrast, is simultaneously male and vulnerable. And it runs, fleeing the narrated violence.

We watch the strips of film disintegrate as they are submerged in water, alluding to the fate of images in the last military dictatorship. The short examines this fate: some of the images are destroyed, while some survive and re-

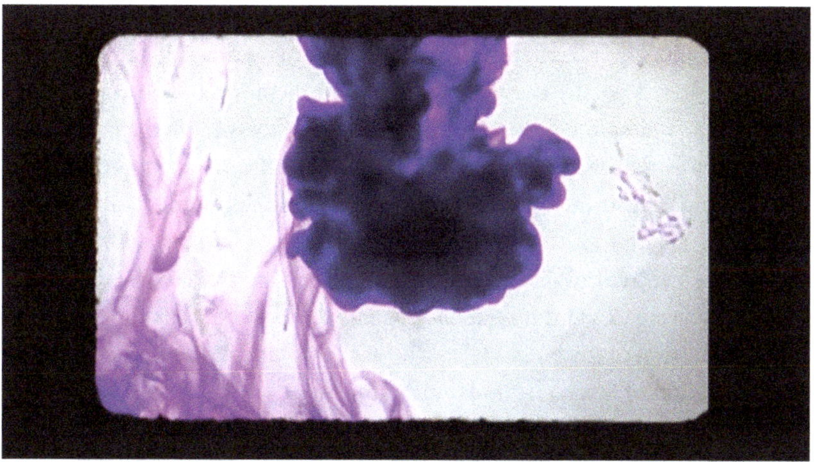

Still Image *Restos* (Dir. Albertina Carri, 2010)

cover the author's signature. At the same time, the short examines the fate of the gaze. The male character holds a camera in his hand, and we see a close-up of the victim's eyes, which are marked by terror. This sequence leads us to question the gaze. His eyes are then smudged out by scratches and become barely visible. The narrative voice refers to the loss of the collective subject: "In this orphanhood in which it is only possible to articulate the first person, I allow myself to be kindled by lost images. Looking for them is a way of resisting this dreamless inclemency." There is subsequently a return to memory through lost images.[42]

The images imply a recovery of what is not narrated, and thus these images intertwine, as Caruth has suggested in her approach to trauma, with those modulations that are lost in the recovery of the historic account. The condensing of elements in Carri's short film allows for a play between images and shots, and the interruption of the narrative thread points, through close-ups and voice-overs, to what remains invisible or outside and to what transcends the form of the close-up or of the voice-over as sound that is desynchronized from the body. However, we can recognize Carri/Couceyro's voice as the

42. For an analysis of the void, see Carla Manzoni and her doctoral dissertation, *Counter-narratives in the Void: Memory in* Los rubios, *Its Aesthetic Heritage and Its Reverberations*. University of Minnesota (2015).

sound that transcends (survives? witnesses?) the terror of the past. In addition, remnants are the red, purple, and blue blotches that fall and disappear into the water. They are the traces, perhaps, of memory, and especially of its images, which are now mere pieces of filmstrips slowly falling. *Restos* points to recovery of the meaning of the metaphorical, of the poetic, of the unrepresentable gap that sustains the core of trauma, violence, and the visual image.

There is an attempt to reexamine those traces that have been wiped away, to look back at a cultural and artistic history through a vision that is capable of encapsulating loss and forced disappearance. The short examines the erasure and survival of traces, as well as the place that cinema has in the historical reconstruction of images, sounds, and meanings.

Hearing Voices

At the center of *Nueva Argirópolis* is the problematic relationship between the image and the strict historical (linear) narrative. As is the case with all of Lucrecia Martel's films, *Nueva Argirópolis* uses the acoustic register to underscore visual fragments and gaps. In the film's historical exploration, Martel puts a series of binaries in counterpoint with one another: past and present, memory and history, writing and acoustic image, articulated voice and murmur, and invisibility and visibility. The film is based on Sarmiento's text *Argirópolis o la Capital de los Estados Confederados del Río de la Plata* [*Argirópolis, or the Capital of the Confederated States of the River Plate*], which preceded Argentina's consolidation as a nation and was published in Chile in 1850. It proposes a solution for pacifying the Rio de la Plata region during the final years of the Juan Manuel de Rosas administration: organizing a congressional meeting and establishing the capital on Martín García Island, an island in the middle of the River Plate estuary, which was under French control at the time. In an interview, Martel refers to this island as a fantasy and a symbol. In her re-vision and re-interpretation, she suggests that the new project is about the islands of the Delta del Tigre, instead of Martín García Island, as Sarmiento had it (Ranzani, 2010). The film returns to the original text by re-interpreting Argirópolis from its edges, which is precisely the space that Sarmiento's Argirópolis placed outside of the nation. (In the short, we see a video in the Wichí language that is circulating on the Internet, in which we hear a woman say, "Argirópolis.") Thus, as different periods are superimposed on one another, we are able to return to Sarmiento's depiction of Argirópolis through the images that Martel offers in the present, and especially how indigenous communities remain "under suspicion" of a watchful gaze that excludes them from the national project.[43]

In the film, Sarmiento and his writings, which were foundational for the Argentine nation, are reflected in a play of mirrors and through images that collapse temporalities. This collapse does not repeat the past in the present, but instead suggests the resonances of the past in the present, its bifurcations and appropriations, and, at the same time, highlights the dissonances produced in repetition. In the short, Sarmiento's text is contrasted with an orality marked not only by the voices that the police officers attempt to translate into Spanish, but also by the voices in Wichí that multiply without translation on the Internet as a platform for organizing and imagining the foundational nature of Nueva Argirópolis.

Martel's short complicates the transparent representation of both memory and history, and calls into question the logic by which the narrative image is subjugated, even though it is only able to narrate the official version of events. The police arrest a group of five people from the Wichí community (who are not carrying their national identification cards) and assume that they are transporting drugs via the Bermejo River. They are arrested and subjected to interrogation and an X-ray scan, which ultimately offer no evidence to confirm the initial suspicion. The gaze, which searches for evidence that might prove the police's assumption, is exerted as a form of monitoring in a dual sense: both as the gaze that regards them with suspicion (as foreigners to the nation) and with the X-ray that scrutinizes the insides of their bodies. The conflict is first revealed through overlapping voices in Spanish and Wichí. The visual presence of the "accused" lies precisely in the way they are made visible only as suspects. The short stresses the colonialism that undergirds Argentine history—Sarmiento's name points clearly to a political project that led to the genocide of indigenous nations in the 1870s—while

43. Martín García Island later became a space used by the liberal nation during the "Conquest of the Desert" (1879) to hold prisoners and captive indigenous people. As such, Argirópolis (despite Sarmiento's emphasis on calling a congress and revising the federal treaties and agreements) represents both the French presence in the national imaginary of writings about Argentina (because the island was in French hands when Sarmiento wrote the text) and a space that would be used (twenty years after the text was written) to hold indigenous captives.

also underscoring the indigenous voices that subvert the visual and acoustic regime and its vigilance. Once again, the whispers in Martel (now of a little girl as she translates the Internet video into Spanish) hint at invisible forms of resistance, which in this case are strengthened precisely by their invisibility. "Indigenous and indigents, don't be afraid to move. We are invisible"—only the spectators hear this translation, not the authorities in the story. The whispers contrast with the voices of the doctors who, after looking at the X-rays, say, "They don't have anything." They also contrast with the police officers' comment ("I hear voices") on the river. They are made visible because they are heard; they are heard because they are suspected. Yet this "visibility" is called into question by the claim "We are invisible," which highlights the conflict between the vigilant gaze and the invisibility of social subjects who are seen only to be criminalized.

Martel produces a double play with framing that reveals the overlap of gazes: the gaze of the camera, which records the incongruencies, and that of the police, which seeks to confirm the drug transport theory as part of the "investigation" process. This investigation takes place by monitoring both the visual and the acoustic realms. Ana Amado suggests that, in the short, the police monitor sounds to be used as "evidence" and to justify the otherization of the Wichí community, which is underscored by the short's final line, "I hear voices." The acoustic realm here plays an important role because, alongside what is translated, we also have the untranslated passages and whispers. When referring to the maternal language, Kaja Silverman does not focus on the subversions of the maternal body or on instances of pre-language or its excesses, as Irigaray and Kristeva do. Instead, she claims that the maternal voice remains anchored in the body, which negates the transcendence of the voice. However, according to Ana Amado (2013), it is possible to interpret this maternal language in contrast with the violence perpetrated by the paternal language (Spanish, the law of the nineteenth-century liberal nation as represented by Sarmiento), which is based on the annihilation of difference. This "difference" survives not in a *pre*-Oedipal space but instead in a present that shows how pre-Oedipal language (and culture and communities and nations) is never entirely erased. Instead, it reappears within the paternal language as untranslatable intermittencies. This tension points to a form of time that is understood to be intermittent and simultaneous, rather than linear. If translation highlights the imposition of the paternal language, which monitors bodies and the modulation of sound-meaning, the untranslatable evokes both the marginalized and excluded, which are controlled via language and biopolitics, and the subversive, or what cannot be assimilated into the norm and as such is the trace of both an exclusion and a belonging that is foreign to the norms used for its exclusion. Martel underscores this tension within language in a close-up that highlights the importance of what is whispered in contrast to what is said out loud. Whispering in another girl's ear, one of the two girls translates the video as we watch it. As such, we hear the voice in Wichí, which says, "Argentina" and "Nueva Argirópolis," and the voice of the girl, which repeats the translation out loud to the authorities, as well as the weak whisper of the girl in close-up while the other girl translates (repeats the translation) for the police to hear. As the camera approaches the girl in the close-up, we hear her say, "Indigenous and indigents, don't be afraid to move. We are invisible." Yet the other girl, who is translating out loud, does not repeat this phrase. The close-up makes the two girls visible and present in order to simultaneously highlight a juxtaposition of voices, including the voice of the leader of the community in the Wichí language, which we see in the image of the video on the TV screen but also hear as an offscreen voice in the close-up of the girls; the voice of the girl who repeats the translation out loud; and the voice of the girl whispering the Spanish translation into the other girl's ear. The close-up emphasizes sight and the possibility of seeing up close. In that close-up of the whisper, we see another kind of transcendence, of the sort highlighted by Silverman. In this case, the transcendence is linked to the body, specifically the girl's mouth as she whispers into another girl's ear. The viewer is thus complicit in this shot, and this complicity is loosed from the space-time coordinates of the image—it is detached from its space to draw nearer the spectator's space. What returns in Martel's *Nueva Argirópolis* is violence in the construction of otherness, in monitoring it, in translating it as a mark of two hundred years of Argentine history. These whispers, which characterize much of Martel's work, point to the limitations of the gaze. These whispered translations record that historical narrative left unrecounted, and make visible the members of those communities who are included only as suspects, and even then, only through a partially audible translation into the logic of Spanish and its dominance.

Voices, Spaces, Times

In Sabrina Farji's *La voz*, the journey through history is accomplished through medium shots and two close-ups of the actress Elena Roger, who is singing

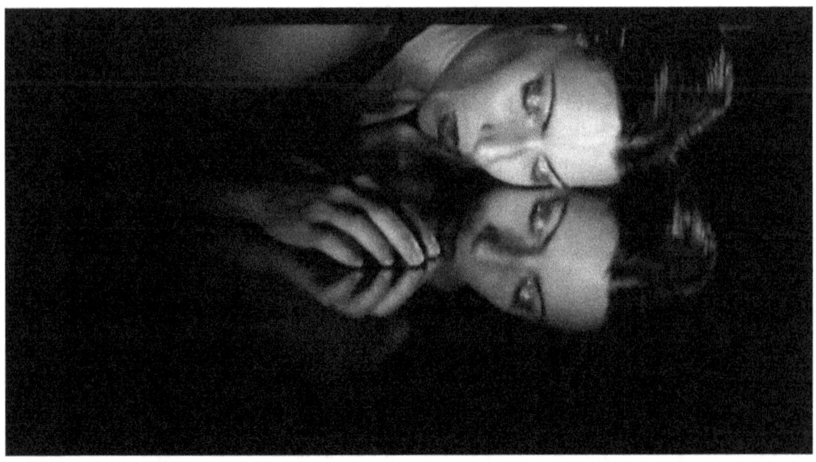

Still Image *La voz* (Dir. Sabrina Farji, Elena Roger performer, 2010)

and reciting the national anthem and who plays different women to tell their stories. The short makes it clear that "the voice" of the nation cannot be represented. Instead, "the voice" (the title of the short is singular, not plural) is depicted as a becoming of different voices, including those of the women who tell their stories and those that seem to be merely intrusions or even involuntary recollections of other people's voices. Farji uses the voice-off/voice-over to inhabit the body of a woman who also represents the nation.[44] A woman ("the voice"?) is possessed by different "voices" from Argentine history, from the most vile and atrocious, such as those of Jorge Rafael Videla and Leopoldo Galtieri, to the most foundational, such as that of José de San Martín. Additionally, we hear the voices of Eva Perón, Juan Domingo Perón, Raúl Alfonsín, Carlos Saúl Menem, Estela Carlotto, and René Favaloro, as well as voices that have a presence across the continent, such as that of Che Guevara. The initial problem posed by *La voz* is identifying the narrated story. At the beginning, we see only a woman who is singing the national anthem, and we

44. I use "voice-over" and "voice-off" in accordance with the distinction that Doane suggests between the two, in which the "voice-over" is associated with the voice without a corporeal or diegetic referent within the film (such as in documentaries) and the "voice-off" designates a voice that evokes a character who is outside the visual frame and thus is connected to the story being narrated.

see her wearing different outfits and hairstyles, each of which evokes a different Argentine woman and her story.

The first voice that possesses her body—the voice of Videla—is an intrusion followed by other intrusive voices that transform the meaning of what comes next and problematize memory as a deliberate exercise by superimposing the different contexts that are invoked by the succession of voices, but which also hamper the historical and linear reconstruction of the past. In *La voz*, the aural dimension is associated with the body, as the actress sings the national anthem and gives first-person accounts of different "characters," including an immigrant, the granddaughter of the immigrant, and the partner of a disappeared person. All of these women have something in common: "I was born in a violent time." Once disappearance is mentioned, the actress is possessed by Videla's voice ("The disappeared person is a mystery. . . . As long as they are disappeared, they cannot be given any special treatment—they're a mystery. They're disappeared. They have no being"). By desynchronizing image and voice, the short superimposes on the image of the woman, as an allegory of the nation, those clashing voices, which intrude on the national anthem and on the performance that tells the stories of Argentine women. At the same time, the voice-off becomes a voice-over and is used as a narrative voice. Though the actress gesticulates in concert with a voice that is not hers (as in a voice-off), she provides the interpretive key for various historical moments (as in a voice-over). In discussing well-known figures, such as the head of the first military junta, Eva Perón, Estela Carloto, and Juan Domingo Perón, the voice inhabits the history recounted in the short. However, these voices, and the virtual images they spark, become audible almost as interferences in the narrative. The short produces, by means of the simultaneity between visual image and virtual image, an image that crystallizes the simultaneity of past and the present—that is, a "crystal-image."[45]

The nation in the present, and especially as it is represented through the singing and recitation of the anthem, is inhabited by these other voices that

45. Deleuze's "crystal-image" implies the collapse of time. For Bergson, time (understood as duration—that is, understood as a seamless continuity) implies a coexistence of the past and the present. For Deleuze, the crystal-image occurs when time "splits into two dissymmetrical jets, one of which makes all the present pass on, while the other preserves all the past. And it is this time, that we see in the crystal" (1981: 81).

tell us about what remains outside the visual frame. The past is emphasized as memory, as a kaleidoscope of images suggested by the voices that become present. Through the contrast between image and sound, the short pierces the nation's history with interruptions and shifts from voice to voice. These shifts sometimes play out as a continuity and sometimes are abrupt. By playing with the harmony and interference of radio or television sounds, the short film marks, through very unpleasant sounds, the intrusion of some voices on others, the gaps as well as the continuities in narration.

The voice of the nation is embodied in the main character who allegorizes Argentina as she recites the national anthem. This same woman portrays other women, who tell their stories as if in an interview. The transcendent voices, both voice-offs and voice-overs, are associated with the nation's political life. This association is often conflicting, as in the moment when the voice of former president Carlos Saúl Menem appears. Nevertheless, the instances of the voice in this short, including the recitation and humming of the national anthem and the fragments that point to the role of testimonial voices in the construction of memory, are expressed through the body as it either quotes a text or is possessed by other voices. This association is also manifested through her body's convulsions whenever she produces these other voices, as if she were a sort of medium. At the end, the images of the actress in her various roles follow one after the other, and we hear the voice of Juan Domingo Perón, now without the actress serving as his medium. In the same way, we hear the voice of Estela Carlotto, which is both embodied by the actress and through images that show the actress singing the anthem in silence (but as a subject of hearing). We then see her saddened as she hears the voices of the Mothers and Grandmothers of the Plaza de Mayo. The short ends with the singing of the anthem and the transformation of the line "We swear to die with glory" to "We swear to live with glory." It concludes with the image of the river, and therefore with the forced disappearances of the last military dictatorship. The short evokes the kaleidoscopic space of the nation, embodied both in the singing of the national anthem and in the many voices that either inhabit or are disassociated from the body, pointing to other spaces and times of the nation outside of the allegorical image. *La voz* reflects on the possibility of representing not the historical (and political) process of 1810 but how memory intrudes on this event in order to revisit it.

Following Hugo Vezzetti's discussions of memory, we can argue that the short reenacts the past as an exercise of memory that attempts to accommodate the past in the present. Yet *La voz*, like the other shorts discussed in this chapter, emphasizes temporality, and more specifically the simultaneity of time periods, past and present. This simultaneity implies another approach to space, in which the return à la Benjamin intersects with the spatial metaphor suggested by Pilar Calveiro in her description of the reconstruction of memory. Calveiro suggests replacing the model of the puzzle, where each piece has only one place, with that of the kaleidoscope, which "recognizes different possible figures and allows for coexistence, rather than suppressing discordant voices" (2005: 14). The kaleidoscope, like the visible world but fragmented and inhabited by ever-shifting parts, is an image that can encapsulate the possibility of representing fragments that do not demand totality.

The bicentennial celebration provides the framework for rethinking the past and the present, insofar as the shorts point to the reflection on and the construction of a collective memory, which perpetuates emotions and images rooted in the social group's identity. At the same time, they also point to the creative (visual and acoustic) reconstruction of the historical past through frames and framing that give meaning to memories and, in some way, stabilize them.[46] It is memory, as remnants, ashes, and especially erasures, that is revealed and translated in images and which exhibits their potential capacity not only for representation but also for poetic alchemy.

These shorts reenvision the reconstruction of memory through their crystal-images. Memory is not, then, a flashback that returns to a historical past that is recognized distinctively as past, but instead, an image that mixes times together, through simultaneity and intermittency. The crystal-image can best be seen through how voice and image are intertwined in the shorts, highlighting not just the coexistence of different time periods, but also the different spaces in which, in parallel, those times are represented. Those spaces are the space of the spectator, inhabited by sounds that are dis-

46. I am using the term "frames" thinking about the classic work by Maurice Halbwachs, as well as of Elizabeth Jelin's analysis, which builds on Halbwachs's approach. The idea of the frameworks of memory emphasizes the present, from which the past finds a place through a selection that collectively gives meaning to the memories of the past and speaks more of the present than of the past. In collective memory, the creativity of the social group is expressed in some way, not to talk about the past but to talk about the present, because, for Halbwachs, anything that does not find its place in the signification of the present is forgotten.

connected from the sound of the image; the space represented by the image; and the spaces of that which remains outside the frame but which can still be heard. Reexamining Argentina's two hundred years as a nation becomes a recollection exercise, a questioning of the historical archives and of the voices of authority that "objectively" narrate the events of the past, and a synesthetic attempt to hear the voices, echoes, returns, and silences with one's own eyes. At the same time, this questioning underscores memory as a process and an exercise that collapses time through images that speak simultaneously of the past and the present. Time becomes an interval in which the voices of the past cross over to the present, producing almost a sort of déjà-vu effect.

In this sense, the shorts point to the return of details that, for Benjamin, serve as context for the exercise of memory but which also allow for a reflection on the aftermath as a core aspect of how the task of memory is rooted in images and voices. Those returning after-effects are implied in Benjamin's image of excavation, and the different layers that contain the images of recollection, which are also interwoven with recent Argentine history. Benjamin uses a comparison to the soil in which the past is interred as a point of departure for his metaphor of excavation in relation with the search for the "buried" past. Benjamin emphasizes the importance of offering an account not only of what has been found but also of the process of memory itself and of the subjects of memory, as well as the images that appear in the process, now stripped of the meaning they once had. That is, images reflect loss, though, at the same time, they are located in a new space that is shaped by visions of the present.[47] In speaking of memory, Benjamin suggests that the layers through which we move when excavating count as much as what is actually found—what matters is not just the place of discovery but also the various spaces that were explored, which also make up part of the search (Benjamin, 1999: 576). The shorts by Farji, Martel, Gugliotta, Carri, and De Luque in *25 miradas, 200 minutos* portray movements of return that aim to, if not create a new meaning, then at least revise (look back at and look again at) the past and the present. The labors of memory are present as an excavation of images, but also as the acknowledgment of the subjects of those visions and revisions

47. That relationship between past and present, also understood in terms of the layers of the palimpsest, is a central part of Andreas Huyssen's argument in *Present Pasts.*

and their silences and voices. Moreover, the acoustic records that are missing from the historical archives also become present in the shorts, and they allow us, as spectators, to understand what remains outside the visual frame and to upend of the meanings of events (or the traces, echoes, and remains) that the shorts themselves depict.

CHAPTER 7

The Voice and the Unlivable

ONE OF THE CHALLENGES with rethinking gender-based violence from a feminist perspective is the difficulty of defying the visibility that such violence receives in the hands of the sexist patriarchy—a visibility anchored in erotic justifications of abuse, the pornographic objectification of women's bodies, and the many pretexts that, in the name of love and passion, normalize violence.[48] As a result, the invisibility of gender-based violence is linked within the heterosexist imaginary to an erasure of violence as such and to the visibility of the pretexts that work to conceal it. Showing violence is not necessarily the same thing as making it visible. Furthermore, making it intelligible implies a shift not only toward making it visible but also toward interpreting the images and norms that justify it. Sound here plays an important role when it comes to thinking about a possible disruption of the image that unfurls new readings of the narrative. This chapter explores some of those disruptions.

In *Las estructuras elementales de la violencia,* Rita Segato argues that what characterizes invisible spaces in which women are deprived of their dignity and rights is the absence of any contract to guarantee relationships of equality—and it is here, in what she calls the "vertical coordinate of violence," that the abuse of women takes place. At the same time, these spaces are "normalized" when they become visible as the result of the conflict over masculinity within

48. For different approaches to gender violence, see, for example, *Rey muerto* (dir. Lucrecia Martel, 1995), *Barbie también puede eStar triste* (dir. Albertina Carri, 2001), *Vagón fumador* (dir. Verónica Chen, 2000), *XXY* (dir. Lucía Puenzo, 2007), *El último verano de la Boyita* (dir. Julia Solomonoff, 2009), and *La mosca en la ceniza* (dir. Gabriela David, 2010).

what Segato calls the "horizontal coordinate of violence." If we think about the spaces generated by gender violence through Judith Butler's arguments in *Bodies that Matter*, we could think of these spaces not only as invisible but also unlivable. Additionally, according to Butler, the subjects that inhabit those unlivable zones constitute the "abject," in contrast with subject/object binarism. These subjects are unrecognized as such because they are excluded by social norms—and while these norms do not kill those subjects, they nonetheless obliterate their subjectivities and control their bodies. Locating the abject in verticality (via Segato) when rethinking the audiovisual representation of gender violence allows us to explore what lies outside the visual field but is often made present through sounds or unarticulated voices. It also allows us to rethink the unlivable flip side of the relationship between subject and object, that double gendered narrative that is made visible on the horizontal coordinate at the expense of the invisibility of violence. In that tense simultaneity, the films I will discuss in this chapter attempt to make visible again (that is, to return them to the political arena) those who have been made invisible and marginalized, those who are unperceivable, and those subjects who emerge by escaping from all dominant languages and articulate a (new) voice/a new silence, even if intermittently.

In this chapter, I will discuss a series of tensions related to the voice and silence: the tension between the authoritarian, violent voice and the silence of suicide in María Victoria Menis's *El cielito* [*Little Sky*], which offers a starting point for thinking about the annihilation of the woman's voice within the frame of gender-based violence. Then, through Lucía Puenzo's *El niño pez* [*The Fish Child*], I explore the tension between the voice that characterizes the subjugation of heterosexist violence and the voices that are able to resist that subjugation. I discuss the third tension in relation to *Por tu culpa* [*It's Your Fault*], by Anahí Berneri, addressing the reestablishment of the prelinguistic voice amid the voices of male authority that only make sense through the exercise of authoritarianism. Finally, I use Gabriela David's *Taxi, un encuentro* [*Taxi, an encounter*] to rethink the tension between silence and the dialogic voice that gives birth to the narration of trauma (that of a teenager who has witnessed a crime, possibly a femicide). In all of these cases, language, whether visual or auditory, repositions horizontally the contractual aspect of grammar, narrative, and dialogue, what is experienced in the unlivable space. In all these cases, the overwhelming traumatic and violent event, characterized, as Segato suggests, by networks of expropriation and surrender, remains outside not only the visible but also the articulable, hence the importance of considering both the narration and the excess that remains outside of language and narrative norms.

From silence to the articulated language of the narration of violence lies a minefield of images, sounds, landscapes, and norms of sexist violence. An audiovisual exploration of sexist violence involves mirror reflections, and their distortions and fragmentations, as well as the presence of sounds and voices that move away from language (by which I mean the language of the moving image as well as language and its grammar) and manage to articulate a post-traumatic narration of the violence endured. What these filmmakers achieve through sound, and especially through the voice, from whispers to screams, is to shake up the subjectivity's sedentarism (that of the victim as a fixed category) and to affirm, instead, its wandering contours. As Rosi Braidotti suggests, this wandering, nomadic subjectivity eludes being pinned down in any way. Instead, as a mere outline of voices and subjectivities, it prowls among dominant paradigms and allows feminized subjectivities to be reconfigured in the gaps, in the flight from sedentarism and from fixed definitions and structured language. While these films' images portray subjectivities in a zombie state (indifferent, slumbering between life and death), voices make them nomadic again. Nomadism allows us to approach gendered subjectivity in terms of the screams, whispers, or stifled breathing that interrupt the articulated language that normalizes violence. At the same time, it allows us to understand the voice's role in constructing, reconstructing, or even imagining a subjectivity that is able to escape, resist, or survive gender-based violence.

The Faded Voice

In María Victoria Menis's *El cielito* (2003), the tension between the authoritarian, violent voice and the silence of suicide offers a starting point for thinking about the annihilation of the subjectivity of the victims of violence. The silence of an oppressed female character who is unable to leave the unlivable space in which she resides anticipates the violence she suffers and her eventual suicide. When capturing her story, the director uses a fixed camera and avoids close-ups, giving the spectator a sense of documentary distance.

The film tells the story of Félix, a young man from the province of Entre Ríos who arrives in a town, probably somewhere in that province, and starts working for a family. The signs of domestic violence in the family gradually become apparent. Worried about Chango, the baby of the household, Félix takes him to Buenos Aires after the mother leaves the home and drowns herself in the river. Nevertheless, this is not where the film actually ends; instead, this ending of sorts gestures toward closure and relocates the story within another context. In this new context, the capital city of Buenos Aires, violence is now completely visible and flagrant.

The structure of the account, which is divided into two clearly differentiated parts (Entre Ríos vs. Buenos Aires), establishes a contrast between the shots. In the first part, the shots are longer, whereas in the second they are shorter, and the silence of the first part contrasts with the noisiness of the second. These contrasts point not just to the differences between the rural and urban experiences but also to two different forms of violence. Even so, there are hardly any voices or dialogue. Menis says in an interview, "The movie portrays the relationship between one character who hasn't yet learned to talk and another who can't" (Soto, 2004). Both in the first context and in the second, the sounds of nature or of the city underscore the voices we do not hear. Mercedes is a victim of her husband's violence; she hardly speaks, and her gaze is distant and lost. In contrast with the silence of the first part, the second part portrays the urban landscape and streets of Buenos Aires. The acoustic emphasis is placed on jarring sounds: the roar of public transport, shouts on the street, car alarms, protests, music, conversations of passersby, all of which contrast with the silence of the hotel room, where the sounds center on little Chango, who is starting to communicate through baby talk.

My focus here will be on the first part of the film and, in particular, on what cannot be seen nor heard about the existing gender-based violence. Mercedes is a woman who is not seen and who suffers an abuse that seems invisible (at least for the spectator) and that remains in complete darkness, as if it did not exist. We do not see gender-based violence, only its outlines—displays of masculinity through boxing, hints of abuse, or a woman's silent depression. In the moment when there actually is violence, the camera records it not with images but with sounds: we hear shouts and the baby's crying (Chango's crying serves as the narrative thread that provides cohesion to the narrative of violence in this first part). When the husband is revealed to be a batterer, the narrative image of *El cielito* remains on the edge of the scene: the sound records it as an unlivable space, which is also invisible and which becomes noticeable only through the acoustic register.

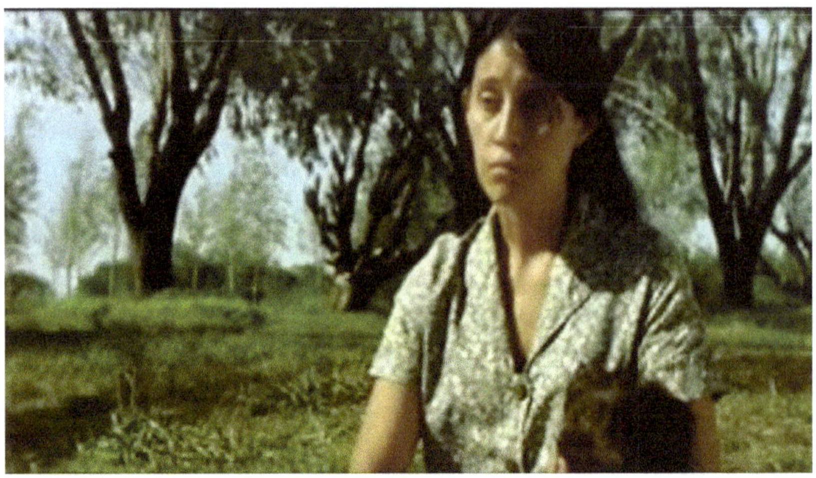

Still image *El cielito* (Dir. María Victoria Menis, 2003)

The story of Roberto, Mercedes, Félix, and Chango exhibits a contained tension that unfolds gradually. The beginning of the scene of domestic violence shows Roberto yelling and carrying Mercedes into the house, and the camera follows Roberto's movements. Then, it shows a close-up of Félix, outside the house, as we hear the blows and Mercedes's sobbing. This scene precedes a fixed camera shot that captures Félix as he walks away and stands motionless at a distance from the door of the house. Félix exits the visual field, and we hear only the sounds of violence. The shots that follow record the witness and then the exterior of the house, leaving us in the foyer, almost as if to resist giving us a visual representation of the violence. Later, the camera moves along with Félix's gaze when he sees one of the marks on Mercedes's arm. In this film, gender-based violence is relegated to the realm of secrets and complicities, with an invisibility that does not erase its violence but which instead serves to portray it as what remains unseen.

Mercedes inhabits a space that is as uninhabitable as it is imperceptible. Her suicide, too, remains in darkness; it remains suspended outside the visual frame. Her son Chango's crying is a clear sign of her absence—and not only her final absence, but her being absent throughout most of the film. His crying is usually surrounded by a silence that mirrors the weakening of her voice—a voice that seemed on the verge of emerging during her first interactions with Félix before fading away—and the weakening of her vital signs, as well as the weakening of any possibility of rebuilding her subjectivity beyond the violence that reduces her to an object.

In these two parts (city and countryside), Menis presents a marked contrast that highlights different forms of violence and marginalization. Two characters, silenced and with limited access to language, are unable to denounce an oppression that no one seem to see. "They may not die, Menis says, but the fates of many Argentine young people without futures are similar to Félix's; they're at a dead end" (Soto, 2004). We could add that *El cielito* reveals the fate of many women who cannot escape domestic violence. Within the film's story, not only does this abuse precede Félix's death in the city and Chango's vulnerability, but it is also the cause of Chango's abandonment. Félix would not be in Buenos Aires with Chango if he had not kidnapped the minor and fled from the household full of gender-based violence that drove the mother to suicide. It is this causality that binds together the two seemingly disparate parts.

Soundwork is key, even the silences, and indicates that *El cielito* is about those characters who cannot speak or who cannot be not heard. The camera accompanies Félix's gaze, but there is also a chain of silences when confronted by violence. Félix looks and listens, but he does not speak. In a film built on silences, the sounds stand out all the more. Mercedes at first talks to Félix, but gradually grows quieter until she is almost mute. Her lack of voice is depicted as a loss. Unlike Martel's whisper, which occurs within a silenced and liberating space, Mercedes's whispers express the weakening or fading of her voice (and, more broadly, the voices of the victims of domestic violence). In contrast, Chango's crying, as pre-language, expresses the neglect, loss, tension, and lack of attention that surrounds him.

The film, narrated with a powerful visuality, privileges the eye: Félix staring out the train window at the beginning of the film; the persistent return to the images of the "little sky" that remind him of his grandmother; the gazes that slowly show the growing relationship between Chango and Félix; the shots in which we see Félix teaching Chango colors, even inviting him to look out the window at a field splashed with the colors of the jam they're eating; the images of the river in which Mercedes loses her life. Sounds interrupt these images and their stillness, so often apparent. Sound exposes the constant violence concealed within these otherwise quiet images, in a marked tension between the increase in violence and the increasingly muted female voice. The first sounds of that violence are shouts and insults, but the camera avoids portraying them visually. Sound interrupts narrative sequences, so we must listen in order to give them meaning. Without sound, violence is represented as a placid image of the exterior of a house. Sound reveals the violence concealed by the household's walls.

The Intrauterine Voice

Lucía Puenzo's *El niño pez* (2009) performs the same gesture of unearthing the violence concealed in intimate spaces, and delves into family secrets and incest as building blocks for gender-based violence, where the female voice, issuing in whispers among other women, is able to transmit the story of the survival of childhood trauma.

When Lala asks her family's domestic worker Ailin ("Guayi") to sing in Guaraní, her father responds, "That's how the Guaraní cast spells on the Spanish, by singing." The sexual tension of the scene—a family dinner with his daughter, his son, and Ailin—is expressed in a series of shots and reverse shots, moving between the father, Ailin, Lala (who is carrying on a relationship with Ailin), and the son, who is uncomfortable and excluded from the situation. We have already learned at this point of the movie that the father is also having a relationship with Ailin. Gender-based violence becomes visible precisely in that tension: it is as if nothing exists outside of it and, at the same time, it seems invisible. As in Puenzo's other films, *El niño pez* centers on the question of whether a secret will be revealed, exposed, or explained. In the case of this film, the legend of the fish child, which evokes the trauma that Guayi herself experienced in her native Paraguay, refers to a child who lives in the depths of the lake and guides those who drown to the bottom. *El niño pez* alludes to Guayi's own pregnancy at thirteen after her father (a telenovela star) raped her. She gives birth to the baby, and, after the baby is born, she takes him to the bottom of the lake and leaves him there.

Narrated through time jumps, the film starts with Lala running away to Paraguay, where the two young women had planned to flee before Lala's father's death, to build a house near a lake. While waiting for Guayi in Ypoá, she hears on the news that Guayi has been accused of killing Lala's father. She also meets Guayi's father there and, from him, learns about the sexual abuse her friend endured. The film revolves around the revelation of secrets and especially hidden violence, in a web of sexual violence and abusive heteronormative masculinity.

The scene of the calm family dinner is the beginning of the tragedy. Presented as a spell or enchantment by the sexist and colonial interpretation of the father, Ailin's voice evokes the dangerous voice of the sirens.[49] It is a voice that, according to the patriarchal reading, attracts and seduces, but which also implies a fear (narrated as danger) of castration and the abyss. For the paternal law, it is the voice of unrestrainable desire: the female voice, represented by the sweetness of the sirens' voices, which is associated not with the maternal body (life) but with pleasure that leads to death and destruction. The story moves from revelation to revelation: Lala finds her father and Ailin having sex. Ailin asks Lala to forget her, and then leaves the house. After Ailin leaves, Lala prepares a glass of milk with sleeping pills. It is not clear whether the glass of milk is for Lala, who is upset after being rejected by Ailin, or her father, nor is it clear, when her father asks Lala for a glass of milk, who switches the glasses around. Yet, the next morning, the father is dead. Ailin is accused and taken away to a juvenile detention facility. After Lala and a friend of Ailin's manage to free her in a sequence that evokes a childish fantasy rather than a realistic sequence, Ailin describes the birth and death of her son. Speaking in whispers, which characterize most of the interactions between Lala and Ailin (many of their conversations take place in the bathtub, evoking both an aquatic context and the maternal aspects of the voice), Ailin tells her painful story. When she was alone and pregnant at fourteen, she took her child swimming in the lake and returned without him. This revelation is narrated through the myth of the fish child, which covers the baby's story and serves as the driving force for the promised journey that finally takes place when the two young women escape at the end of the movie. This ending shows us—that is, reveals to us—the other face of bewitchment, which is associated with the muses rather than the sirens and, as such, is tied to creation, and especially to the narration of history. Associated with motherhood and life, hexes here are a poetics, a creation, that contrasts with the figure of Ailin in Lala's father's eyes (and those of her own father and the harm caused by sexual assault, harassment, and abuse). Only Lala brings her to life, through the maternal realm, the space of a desire that eludes heterosexist violence.

The association of sound with femininity as an intrauterine element is key for thinking about this film, in which the water through which the fish child

49. See Adriana Cavarero, *For More than One Voice*, in the chapter titled "The Fate of the Sirens."

swims symbolizes the return to the intrauterine. In addition to telling the love story of Lala and Ailin, the film also tells the story of the wound inflicted on the female subjectivity by violence and cis-heteronormative patriarchy, which is represented by the two paternal figures who also symbolize, as in the case of Lala's father, the intersection of colonial and patriarchal violence. The fear that Guarani women once cast spells on the colonizers through songs—and may still cast them on their descendents—is still used to justify abuse and violence. And yet there is another voice: the whispers that serve as an anchoring point for the imagination and for survival to the end, when Lala and Ailin imagine their future house. These whispers later serve to recount that traumatic event, or at least its contours, and posit memory as a creative act. Through these whispers, voice is associated no longer with a hex that leads to death but with the imagination and narration, which lead to life.

The Suffocated Voice

The tension between the prelinguistic voice (assigned to the feminine) and the articulated voice (assigned to the masculine) can be explored in *Por tu culpa* (2009) by Anahí Berneri. In this film, the labored breathing of the woman protagonist makes more sense than the well-articulated language of all the male characters, particularly the husband. Additionally, it exposes that the dominance of masculinity associated with *logos* is based not on rationality (as opposed to its lack in the feminine counterpart) but solely on violence perpetrated by patriarchal institutions (the family, the hospital, the police). From silence to the articulated language, the film inhabits a terrain sown with sexist violence.

The first sequence starts with an extreme close-up of a woman, which shows the lower part of her face and a hand on her neck grabbing her from behind. A scream breaks out, and, then there is a physical struggle between the woman and a child. We cannot see clearly because the shot is too close to their bodies. We hear the shouts and sense the bodies and the violence. It seems to be a hand game between two children and their mother, which ends when the mother complains, "I'm not playing anymore." Violence is a game, and that is where everything begins. We hear shouts, a complaint, and the panting of Julieta, the mother—and these sounds will be almost constant throughout the film.

The sound of the telephone intrudes on this opening family scene. Julieta's ex-husband's voice reproaches her because the children are not in bed and because the mother is yelling. The voice we hear on the phone—paternal, calm, absent, distant—tries to give solutions that fail to take into account the mother's overwhelmed mental state. She is clearly in a moment of crisis, perhaps due to her recent divorce. The paternal voice on the telephone starts out well articulated, but, as it gets farther from Julieta's reality (she provides the point of view for the scene), it starts to make no sense. The supposedly well-articulated voice of the father becomes a repetitive sound that berates the mother and is detached from what we can see as spectators. From the beginning, Berneri gives us clues to make sense of this tension. There is a distance, a vast gap, between the voice of authority figures, such as the father, the doctors, or the police officer, and the voices, such as Julieta's voice and the voice of her youngest son, who does not yet have an articulated voice, that provide a different meaning, but only outside the norms of grammar and order. There is a tension between shouts and phallocentric language, or between heavy breathing and *logos.* It is not that Julieta does not speak but that nobody listens to her.

The narrative sequence before one of the children falls relays a very simple story: one night, a mother, alone with her two children, is trying to finish a job and cannot. Sound marks this interruption, or series of interruptions: shouting, noise, a ringing telephone, the father's voice—and then yelling and a slap. The camera does not allow us to see clearly. That is, it signals to us that we cannot see everything, and therefore it signals the need to listen. When Julieta manages to work on the project she is supposed to deliver to a consultant, she uses her headphones to listen to some interviews, which we can faintly hear. Through extreme close-up shots that are often out of focus and close-ups that fragment rather than trying to show her face, as well as through framing that leaves most of what is happening outside the visual field, the film makes the acoustic element central.

Throughout the film, Julieta's voice consists of unarticulated sounds: her panting, which is contrasted with the very few moments of calmer breathing that she has in the few minutes of serenity and silence during the film, as well as her shouting, moans, and weeping. The greatest contrast is not silence, which can be a relief for the spectator in the few moments it does occur, but rather supposedly articulated language, which is represented by her ex-husband, the doctors, and the police personnel who will appear later (although, paradoxically, it is also represented by Julieta's mother, a psychoanalyst). And I say *supposedly* articulated language because the soundwork in the film suggests a challenge to the articulated voice—that is, those voices associated with the language of authority in terms of its coherence. Instead, the film emphasizes the incoherence of the articulated voice and proposes to read its authority as authoritarianism.

The atmosphere of the film is characterized by suffocation, asphyxiation, possibly the crisis of a divorce, endless moments of impotence, and frustration. Julieta acts like a zombie, disconnected from the supposed coherence and logic of her surroundings and from the paternal voice that narrates them. That asphyxiation becomes visible/audible through the close proximity of the camera, which is so close that it makes seeing difficult, and through the sound that reverberates in our ears. All of the voices in the domestic space verge on the incomprehensible: the mother shouts or slaps, then immediately starts to play with one of the boys; nine-year-old Valentín and two-year-old Tao shout, fight, and whine; the voices of the husband and grandmother issue rules that have nothing to do with Julieta's reality. A truly articulated voice does not seem to exist; it vanishes when exposed to the sexist authoritarianism of the voice that monitors, represses, and punishes. The sound of her labored, almost smothered breathing is disturbing and unsettling, perhaps even more so than the fighting and shouting. The camera captures these everyday domestic moments, focusing on details so we cannot make out the scene, and on the vague outlines that keep us from seeing. The visible, in its own invisibility, becomes more visible only if we focus on sound.

When the boys fight over a toy car, and Tao injures Valentín, the mother rushes over and, as if in a body-against-body, tries to separate them. Tao's fall occurs outside the visual field, with the camera recording it only after it has happened. We see him on the floor with his mother taking care of him and, later, in her arms with his brother asking him where it hurts. From this point until the very end, the film moves into the street and then into the hospital, before returning to the house in the last sequence. The car, too, is a closed, suffocating space: the mother drives, fumbles to answer the phone, and turns around, trying to keep her son awake. The scolding voice belongs to her ex-husband: "Didn't you see him? Weren't you watching? . . . I told you to put him to bed." The reproach alludes to the title: *it's your fault*. After they arrive at the hospital, the doctor examines the boy, and, when he sees the boy's bruises, the older brother blames the mother. Believing that he is dealing with a case of domestic violence, the doctor consults with another doctor and, without offering any explanation, tells the mother they have to stay at the hospital. Unlike the first part of the film, these sequences are narrated with much more conventionally coherent narrative images, and they show the institutional gender-based violence through the voice of male authority—in this case, the doctor's. Though the doctor's suspicion and his effort to protect the child are understandable (and plausible), the way that protection plays out clearly reveals the sexist paradigms of interpretation. This authoritative voice materializes in a series of accusations leveled at the mother, revealing the tentacles of sexism that are surrounding (suffocating?) her.

The ex-husband's arrival serves only to amplify this atmosphere. He wants to take the boys home, but the doctors report the case to the police. The paternal voice blames the mother ("What did you do?"). Despite "defending" her in front of the authorities when the police are called over the accusations, he tells his ex-wife, "My children don't have a mother who looks after them.... You hand them back to me all messed up.... You're such an idiot." Is this the voice associated with *logos*? Here the challenge to the patriarchal voice begins. At first, during the first reprimands, it seems to make more sense; maybe the boys should have been in bed so Julieta could work in peace. Yet, as they head to the police station to deal with the abuse report, any pretense of rationality or coherence of the father's voice falls apart—particularly when he says, "I'm on my own, I'm on my own with everything." After all, the film serves as evidence: the camera is witness to the mother, who is on her own with the children, overwhelmed, and unable to defend herself from the (masculine) articulated voices that surround her, scold her, and oppress her. Where is violence? Is it only in the shouts of the first part? In the slap? In the husband's insults and verbal abuse? In the shouting voice of the violent patriarchy? In the articulated voice that acts as a disciplinary rationality? Julieta's shouting at the beginning and her heavy breathing throughout most of the film signal not just her mistreatment and agitation, but also her inarticulable (and untranslatable) voice within her family and the social environment that surrounds her.

The final sequences in the film show the dead end that facilitates the return of the father to the household to "restore order" to the disorder characterized by the zombified subjectivity of the mother. This zombified subjectivity is both a consequence of her repression and a form of distancing as resistance. The explosion of the senselessness of masculine rationality, which conceals violence with excuses, is the clearly audible voice of authority, as evidenced by the police. According to the police, "If your husband promises to make sure that nothing happens to the boys, you can go home with them." The voice here makes visible the patriarchal pact, the alliance associated with meaning and authority. It is a watchful voice that makes pacts only horizontally with other men while reinforcing the hierarchies of power. And this vigilant voice that claims to guarantee well-being exposes its inconsistency with respect to well-being from a woman's point of view. The voicework calls into question the voice's association with the patriarchal norm in order to uncover the violence the patriarchal norm inflicts. It is this voice that sets the trap and marginalizes, silences, and abuses women. The last sequence, when the ex-husband returns to Julieta's house and there is a final silence, shows the authoritarian restoration of order and "sense" at the expense of the mother's dignity. The restored order comes from that quashing of a disobedient voice, with its agitated breathing, subjugating it and making it invisible and unlivable. Whereas, at the beginning, we heard Julieta, at the end we can no longer hear her. Her voice has gone quiet.

The Dialogic Voice

Gabriela David's *Taxi, un encuentro* (2001) tells the story of a young woman's survival after she flees the scene of a family crime. The film focuses on the complex process of witnessing, and it affirms the centrality of the voice in the reconstruction of a narrative that is visually presented as blurry and confusing. Laura is the sole survivor of a femicide: her father kills her mother and, before committing suicide, shoots his daughter. Laura escapes and gets into a taxicab. She is visibly traumatized and, in the very moment of her survival, cannot express in words what happened. She can speak only in moans, cries, and screams. It is almost as if the camera is looking for clues about the possible crime; we hear gunshots, and we know that Laura is wounded. The narrative images return several times to the corner where she gets into a taxi and where the encounter between her and the taxi driver takes place. Only later on, toward the end of the film, does she provide a brief and concise narration of her own recollection of the crime. Laura's narration reconstructs what the camera is not able to capture, and so the viewer does not know about the details of the crime until later. Her narration also reconstructs the puzzle for Esteban, the taxi driver, who attempts to understand her story, but cannot piece it together. The acoustic anchor of the traumatic event is the triple gunshot.

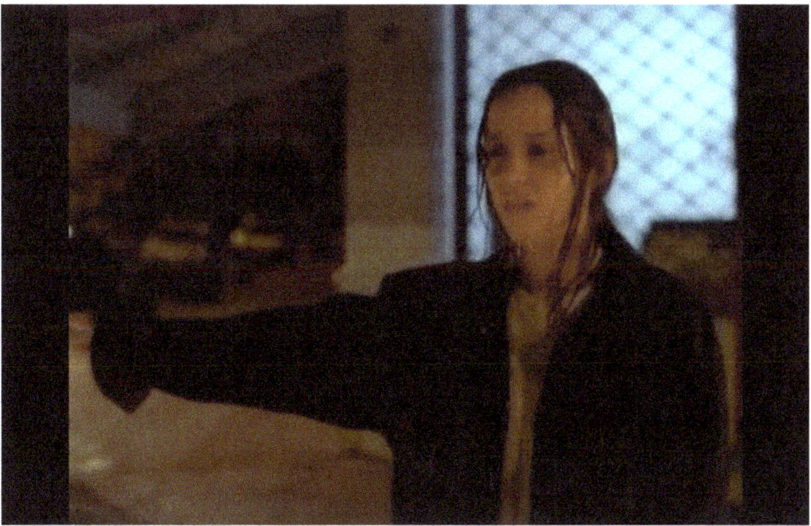

Still Image, *Taxi, un encuentro* (Dir. Gabriela David, 2001) – Script, Prod. and Dir. Gabriela David (1960–2010)

The visual anchor is the encounter and Esteban's attempt to save the life of a wounded teenager. The camera insists on returning back to the corner where Laura catches the cab. The film starts there, on that street corner. The other recurring scene is that of the narration: medium shots of the male protagonist interrupt the narrative images and show him telling the story.

From the beginning, we see Esteban (or "Gato") telling a story and looking at the camera and, therefore, at the viewer. Later on, we realize that he is talking to Laura and that the camera, positioned from her perspective, is focused on Esteban telling the story as the narrative voice. Only at the end does Laura describe her trauma and the crime she witnessed: "My dad, looking at a gun, holding it in his hands. I called to him, but I think he didn't hear me. He lifted the gun and looked at us in fear. Mom leaped on top of me. He shot me and I saw him bring the gun to his mouth. There was a noise. Like the whole house was exploding."

The opening of the film foreshadows everything. From the corner where the encounter takes place, a fixed camera records different moments of the day and night. Suddenly, there are three gunshots. Then, a taxi pulls up, into which a still-unknown passenger climbs. The male protagonist, in a medium shot, kicks off the narration: "Do you want me to tell you what happened that night?" El Gato/Esteban's narrative voice, in its intrusions, speaks in the past tense. The story of what happened to Esteban that night starts with the theft of the taxi. Then we see Esteban, who stole the taxi, picking up passengers and talking to them. Again, we return to the gunshots. Esteban moves away from the area after hearing them, but he has to get closer again and drives by the corner shown in the opening shots. There we see a young woman (Laura), who climbs in. Her breathing is halting and agitated, and she asks him to go around the block and drive past the door of her house, where the crime took place.

Believing she was shot during a robbery, El Gato takes her to his house to heal her wound. Laura does not seem to get any better, so he leaves her on the street and calls an ambulance to pick her up. The next morning, Esteban's father reads about the incident in the newspaper, which describes the mother's murder, the father's suicide, and the daughter's survival. As the narrative voice, Esteban seeks to reconstruct the different pieces and put them in order so that they make sense. However, the narration (the male voice that acts as the narrator of/witness to Laura's survival) is interrupted by something that exceeds language: a traumatic experience that becomes present in breathless sobs and cries of pain.

The shots that capture the spectator's returns to the corner vary, being taken from a greater or lesser distance. When, in one of those returns, the camera captures Laura in a medium shot, we can finally identify the face we were at first unable to recognize. We see her wait on the corner, hail the taxi, and, once inside, cry as they drive past the house where the crime took place. The camera repeats the opening shots and returns to the same corner. The encounter means that El Gato's night changes course as he, compelled by Laura's situation, takes care of her. It is Laura's body that becomes visible: a wounded body that is unable to speak with words.

At some point after the night of the tragedy, and after she recovers, Laura manages to return to Esteban's house using her memory of what she saw and heard through the taxi window the night of the crime. She recalls the image of a highway and the sound of the train, which guide her to his house. Once there, she asks him what happened that night, and then we see the sequence of the film's opening minutes. Yet, this time, the camera provides us with a medium shot of Laura while blurring the image of the taxi driver. Then the camera frames both of them within the visual field as he repeats the same

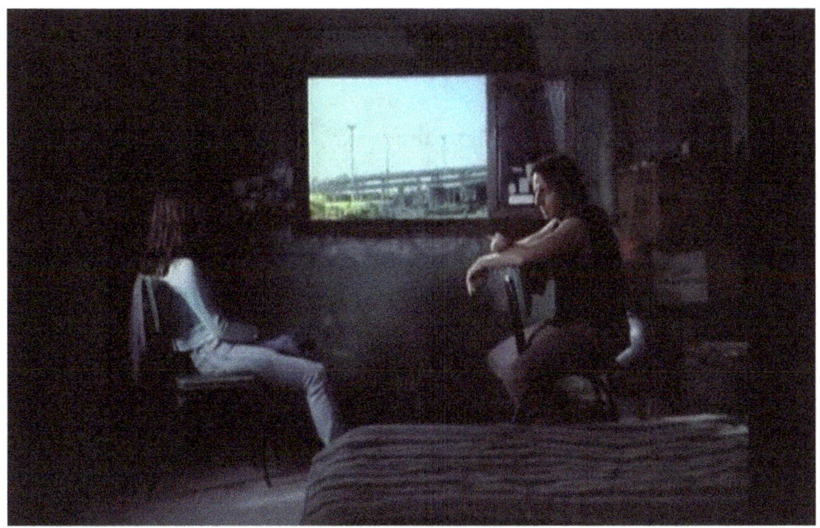

Still Image, *Taxi, un encuentro* (Dir. Gabriela David, 2001) –
Script, Prod. and Dir. Gabriela David (1960–2010)

words he said at the beginning: "You've got to learn to survive, to adapt to life." Then, we hear Laura's story. She mentions her parents' fights, and she returns to that day and their final argument. At that point, she describes the crime, which she summarizes as a noise and an explosion. According to Laura, her father aimed at her mother and fired, then he repeated the action with Laura before lifting the gun to his mouth. Laura fled the crime scene. And only when she relates what happened that night does her voice become visible, does she become a witness. Now her voice describes the crime.

Esteban's voice, which is initially the narrative voice, is more powerful, or at least more audible, than Laura's voice. Hers is, at first, a voice of sounds, in which meaning is not articulated until the final sequences of the film, when she becomes the narrative voice in dialogue with Esteban. Though these initial sounds are not articulated as language, they do convey her pain and anguish. Her weeping and shouts are part of what Dolar understands, following Lacan, as pre-symbolic sounds, which carry meaning as gesture and which wait to be heard or understood. Only at the end does Laura recount what she saw, and in that moment, she becomes the narrator of what the newspaper calls a *family tragedy*. From the beginning, with the three gunshots and the ambulance siren, sound connects us to the scene, and we return again and again to the corner where the encounter with Esteban takes place. The three gunshots point to that other setting of survival—Laura's house, where her father kills her mother and shoots his daughter before committing suicide. The film accompanies—you might almost say *seeks*—the emergence of Laura's narrative voice. Only when she manages to speak can we reconstruct the event, and her voice gives existence to the crime she witnessed and survived.

Mirror Sounds: The Invisible and the Unlivable

The films discussed here explore female subjectivities, their fragments, their remnants, their incipient manifestations, and even their annihilations. In particular, they explore those subjectivities that inhabit not entirely livable worlds. All these films challenge the dominant language of the narrative image and focus instead on what remains invisible of those subjectivities. The wound produced by gender-based violence exceeds the limits of the narrative image, and it is the tension between image and voice that often succeeds in providing an account of heteronormative violence and the annihilation it provokes. These directors propose, I argue, a reconnection that takes place in the realm of the voice, from "minor" sounds (breathing, shouts, sobs, whispers) to singing and articulated voices. In the case of the former, this reconstruction is intermittent, whereas it is more sustained in the latter, and in both cases it reveals the survival of and resistance to violence. It is through the aural dimension that the new form of subjectivity is reconstructed.

One might say that the new Argentine cinema, which first kicks off in *Historias breves*, starts with a portrayal of the invisible as unlivable, marked by gunshots that put an end to a string of insults, threats, and blows. I am referring here to Lucrecia Martel and her short *Rey muerto* (1995). Toward the end of the short, we see the end of the violent relationship, when a woman responds to her husband's humiliations and coercions with a gunshot before fleeing with her children. The short, which I previously mentioned in the chapter on Martel, depicts the scene of violence visually. It lingers, with a slow camera that constantly distorts any clear view of the scene, and emphasizes the opacity of the shots and the shakiness of the images, which tremble from the effects of violence. The short film explores two dimensions of the voice. First, it explores the gossip that starts up around town when it becomes clear that Juana is going to leave with her children and abandon her violent husband, and this gossip features markedly male voices, which are set apart from the single female voice that asks them to leave the protagonist alone. Second, the short explores the voices that issue from the TV and the comments in town about an incident in which a female journalist was assaulted by a man on the street. That incident, and the discussions it provokes, offers a contrast between the argument about violence, in which some of the men in town engage, and the scene of violence itself. The final gunshots reveal the emergence of a new voice in the protagonist, who, while walking with her children, leaves Rey Muerto, a town and a space that encapsulates the context of pervasive sexist violence.

The very attempt to portray that which is not seen privileges the acoustic register because, through certain voices that remain not fully subjugated to the image, it is possible to play out sounds that are not fully articulated, such as screams, babbling, panting, suffocation, and even silence. Nevertheless, pre-language, even if it takes place outside of articulated language and even if it still has meaning, belongs to the invisible world, to the wound inflicted on the subject who is a victim of sexist violence. This subject is a posttraumatic female subject, often nearly motionless, who uses articulate words and grammar or a voice that does not translate well to articulated language and who makes gender violence both visible and audible—at least for us, as viewers.

Coda

In a provocative discussion about the intersections of the gaze and gender, Teresa de Lauretis wonders about Medusa's fate upon seeing herself in Perseus's mirror. "Seeing herself" is the reflexive action I wish to highlight because Medusa's power resides precisely in her gaze. Perseus decapitates her and holds her head next to his hero's shield. Medusa is not only vanquished by Perseus, or at least by the reflection off his armor, but she is also captured by the hero for his own benefit. On his shield, her gaze continues to have power, but now she turns Perseus's enemies, rather than her own, into stone. De Lauretis lingers on this portrayal of Medusa and her gaze, especially on her defiance of masculine visions, and argues that the power of her eyes implies a long-term effect. The threat highlights the male power of the gaze that reduces women not only to objects to be looked at but also to a place of mystery (De Lauretis, 1984: 110).

The metaphor of Medusa as a monster-woman, whose gaze is the root of her monstrosity, condenses the danger embodied by the feminine gaze (as both marginalized and subversive) within masculine culture. Medusa survives as a monstrous being within male heroic narratives—that is, she does not have her own story but instead remains as a vestige inside male history, buried among different layers of narrations and fantasies that are not her own (De Lauretis, 1984: 109). It is within this capture of the dangerous female, who is also the powerful female, that the process of domesticating the female image takes place, making her domestic, or at least domesticated, in heroic narratives, and this process is paradigmatic of masculinity and patriarchy.[50] At the heart of domination lies the projection of male fantasy through the

50. When Perseus tries to kill Medusa, some versions relate that he cannot look at her directly. Nobody can look at the Medusa because her gaze turns people to stone. So, instead he looks at Medusa's reflection in his own shield, and only then is he able to decapitate her.

monstrous woman, who is accompanied by certain voices, such as the sirens' deadly singing, that must be defeated so that the hero can complete his journey. In the case of the sirens, the hero's journey is that of Ulysses, who hears the sirens while lashed to a mast—a self-evident part of the phallocentric economy, by the way. In the case of Medusa, the hero's journey is that of Perseus, who cuts off Medusa's head and uses it on his own shield.

This book has discussed several examples of how filmmakers have explored gender in terms of the gaze and its limits, examples that emphasize the fragmentary nature of images and the difficulty of narrating visually. This preoccupation is expressed through the cropping and framing of bodies; the use of a fixed camera that records only the movements that take place in front of it, underscoring the invisibility of subjects that remain outside the visual field; cuts in the conventional narrative sequence to emphasize visual images that halt the narration; explicit images that show us characters or directors with their cameras, repeating shots, going out into the street to look for a story by happenstance; and even constant references to seeing, to knowing how to see, or being unable to see. In different ways, María Luisa Bemberg, Lita Stantic, Lucrecia Martel, Albertina Carri, María Victoria Menis, Lucía Puenzo, Sabrina Farji, Paula de Luque, Anahí Berneri, Sandra Gugliotta, and Gabriela David explore the visual realm through the continuities, intrusions, irrelevancies, harmonies, and desynchronizations of the voice. Or, rather, they explore voices (plural) and their different modulations, including whispers, screams, singing, echoes, breathing, resonance, sighs, the transcendent voice, the narrative voice, the silenced voice, the articulated and unarticulated voice, and that which is none of the above. The voice suggests another sort of relationship with the audiovisual realm, one that seems to include a closeness that erases, if only intermittently, the unalterable relationship between subject and object that characterizes the patriarchal visual regime.

The acoustic record, especially through the voice, allows for the possibility of reviewing images through a contact anchored in feminine sound, rather than paternal languages, and in the proximity of touch. The voice touches the ear, whether it comes from a nearby and extreme close-up or from the suspension of perspective that allows for a view from a distance. Hearing and touching bring that closeness, which, as in Sor Juana's poetry and Albertina Carri's installation *Punto impropio*, as well as in Carri's *Operación fracaso y el sonido recobrado*, invades and undermines the remoteness of eyes, camera, and shots.

This book has attempted to show some of these routes, not to propose a dismantling of the patriarchal regime of the gaze or the articulation of the voice, but to point to a number of fleeting interventions in cinematographic language and to some of the interstices through which many Argentine women filmmakers express their dissent in the face of the norms of the visible and the audible. They do not create a new visual or auditory regime but, instead, gesture toward the limits (insecurities, impotencies, vulnerabilities) of dominant images and voices. Of course, this dissent could be translated into the logic of castration, but that would transport dissident images and sounds into patriarchal, heteronormative territory and into the defense of the fantasy of masculinity and its inherent superiority (power, rationality, and invulnerability). The work of feminist critics and filmmakers is to punch a hole in the scenography of the visible and the audible and to give us models for other forms of reading, seeing, and listening. Certainly, as spectators, we can choose our keys of interpretation. And, even so, it is possible to say, recalling Clarice Lispector's words in *A hora da estrela*, that these directors' names are located between the "right to shout" and the uncertainty of how to shout (or "the blues lament," or "a sense of loss"), just as Lispector asserts her own voice between those two options that evoke not only the ability to speak but also the mute and untranslatable voice that remains silenced.

In this book, the maternal voice, in a wide range of different instances, was useful for rethinking subversion in a space closer to the body than the transcendence of the desynchronization of the voice that takes place in the voice-over or in acousmatic sound, or sound without a visual referent. In this sense, the book implies an intersection between masculinization and feminization at the moment of their becoming intelligible. It is not merely a matter of being able to see or being able to hear the female voice as a voice detached from the body, as a transcendent voice in a male key. It has to do with showing that the desynchronized male voice is also vulnerable, is also an echo, is also meaningless, because it has to do with showing that the voice closest to the body is, or may be, a disobedient voice that reconstructs untranslatable meanings into the paternal language, the flat mirror, or the voice that evokes *logos*. I invoke once more Albertina Carri and her attempt to restore the articulated voice of her disappeared mother's letters, but also those other sounds that can be linked to intrauterine modulations. The sound that Carri uses to recover that voice, the voice of the letters her mother wrote, has modulations, echoes, and undulations.

This book also attempts to immerse itself in contact with voices and with their explosions and magical plasticities, with which images fuse and switch places. It has aspired to see, or at least imagine, an auditory (re)encounter with the feminine in order to hear with the eyes those voices of denunciation, of protest, as well as that bodily resonance and that love letter.

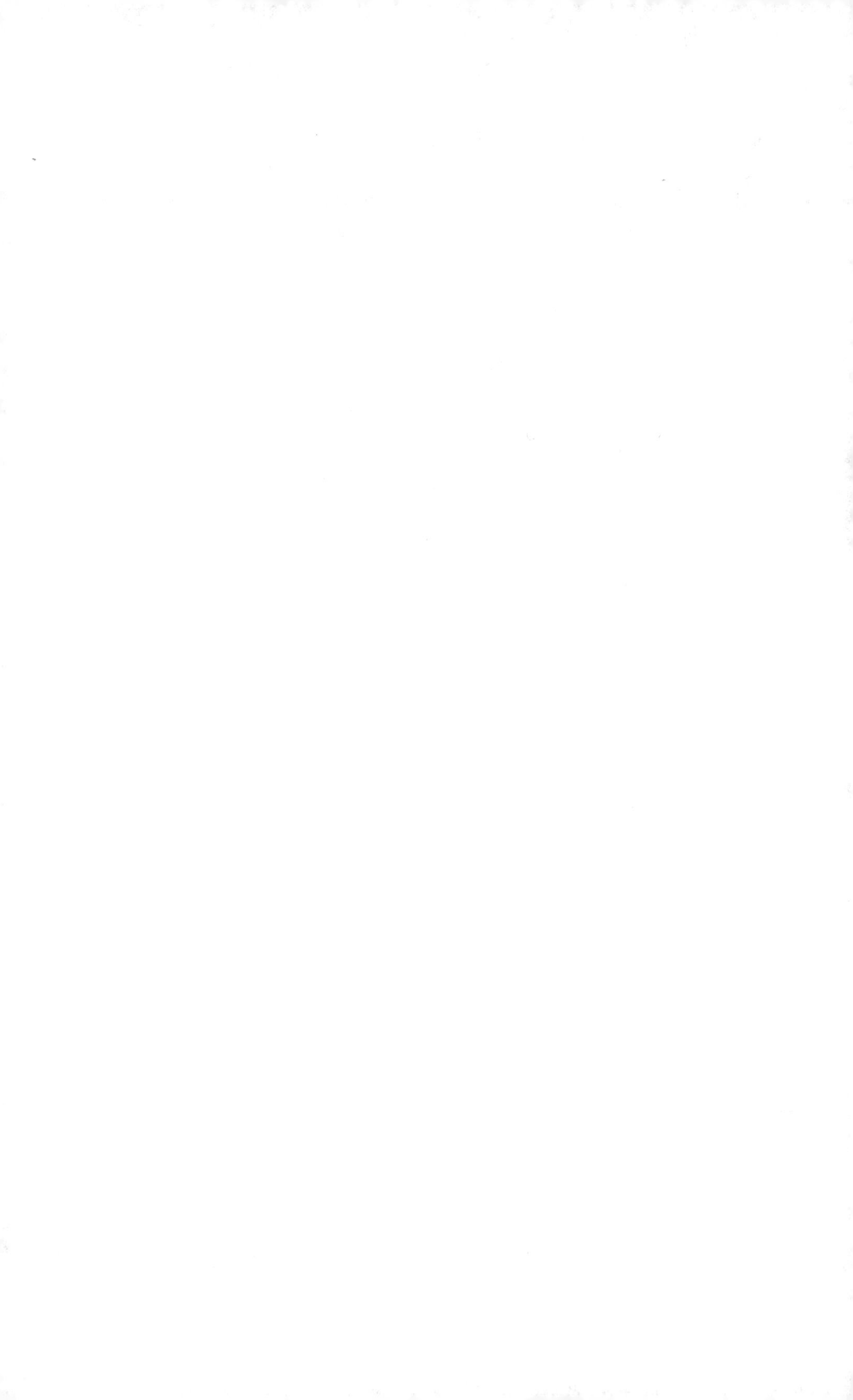

BIBLIOGRAPHY

Agamben, Giorgio: *Homo Sacer: Sovereign Power and Bare Life.* Stanford: Stanford University Press, 1998.

Aguilar, Gonzalo: *Otros mundos: Ensayo sobre el nuevo cine argentino.* Buenos Aires: Santiago Arcos, 2006.

Amado, Ana: *La imagen justa: Cine argentino y política 1980–2007.* Buenos Aires: Colihue, 2007.

———: "No son como nosotros. Lenguas aborígenes, género y memoria en el cine argentino." International Symposium *Erasures: Gender Violence and Human Rights.* University of Minnesota, October 24–25, 2013.

Bach, Caleb: "María Luisa Bemberg Tells the Untold." *Americas* 46 (1994): 21–27.

Batlle, Diego: "De la virtual desaparición a la nueva ley: El resurgimiento." In Horacio Bernades, Diego Lerer, and Sergio Wolf, *El nuevo cine argentino: Temas, autores y estilos de una renovación,* 17–28. Buenos Aires: Tatanka, 2002.

Beauvoir, Simone De: *The Second Sex.* Trans. H. M. Parshley. New York: Alfred A. Knopf, 1957.

Benjamin, Walter: *Selected Writings. Volume 2, 1927–1934.* Edited by Michael W. Jennings, Howard Eiland, and Gary Smith. Cambridge, MA: Belknap Press of Harvard University Press, 1999.

———: *The Work of Art in the Age of Its Technological Reproducibility, and Other Writings on Media.* Cambridge, MA: Belknap Press of Harvard University Press, 2008.

Bernades, Horacio, Diego Lerer, and Sergio Wolf (eds.): *El nuevo cine argentino: Temas, autores y estilos de una renovación.* Buenos Aires: Tatanka, 2002.

Bettendorff, Paulina, and Agustina Pérez Rial (comps.): *Tránsitos de la mirada: Mujeres que hacen cine.* Buenos Aires: Libraria, 2014.

Bhabha, Homi: *The Location of Culture.* New York: Routledge, 1994.

Braidotti, Rosi: *Sujetos nómades.* Buenos Aires: Paidós, 2000.

Burton-Carvajal, Julianne: "María Luisa Bemberg's *Miss Mary*: Fragments of Life and Career History." In *Redirecting the Gaze: Gender, Theory, and Cinema in the Third World*, edited by Diana Robin and Ira Jaffe, 331–52. Albany: State University of New York Press, 1999.

Butler, Judith: *Bodies that Matter: On the Discursive Limits of "Sex."* New York: Routledge, 1993.

Calveiro, Pilar: *Política y/o violencia: Una aproximación a la guerrilla de los años 70*. Buenos Aires: Grupo Editorial Norma, 2005.

Calvera, Leonor: *Camila O'Gorman o el amor y el poder*. Buenos Aires: Leviatan, 1986.

———: *Mujeres y feminismo en Argentina*. Buenos Aires: Grupo Editor Latinoamericano, 1990.

Carbonetti, María: "Deseos argentinos: *Miss Mary*." *Revista Canadiense de Estudios Hispánicos* 27, no. 1 (2002): 87–98.

Carri, Albertina: Los rubios: *Cartografía de una película*. Buenos Aires: Ediciones Gráficas Especiales, 2007.

———: *Operación fracaso y el sonido recobrado*. Buenos Aires: Parque de la Memoria, 2015.

Caruth, Cathy: *Unclaimed Experience: Trauma, Narrative, and History*. Baltimore: Johns Hopkins University Press, 1996.

Castagna, Gustavo: "De una vanguardia a otra, ¿hay una tradición?" In *El nuevo cine argentino: Temas, autores y estilos de una renovación*, edited by Horacio Bernades, Diego Lerer, and Sergio Wolf, 105–10. Buenos Aires: Tatanka, 2002.

Cavarero, Adriana: *For More Than One Voice: Toward a Philosophy of Vocal Expression*. Stanford: Stanford University Press, 2005.

Chion, Michel: *Audio-Vision: Sound on Screen*. Columbia University Press, 1994.

———: *The Voice in Cinema*. New York: Columbia University Press, 1999.

Cixous, Hélène: "The Laugh of the Medusa." Translated by Keith Cohen and Paula Cohen. *Signs: Journal of Women in Culture and Society* 1, no. 4 (1976): 875–93.

——— and Catherine Clément: *The Newly Born Woman*. London: I. B. Tauris, 1986.

Cruz, Sor Juana Inés de la: *Obras completas*. Mexico City: Porrúa, 1969.

Deleuze, Gilles: *Cinema 2*. Minneapolis: University of Minnesota Press, 1989.

Deleuze, Gilles and Félix Guattari: *Anti-Oedipus: Capitalism and Schizophrenia*. Minneapolis: University of Minnesota Press, 1983.

Derrida, Jacques: *Mémoires: For Paul de Man*. New York: Columbia University Press, 1989.

———: *Specters of Marx: The State of the Debt, the Work of Mourning and the New International*. New York: Routledge, 1994.

Doane, Mary Ann: "The Voice in the Cinema: The Articulation of Body and Space." *Yale French Studies* 60 (Fall 1980): 33–50.

———: "Film and the Masquerade: Theorizing the Female Spectator." In *Issues in Feminist Film Criticism*, edited by Patricia Erens, 41–57. Bloomington: Indiana University Press, 1990.

———: "The Close-Up: Scale and Detail in the Cinema." *Differences: A Journal of Feminist Cultural Studies* 14, no. 3 (Fall 2003): 89–111.

Dolar, Mladen: *A Voice and Nothing More*. Cambridge, MA: MIT Press, 2006.

Enríquez, Mariana. "La mala memoria," Radar, *Página 12*, August 17, 2008.

Escudero, Mónica: "The Tragedy in María Luisa Bemberg's *De eso no se habla*." *Revista Canadiense de Estudios Hispánicos* 27, no. 1 (2002): 193–206.

Falicov, Tamara: *The Cinematic Tango: Contemporary Argentine Film*. London: Wallflower Press, 2007.

Fontana, Clara: *María Luisa Bemberg*. Buenos Aires: Centro Editor de América Latina, 1993.

Forcinito, Ana: "Mirada cinematográfica y género sexual: Mímica, erotismo y ambigüedad en Lucrecia Martel." *Chasqui* 35, no. 2 (2006): 109–30.

———: "Lo invisible y lo invivible: El Nuevo Cine Argentino de mujeres y sus huellas acústicas." *Chasqui* 42, no. 2 (2013): 37–57.

———: "Óyeme con los ojos: Miradas y voces en el cine de María Luisa Bemberg." In *Tránsitos de la mirada: Mujeres que hacen cine*, edited by Agustina Pérez Rial and Paulina Bettendorff, 41-68, Buenos Aires: Libraria, 2014.

———: "Los cristales de la memoria: Voces y miradas frente a la historia argentina." *Revista Iberoamericana* 251 (2015): 409-434.

Foster, David William: *Contemporary Argentine Cinema*. Columbia: University of Missouri Press, 1992.

———: "*De eso no se habla:* A Film of Queer Difference." *Revista Canadiense de Estudios Hispánicos* 27, no. 1 (2002): 177–92.

Franco, Jean: *Las conspiradoras: La representación de la mujer en México*. Mexico City: El Colegio de México/Fondo de Cultura Económica, 1993.

Friedan, Betty: *The Feminine Mystique*. New York: W. W. Norton & Company, 1963.

Grandis, Rita de: "Introducción: María Luisa Bemberg o las trampas de la clase." *Revista Canadiense de Estudios Hispánicos* 27, no. 1 (2002): 3–14.

Grant, Catherine: "Camera Solidaria." *Screen* 38, no. 4 (1997): 311–28.

———: "Intimista Transformations: María Luisa Bemberg's First Feature Films." In *An Argentine Passion*, edited by John King, Sheila Whitaker, and Rosa Bosch, 73–109, London: Verso, 2000.

Halbwachs, Maurice: *On Collective Memory*. New York: Harper and Row, 1980.

Hart, Stephen: "Bemberg's Winks and Camila's Sighs: Melodramatic Encryption in Camila." *Revista Canadiense de Estudios Hispánicos* 27, no. 1 (2002): 75–86.

Huyssen, Andreas: *Present Pasts: Urban Palimpsests and the Politics of Memory.* Stanford: Stanford University Press, 2003.

Irigaray, Luce: *Speculum of the Other Woman.* Ithaca: Cornell University Press, 1985.

———: *This Sex Which Is Not One.* Translated by Catherine Porter and Carolyn Burke. Ithaca: Cornell University Press, 1985.

———: *I Love to You: Sketch for a Felicity within History.* New York: Routledge, 1996.

Jelin, Elizabeth: *State Repression and the Labors of Memory.* Minneapolis: University of Minnesota Press, 2003.

Kantaris, Elia Geoffrey: "Re-engendering History: María Luisa Bemberg's *Miss Mary.*" In *An Argentine Passion*, edited by John King, Sheila Whitaker, and Rosa Bosch, 122–36. London: Verso, 2000.

Kaplan, E. Ann: *Women and Film: Both Sides of the Camera.* New York: Methuen, 1983.

———: *Looking for the Other: Feminism, Film and Imperial Gaze.* New York: Routledge, 1997.

———: "Global Feminisms and the State of Feminist Film Theory." *Signs: Journal on Women in Culture and Society* 30 (Autumn 2004): 1236–46.

King, John: *Magical Reels: A History of Cinema in Latin America.* London: Verso, 2000.

King, John, Sheila Whitaker, and Rosa Bosch, eds., *An Argentine Passion: María Luisa Bemberg and Her Films.* London: Verso, 2000. 1–72.

Kohan, Martín: "La apariencia celebrada." *Punto de vista* 78 (2004): 24–30.

Kristeva, Julia: *Revolution in Poetic Language.* New York: Columbia University Press, 1984.

———: *The Sense and Non-sense of Revolt.* New York: Columbia University Press, 2000.

———: *Intimate Revolt: The Powers and Limits of Psychoanalysis.* New York: Columbia University Press, 2002.

Lauretis, Teresa de: *Alice Doesn't.* Bloomington: Indiana University Press, 1984.

———: *Technologies of Gender: Essays on Theory, Film and Fiction.* Bloomington: Indiana University Press, 1987.

———: "Rethinking Women's Cinema: Aesthetics and Feminist Theory." In *Multiple Voices in Feminist Film Criticism*, edited by Diane Carson, Linda Dittmar, and Janice R. Welsch, 140–61. Minneapolis: University of Minnesota Press, 1994.

Mahieu, José Agustín: "Cine argentino: Nuevas fronteras." *Cuadernos Hispanoamericanos* 517–19 (1993): 289–304.

Malabou, Catherine. *Changing Difference: The Feminine and the Question of Philosophy*. Cambridge, MA: Polity Press, 2011.

Manzoni, Carla: "Decapitaciones poderosas: "paraespacios" surrealistas y poder de gestión feminista." *Ámbitos Feministas* 3 (2013): 123–36.

———: "Counter-narratives in the Void: Memory in *Los rubios*, Its Aesthetic Heritage and Its Reverberations." Doctoral dissertation. University of Minnesota, 2015.

Mennell, D. Jan: "Eloquent Elisions: The Expressive Play of Silence in María Luisa Bemberg's *De eso no se habla*." *Revista Canadiense de Estudios Hispánicos* 27, no. 1 (2002): 157–76.

———: "Jane Eyre Goes to Argentina: Cultural Imperialism in María Luisa Bemberg's *Miss Mary*." *Revista Canadiense de Estudios Hispánicos* 27, no. 1 (2002): 99–118.

Monteagudo, Luciano: "Lucrecia Martel: Susurros a la hora de la siesta." In *El nuevo cine argentino: Temas, autores y estilos de una renovación*, edited by Horacio Bernades, Diego Lerer, and Sergio Wolf, 69–78. Buenos Aires: Tatanka, 2002.

Mulvey, Laura: "Visual Pleasure and Narrative Cinema." *Visual and Other Pleasures*. Bloomington: Indiana University Press, [1975] 1989.

———: "Afterthoughts on 'Visual Pleasure and Narrative Cinema.'" *Visual and Other Pleasures*. Bloomington: Indiana University Press, [1981] 1989. 29–38.

Newman, Kathleen: "'Convocar tanto mundo': Narrativising Authoritarianism and Globalisation in *De eso no se habla*." In *An Argentine Passion: María Luisa Bemberg and Her Films*, edited by John King, Sheila Whitaker, and Rosa Bosch, 181–92. London: Verso, 2000.

Oubiña, David: *Estudio crítico sobre* La ciénaga. Buenos Aires: Picnic Editorial, 2007.

Page, Joanna: *Crisis and Capitalism in Contemporary Argentine Cinema*. Durham, NC: Duke University Press, 2009.

Paulinelli, María (ed.): *Poéticas en el cine argentino (1995–2005)*. Córdoba: Comunicarte, 2005.

Pauls, Alan: "On *Camila*: The Red, the Black and the White." In *An Argentine Passion: María Luisa Bemberg and Her Films*, edited by John King, Sheila Whitaker, and Rosa Bosch, 110–21. London: Verso, 2000.

Paz, Octavio: *Sor Juana Inés de la Cruz o las trampas de la fe* (2nd. ed.). Mexico City: Fondo de Cultura Económica, 1983.

Peña, Fernando Martín (ed.): *60/90: Generaciones de cine independiente*. Buenos Aires: Fundación Eduardo Constantini, 2003.

Pinto Veas, Iván: "Entrevista a Albertina Carri: A propósito de *La rabia*." *La fuga*. n.d. Web. August 15, 2011.

Pratt, Mary Louise: *Imperial Eyes: Travel Writing and Transculturation*. New York: Routledge, 1992.

Quintín: "Lucrecia Martel, antes de la largada. Es de Salta y hace falta." *El amante*. http://www.elamante.com/nota/0/0488.shtml.

Rancière, Jacques: *Disagreement: Politics and Philosophy*. Translated by Julie Rose. Minneapolis: University of Minnesota Press, 1999.

———: *The Politics of Aesthetics: The Distribution of the Sensible*. Translated by Gabriel Rockhill. London: Continuum, 2004.

Ranzani, Oscar: "Un mapa de la diversidad de las imágenes." *Página/12*. June 17, 2010.

Richard, Nelly: *Masculino/femenino: Prácticas de la diferencia y cultura democrática*. Santiago: Francisco Zegers, 1993.

Rocha, Carolina, and Elizabeth Montes Garcés: *Violence in Argentine Literature and Film (1989–2005)*. Calgary: Univeristy of Calgary Press, 2010.

Rodríguez, Omar: "Poder, institución y género en *Yo, la peor de todas*." *Revista Canadiense de Estudios Hispánicos* 27, no. 1 (2002): 139–156.

Rojas, Eduardo: "*Momentos* y *Señora de nadie*: Señoras de nadie, nada, nunca." *Revista Canadiense de Estudios Hispánicos* 27, no. 1 (2002): 59–74.

Romano, Evelina: "Mujer que sabe de cine: Una entrevista con Lita Stantic." *Revista Canadiense de Estudios Hispánicos* 27, no. 1 (2002): 207–15.

Ruffinelli, Jorge: "María Luisa Bemberg y el principio de la trasgresión." *Revista Canadiense de Estudios Hispánicos* 27, no. 1 (2002): 15–44.

Sarabia, Rosa: "Sor Juana o las trampas de la restitución." *Revista Canadiense de Estudios Hispánicos* 27, no. 1 (2002): 119–38.

Sarmiento, Domingo F.: *Argirópolis*. Rio de Janeiro and Buenos Aires: Editorial Tor, 1938.

Scarry, Elaine: *The Body in Pain: The Making and Unmaking of the World*. New York: Oxford University Press, 1985.

Silverman, Kaja: *The Acoustic Mirror: The Female Voice in Psychoanalysis and Cinema*. Bloomington: Indiana University Press, 1988.

———: *The Threshold of the Visible World*. New York: Routledge, 1996.

Spivak, Gayatri: "Echo." In *The Spivak Reader*, edited by Donna Landry and Gerald Maclean, 175–202. New York: Routledge, 1996.

Soto, Moira: "El paraíso perdido." *Página/12*. *Las 12*. October 15, 2004.

Tesler, Mario: *Tres mujeres en Pilar*. Buenos Aires: Dunken, 2000.

Torrents, Nissa: "One Woman's Cinema: Interview with María Luisa Bemberg." In *Knives and Angels: Women Writers in Latin America*, edited by Susan Bassnett, 171–75. London: Zed Books, 1990.

Treibel, Guadalupe: "La mirada indiscreta." *Página/12. Las 12.* October 10, 2008.

Vezzetti, Hugo: *Pasado y presente: Guerra, dictadura y sociedad en la Argentina.* Buenos Aires: Siglo XXI, 2002.

Vilaboa, Daniela: "La educación sentimental." In *Otro campo: Estudios sobre cine.* http:// www.otrocampo.com/críticas2/laninasanta/html.

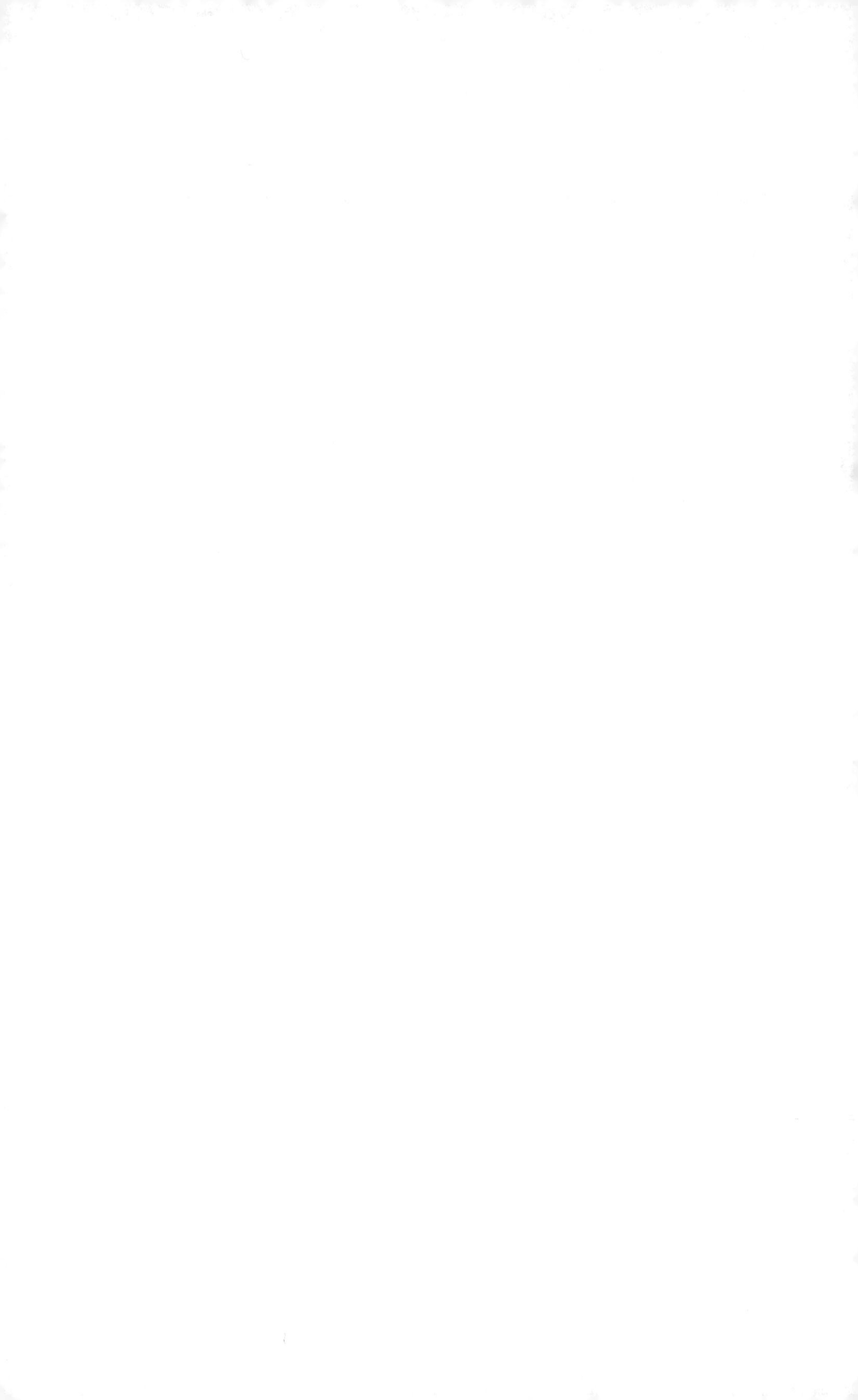

FILMOGRAPHY

25 miradas, 200 minutos: los cortos del bicentenario. Secretaría de Cultura de la Nación/Universidad de Tres de Febrero, 2010 <mediateca.filo.uba.ar/content/25-miradas200-minutos>.

Bemberg, Maria Luisa (dir.): *Señora de nadie* [1982]. Facets Multimedia, 2003.

———: *Camila* [1984]. Facets Video. 2002.

———: *Miss Mary* [1986]. New World Video, 1987.

———: *Yo, la peor de todas* [1990]. First Run, 2003.

———: *De eso no se habla* [1993]. Columbia: TriStar Home Video, 1995.

Berneri, Anahí (dir.): *Por tu culpa*. Argentina 791 Cine. 2009.

Carri, Albertina (dir.): *Barbie puede eStar triste*. Buenos Aires, 2001.

———: *Los rubios*. New York: Women Make Movies, 2003.

———: *Géminis*. Buenos Aires, AVH, San Luis, S.R.L, 2005.

———: *La rabia*. Buenos Aires: Matanza Cine, 2008.

———: "Restos." *25 miradas, 200 minutos: los cortos del bicentenario*. Secretaría de Cultura de la Nación/Universidad de Tres de Febrero, 2010 (<mediateca.filo.uba.ar/content/25-miradas-200-minutos>). Online. November 22, 2013.

David, Gabriela (dir.): *Taxi, un encuentro* [2001]. Strand Releasing Home Video, 2006.

———: *La mosca en la ceniza* [2010]. SP films, 2012.

Farji, Sabrina (dir.): *Cuando ella saltó*. Buenos Aires: Industria Argentina, SBP S.A. Worldwide, 2008.

———: "La Voz." *25 miradas, 200 minutos: los cortos del bicentenario*. Secretaría de Cultura de la Nación/Universidad de Tres de Febrero, 2010 (<mediateca.filo.uba.ar/content/25-miradas-200-minutos>).

Gugliotta, Sandra (dir.): "Posadas." *25 miradas, 200 minutos: los cortos del bicentenario*. Secretaría de Cultura de la Nación/Universidad de Tres de Febrero, 2010 (<mediateca.filo.uba.ar/content/25-miradas-200-minutos>).

Luque, Paula de (dir.): "Leyenda del Ceibo." *25 miradas, 200 minutos: los cortos del bicentenario*. Secretaría de Cultura de la Nación/Universidad de Tres de Febrero, 2010 (<mediateca.filo.uba.ar/content/25-miradas200-minutos>).

Luque, Paula de and Sabrina Farji (dirs.): *Cielo azul, cielo negro*. Buenos Aires: SBP, [2003] 2009.

Martel, Lucrecia (dir.): *La ciénaga*. Buenos Aires: Transeuropa Video Entertainment, 2001.

———: *La niña santa*. Buenos Aires: Lita Stantic Producciones, 2004.

———: *Rey muerto* [1995]. Included in *La ciénaga*. New York, NY: Criterion Collection, 2005.

———: *La mujer sin cabeza*. Culver City, CA: Strand Releasing Home Video, 2009.

———: "Nueva Argirópolis." *25 miradas, 200 minutos: los cortos del bicentenario*. Secretaría de Cultura de la Nación/Universidad de Tres de Febrero, 2010 (<mediateca.filo.uba.ar/content/25-miradas-200-minutos>).

———: *Pescados*. NotodoFilmFest, 2010.

Menis, María Victoria (dir.): *El cielito*. Buenos Aires: Todo Cine, 2003.

———: *La cámara oscura* [2008]. National Center for Jewish Film, 2009.

Puenzo, Lucía (dir.): *El niño pez*. Peccadillo Pictures, 2009.

Stantic, Lita (dir.): *Un muro de silencio*. Aleph Producciones S.A., 1993.

www.ingramcontent.com/pod-product-compliance
Lightning Source LLC
LaVergne TN
LVHW050534100826
845148LV00002B/556